The Service Profit Chain

How Leading Companies Link Profit and Growth to Loyalty, Satisfaction, and Value

JAMES L. HESKETT

W. EARL SASSER, JR.

LEONARD A. SCHLESINGER

THE FREE PRESS

THE FREE PRESS
A Division of Simon & Schuster Inc.
1230 Avenue of the Americas
New York, NY 10020

Manufactured in the United States of America

10 9

Library of Congress Cataloging-in-Publication Data

Heskett, James L.
The service profit chain : how leading companies link profit and growth to loyalty, satisfaction, and value / James L. Heskett, W. Earl Sasser, Jr., Leonard A. Schlesinger.
p cm.
Includes bibliographical references and index.
1. Customer services. 2. Customer satisfaction. 3. Employee loyalty. 4. Industrial productivity. I. Sasser, W. Earl. II. Schlesinger, Leonard A. III. Title.
HF5415.5.H47 1997
658.8′12—dc21 96–44611
CIP

ISBN 0–684–83256–9

To Marilyn, Connie, and Phyllis—
the loves of our lives

Contents

PART III: PUTTING IT ALL TOGETHER

Preface

Why are a select few service organizations better year in and year out at what they do than their competitors? This is a question that has prompted any number of "how to do it" books presenting keys to successful competition. Often based on anecdotal or case information of a sketchy nature, these books either leave unanswered a number of questions or room for a wide range of interpretations, actions, and judgments based on the "theories" espoused. (One outstanding exception to this statement is the work reported by James C. Collins and Jerry I. Porras in their book *Built to Last.*)

Several years ago, we decided to try to approach this question from another angle, the development and testing with quantifiable measures of a set of relationships that we have come to call the service profit chain. The "chain" represents a related set of strongly held convictions. The more we explored these convictions, the more we became convinced that they were not just ours, they were shared by managers leading some of the best-performing service organizations in the world. Some of them had fragments of data to support their convictions. No one had either the complete picture or all of the data in hand to support their views, but they clearly were managing by tenets similar to those in the service profit chain. In fact, we concluded that the chain was not our invention, but rather the assembled judgment of several dozen outstanding service managers and academic researchers with whom we have had the pleasure of interacting over the years.

The result of our efforts is a view, backed up with facts, of relationships that describe the achievement of success, measured ultimately in terms of growth and profitability, in a service organization. At the core of service profit chain management is the principle of "managing by fact," an admonition heard more frequently than it has been practiced during the past decade of emphasis on continuous quality improvement.

This book presents both fact and anecdote. Without the latter, facts have little life. And some elements of the service profit chain cannot be explained by fact alone. Further, merely understanding the nature of the links in the chain does not dictate any one method for achieving high levels of performance in each. That's where anecdotes can provide rich examples of the various ways that strong service profit chain performance can be attained, an important objective of this book.

In particular, our interest turned not just to behavior achieved through extraordinary effort of the kind difficult to duplicate, but, more importantly, to those mechanisms and behaviors that can be sustained over time. After all, organizations practicing things that truly separate them from their competitors do so one day at a time on the competitive frontline, not just through occasional brilliant strategies or insights from headquarters. The anecdotal evidence we have included is intended to convey both the extraordinary actions and accomplishments of the organizations we describe but also, as the chairman of one of the companies in our sample likes to put it, "the importance of the mundane" in these same organizations.

The service profit chain, like any good product or service, is an evolving set of ideas. We are constantly learning new things about it with each new set of data we obtain, although the data have long since conformed to a consistent pattern. This book reflects our most recent thinking, but it also is written to convey the sense that more work on this set of ideas is required, just as is true of any useful management concept.

Several colleagues have worked closely with us in the development and testing of these ideas. Fred Reichheld of Bain & Co. management consultants, working with one of us, developed the early thinking on the importance of customer loyalty. Jeff Zornitsky and Alan Grant of Exchange Partners, with the help of one of us, developed data showing the influence of frontline capability on employee satisfaction as well as differences between current and full potential performances. A number of our associates at the Harvard Business School have provided important inputs to our thinking. These include Gary Loveman, Jeffrey Rayport, and Roger Hallowell, members of the service management interest group, who have helped us hone a number of the ideas expressed here. Bob Kaplan has provided important stimulation with his work on what has come to be known as the balanced scorecard, a concept compatible with much of the service profit chain. The work of Mike Jensen, George Baker, and Karen Wruck has confirmed some of our thinking about pay-for-performance and other reward schemes. And Bob Simons, also of the HBS faculty, has stimulated us with his thinking about designing control systems with different degrees of latitude and limits. We have benefited as well from the contributions of our former colleagues Chris Hart, Christopher Lovelock, Tom Jones, and David Maister. And the support of Nancy Lund and Kathy Ivanciw at HBS was critical to the preparation of the book manuscript.

Perhaps most important of all, a number of organizations have cooperated more than we could have expected in supplying evidence that the service profit chain exists in practice. They include the Merry Maids subsidiary of The ServiceMaster Company, the Taco Bell division of Pepsico, Banc One, Southwest Airlines, American Express, Waste Management, USAA, MBNA, Intuit, British Airways, The Ritz-Carlton Hotel Company, and the Fairfield Inn subsidiary of the Marriott Corporation. We are indebted to all of these people and organizations for helping to shape the thinking described here.

In a sense, then, this is an account of our investigational odyssey, one that has taken surprising turns. In the process, marketing ideas we have nurtured and taught for years have been turned upside-down, conceptions of what drives employee performance have changed, the real value of process assessment such as continuous quality improvement or reengineering has become apparent, and the role of leadership in all of this has become clearer.

James L. Heskett
W. Earl Sasser
Leonard A. Schlesinger

Boston, Massachusetts
December 1996

Part I

The Service Profit Chain

A Rationale for Excellence

1

Setting the Record Straight

How many of us have attended seminars or read recently written books that admonish us to: (1) treat customers like royalty, (2) exceed customers' expectations, (3) either seek low operating costs or some means of differentiating our businesses from competitors, and (4) assume that the customer is always right. They are led by master storytellers who move with ease among the audience and are filled with enjoyable anecdotes that seem relevant at the time. We know. We've given our share of these presentations.

Who hasn't heard a Nordstrom story at one of these seminars? Most often it's the one about the Nordstrom store that accepts the return of a set of tire chains by someone claiming to have bought them there even though Nordstrom doesn't sell tire chains. The misguided moral is that by wowing the customer in that manner, Nordstrom will gain a new customer and possibly great word-of-mouth advertising. However the story is designed to make a point that is not only illogical, but is supported by no substantial evidence, quantitative or otherwise. Fortunately, few of us try to act on the implied advice. And yet we remember the story, if not the point it is designed to make.

A WORLD OF MISLEADING ADVICE

Why is it that the advice implied by these storytellers is so difficult to apply? Or worse yet, leads to the opposite results that they forecast? It's because the advice too often is sometimes totally inappropriate and always partially wrong. It nearly always is offered out of context, is based on incorrect assumptions, emphasizes symptoms instead of real causes, in the process trivializes service issues by confining them to the front line, and overemphasizes process quality while underemphasizing results.

Too Much Advice out of Context

Too much anecdote-peppered advice is given by many service gurus today without a context. We're not told that what worked in one organization may not be appropriate for another. The advice is so overly simplistic that it leads us as managers to seek the elusive "one big idea" that can help us improve performance. It is offered with little real supporting evidence other than the fact that the subjects of the anecdotes are often regarded as successes.

On the other hand, how often are we told that Nordstrom actually "fires" customers? We rarely, if ever, hear that side of the story. In fact, Nordstrom wows some customers and fires others who may be especially difficult for its staff to deal with (by advising them that, because of Nordstrom's failure to find a way to meet their needs, they should perhaps seek out other stores) as part of a careful strategy to target people with a particular profile and a record of outstanding loyalty to the company. If the tire story ever did occur, you can bet that it involved a customer that Nordstrom's people, based on facts, knew they did not want to alienate. In the context of a more carefully planned strategy, it could have made sense, although one could question the loyalty of a customer who would pull such a stunt on the company and expect to get away with it.

The Tyranny of the Trade-off

Ever since the popularization of Michael Porter's research on competitive strategy, we have been advised to seek either the lowest costs or a significant means of differentiation from competition for our businesses.[1] The assumption here is that managers must choose, because both can't be achieved. In some cases, this is simply wrong. In fact, there is little evidence that it was the message that Porter himself intended. Furthermore, it leads us to achieve "merely good" performances as opposed to outstanding achievements that can result from strategies designed to achieve both low cost and competitive differentiation, strategies that are more achievable than is generally believed.

James Collins and Jerry Porras, in their fascinating book *Built to Last,* which reports their study of companies with long-term staying power in the marketplace, call this "the tyranny of either/or." They point out that many companies with long records of success practice the policy of "and/also," assuming they can "have it all."[2]

Management by trade-offs reached its peak during an era in which the price of low inventory investments was thought to be poor customer service, or in order to achieve the economies of long production runs, factories had to stop trying to supply "one-of-a-kind" items to customers. Information systems, computer-aided design and manufacture, and robotics have killed, or at least seriously crippled, assumptions underlying trade-off management. Yes, trade-offs are a part of some businesses. But truly outstanding competitors, often limited to one or two in any one industry, achieve both outstanding results for customers and the lowest costs. A good case in point is USAA, an organization offering casualty insurance and other financial services.

USAA (United Services Automobile Association) was founded by a group of military officers to provide casualty insurance only to other officers. Given the transient nature of military duty, the service delivery system best suited to military personnel was direct mail and telephone. In fact, few USAA policy holders have ever seen a representative of the company. Nevertheless, it is hard to find anyone who has ever received less than outstanding service from the company. "War stories" abound about how USAA sends checks to repair damage based entirely on the word of the policyholder, or how a USAA claims adjustor may have pointed out damage that the policyholder had not seen and written a check on the spot for a larger-than-expected amount. At the same time, the company's system of selling through word-of-mouth recommendations to a trustworthy, disciplined group of customers prescreened by the military has led to some of the lowest sales, administration, and total costs in the business. Although the company has expanded its line of financial services and offers some of them to nonmilitary customers, its core business continues to be a refutation of "either/or" thinking. USAA offers a differentiated service at some of the lowest rates (prices) and costs in its industry.

Emphasis on Symptoms vs. Causes

Many of the great service stories are downright misleading—for example, the one involving the Southwest Airlines counter agent who encountered a customer who had just missed the flight that would take him to his most important business meeting of the year. The attendant decided to have his own light plane pulled out of the hangar and fueled in order to fly him to the customer's destination. We're supposed to believe that it's just part of the great service at Southwest, an airline that charges no more than $39 for many of its tickets. If so, it's the kind of great service that, offered repeatedly, will put a company out of business.

The story behind the story is much more important. It is that the counter agent knew the customer by his first name because the agent had been at his job for seven years. He knew that the customer flew over 300 segments per year and was worth more than $18,000 a year in revenue to his airline. He regarded it as *his* airline because he, like all other Southwest employees, had owned stock in it since his first full year of employment. And he knew that Southwest's policy for frontline personnel was "do whatever you feel comfortable doing for a customer." As an owner, he felt comfortable flying this customer to his destination. But a run-of-the-mill customer at Southwest certainly shouldn't expect this kind of service. In fact, Southwest Airlines, the paragon of good service, also fires customers, especially if they are drunk or unruly. It doesn't just put them off its planes, it tells them it never wants to see them again. But rarely do the great stories go much below the surface to suggest causes rather than symptoms of great service.

The "Trivialization" of Service

Many services occur, are marketed and produced, at the point of contact with the customer. Thus, the service "encounters" between customers and frontline service providers or electronic media are central and critical to successful results. It is entirely appropriate that a great deal of attention be drawn to the challenge of producing successful service encounters. But too much research, including some of ours, tends to confine service to the front line, neglecting the broader strategies of which the encounter and its design are a part. It overlooks the fact that frontline services are products of fundamentally strategic issues, issues that have to be understood and addressed by top management.

For example, Southwest Airlines is known for its ability to turn its planes, from arrival at the terminal gate to departure from the gate, much more rapidly than other airlines. This is undoubtedly in part due to the fact that Southwest's ground services employees work as teams, helping each other out as needed in an effort to turn two out of three flights in less than twenty minutes, less than half the time required by other major airlines.

But it is due also to the fact that Southwest's management has shunned the hub and spoke system used by other airlines, a system that slows aircraft turnaround in order to provide a larger time "window" for the arrival of connecting flights. Southwest also has structured its routes to utilize less-congested airports and cater to short-haul flyers expecting little in the way of baggage handling, catering, and other amenities that eat up ground time. The route structure and market to which it is targeted are strategic decisions made by top management. Without those decisions, the outstanding accomplishments of the frontline personnel would not be possible.

Fixation on Service Process Quality

Pick up any trade journal, management magazine, or even academic journals devoting space to service, and you rapidly conclude that service quality is the key to success. Too often, service quality is defined solely in terms of those things that contribute to process quality: dependability, timeliness, the authority and empathy (identification with the customer) with which a service is delivered, and the extent to which tangible evidence is created that a service has been delivered.

Rarely is any mention made of results delivered to customers in these reports. Carl Sewell describes this in his book *Customers for Life,* as follows: "Being nice to people is just 20% of providing good customer service. The important part is designing systems that allow you to do the job right the first time. All the smiles in the world aren't going to help you if your product or service is not what the customer wants."[3]

Michael Hammer of reengineering fame is even more pointed. As he puts it, "A smile on the face of a limousine driver is no substitute for an automobile."[4]

In fact, customers report time and again that both results and process quality are important to them in their selection of service providers. These are important elements in what we call the value equation, a concept on which we will elaborate later.

THE SERVICE PROFIT CHAIN AND OUR SEARCH FOR EVIDENCE

In part as a reaction to the repeated service stories that we got tired of hearing and the frustrated managers who have tried to apply the advice they were supposed to illustrate, we sought to understand why some service organizations succeed year-in and year-out. In addition to collecting lore and listening to countless stories emanating from outstanding service organizations, we did a risky and audacious thing. We started to collect data. Our work has grown a data base comprising inputs from several dozen well-known service organizations operating in a number of different competitive environments.

In addition to seeking facts, we developed measurements and began looking for relationships in our data that could shed light on ways of achieving service excellence and organizational success. Our work covered three phases: (1) discovery, (2) naïve and simple-minded revelation, and (3) selective rejection and application. The first phase was the most exciting. The second phase was frankly exploitative. But the third, still ongoing, has yielded the deepest insights and most practical output for managers. This book is a record of our odyssey, the fact-based insights it has yielded for managers, and the translation of those insights into action in outstanding service organizations. We came to these conclusions from three very different directions.

Heskett and the Strategic Service Vision

In the mid-1980s, James Heskett set forth a set of relationships, based on a number of observations, called the strategic service vision.[5] The "vision" comprised four important elements: (1) markets targeted on the basis of psychographic (how people think and act) as well as demographic (who people are, where they live, and how well they are educated) factors, (2) service concepts, products, and entire businesses defined in terms of results produced for customers, all positioned in relation to the needs expressed by targeted customers and the offerings of competitors, (3) operating strategies comprising organizations, controls, operating policies, and processes that "leverage" value to customers over costs to the offering organization, and (4) service delivery systems comprising bricks and mortar, information systems, and equipment that complement associated operating strategies. Questions characterizing the strategic service vision are shown in Figure 1–1.

Heskett concluded that companies achieve high profitability by having either market focus (as in ServiceMaster's almost single-minded concentration on providing cleaning and related support services to hospitals in the early years of the development of its institutional service business) or operating focus (as in United Parcel Service's long-time insistence that all packages it handled in its retail and consumer package delivery service had to weigh less than seventy pounds and have a combined length and girth of 130 inches). Organizations that achieve both market and operating focus are nearly unbeatable.

One interesting symptom of market focus is a small, but vocal group of dissatisfied customers. In fact, one of the phenomena we've observed in recent months is the growing number of pages on the Internet de-

FIGURE 1–1
Elements of the Strategic Service Vision

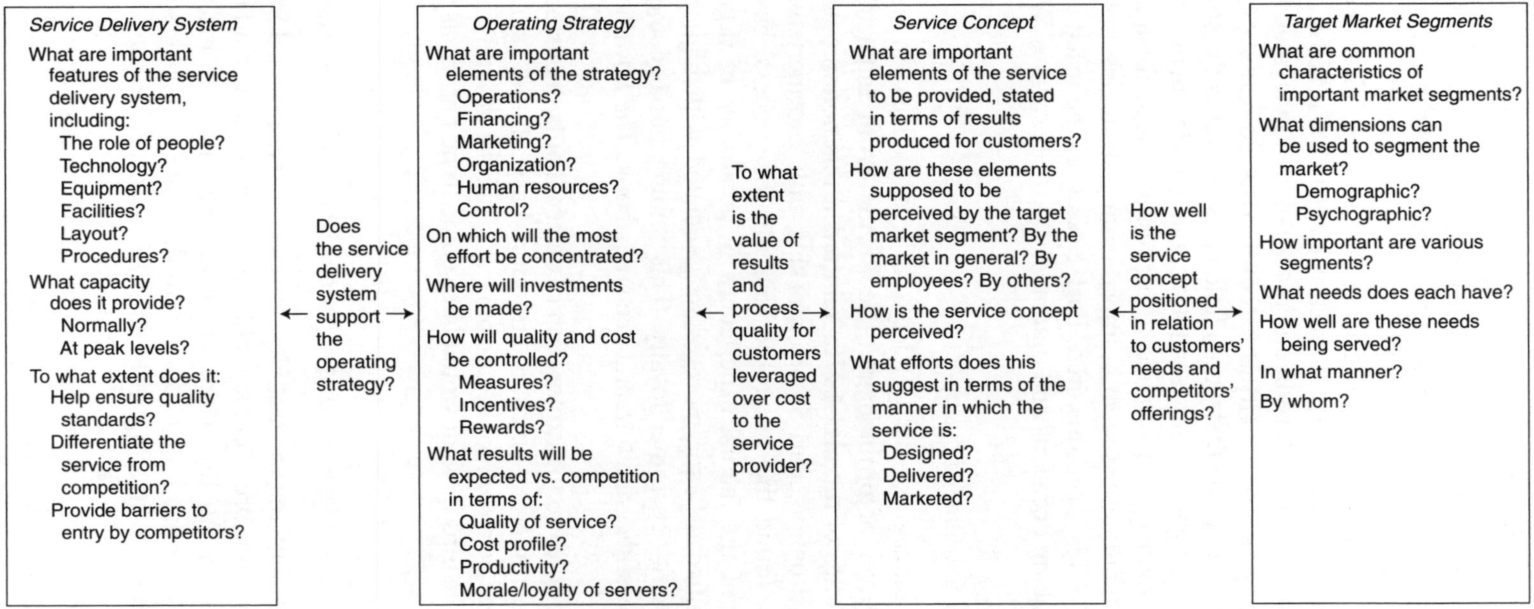

Service Delivery System

What are important features of the service delivery system, including:
- The role of people?
- Technology?
- Equipment?
- Facilities?
- Layout?
- Procedures?

What capacity does it provide?
- Normally?
- At peak levels?

To what extent does it:
- Help ensure quality standards?
- Differentiate the service from competition?
- Provide barriers to entry by competitors?

← Does the service delivery system support the operating strategy? →

Operating Strategy

What are important elements of the strategy?
- Operations?
- Financing?
- Marketing?
- Organization?
- Human resources?
- Control?

On which will the most effort be concentrated?

Where will investments be made?

How will quality and cost be controlled?
- Measures?
- Incentives?
- Rewards?

What results will be expected vs. competition in terms of:
- Quality of service?
- Cost profile?
- Productivity?
- Morale/loyalty of servers?

← To what extent is the value of results and process quality for customers leveraged over cost to the service provider? →

Service Concept

What are important elements of the service to be provided, stated in terms of results produced for customers?

How are these elements supposed to be perceived by the target market segment? By the market in general? By employees? By others?

How is the service concept perceived?

What efforts does this suggest in terms of the manner in which the service is:
- Designed?
- Delivered?
- Marketed?

← How well is the service concept positioned in relation to customers' needs and competitors' offerings? →

Target Market Segments

What are common characteristics of important market segments?

What dimensions can be used to segment the market?
- Demographic?
- Psychographic?

How important are various segments?

What needs does each have?

How well are these needs being served?

In what manner?

By whom?

Adapted and reprinted by permission of the Harvard Business School Press. From *Managing in the Service Economy,* by James L. Heskett, p. 30.

voted to "clubs" of disaffected customers from service organizations with highly targeted and focused strategies. Clearly, these customers represented a poor match with the service in the first place. They should have been discouraged from utilizing the service or given the opportunity to select themselves out at an early stage in the process.

The strategic service vision embraces the idea that value is achieved by leveraging results for customers over costs, something that is integral to other concepts that would follow. As helpful as the strategic service vision might be in facilitating the development of strategy, practicing managers continued to express the need for a set of concepts that would assist them in implementing strategies, not formulating them. This need inspired Earl Sasser as he tried to identify money-making decisions and outcomes.

Sasser and Customer Loyalty

For years, managers have been led to believe that share of market is the primary driver of profitability. The PIMS (Profit Impact of Market Share) studies of the mid-1970s reinforced this notion.[6] But in situation after situation, Earl Sasser, working with a former student, Fred Reichheld, found this not to be true.[7] In the process, based on the collection of the factual experiences of a number of organizations, they identified a factor more often associated with high profits and rapid growth—customer loyalty. This finding has become the basis for a successful consulting practice and a book, *The Loyalty Effect,* for Reichheld.[8]

This work led to the exploration of determinants of customer loyalty such as customer satisfaction, and more basically the value of goods and services delivered to the customer.[9] It laid the groundwork for several relationships in what would later come to be known as the service profit chain.

Schlesinger and Determinants of Employee and Customer Loyalty

Concurrent with the work of Heskett and Sasser, Leonard Schlesinger, as executive vice president and chief operating officer of a French bakery cafe chain, Au Bon Pain, was experimenting with incentives and other ideas designed to encourage Au Bon Pain's managers to exercise wide latitude in creating differentiated services for their customers while delivering exceptional profits for the company. They were designed to break what Schlesinger and his colleagues called the "cycle of failure" practiced by many of Au Bon Pain's competitors who paid their employees and managers low wages, offered them little training and other support, and suffered high turnover of employees and limited customer loyalty as a result.

During Schlesinger's tenure with Au Bon Pain, the company implemented a Partner/Manager Program that enlisted unit managers in a program in which they would split with the company on a 50/50 basis all operating profits over an agreed-on sum. In return, Au Bon Pain gave managers greater latitude to manage as they might choose, taking responsibility as well for all physical changes to the premises of their respective stores, subject only to quality control limits and certain matters, such as standard signage and standard "core" products, that every store had to practice.[10] The results were so good that he knew he was onto something. The "something" consisted of a set of ideas examined in field studies with Heskett and others that is described in detail later in this book as the "cycle of capability," making up a significant part of the service profit chain.[11] The philosophy behind the cycle of capability is that satisfied employees are loyal and productive employees. Their satisfaction stems, at least among the best frontline employees, from their desire to deliver results to customers. In order to deliver results to customers, they must have the ability to relate to customers, the latitude (within well-specified limits) to use their judgment in doing so, the training and technological support needed to do so, and recognition and rewards for doing so.

Schlesinger and his colleagues applied this philosophy to managers, some of whom extended it to frontline employees in Au Bon Pain restaurants, greatly reducing the turnover of employees and increasing customer satisfaction in the several restaurants where it was implemented. The results of the Partner/Manager Program related to findings from other research studies that there were direct links between customer and employee satisfaction and loyalty.[12] By now a compelling body of evidence was being accumulated that suggested that the cycle of capability was a significant management tool, one that encompassed several additional important relationships in the service profit chain to come.

THE SERVICE PROFIT CHAIN

Simply stated, service profit chain thinking maintains that there are direct and strong relationships between profit; growth; customer loyalty; customer satisfaction; the value of goods and services delivered to customers; and employee capability, satisfaction, loyalty, and productivity.[13] These relationships are shown in Figure 1–2. Notice that market share is not mentioned in these relationships. In few industries studied by Sasser and Reichheld was market share a more important predictor of profitability than customer loyalty.

FIGURE 1–2
Elements of the Service Profit Chain

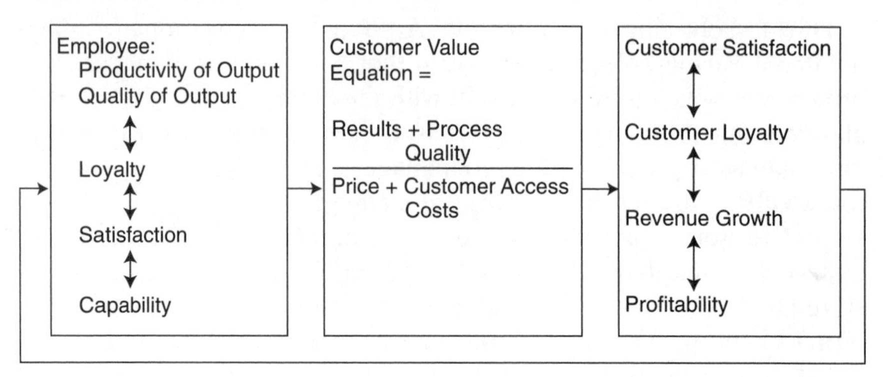

The strongest relationships suggested by the data collected in early tests of the service profit chain were those between: (1) profit and customer loyalty, (2) employee loyalty and customer loyalty, and (3) employee satisfaction and customer satisfaction. They suggested that in service settings, the relationships were self-reinforcing. That is, satisfied customers contributed to employee satisfaction, and vice versa.

The Centrality of Value

Central to the chain, as shown in Figure 1–2, is the customer value equation, suggesting that the value of goods and services delivered to customers is equivalent to the results created for them as well as the quality of the processes used to deliver the results, all in relation to the price of a service to the customer and other costs incurred by the customer in acquiring the service. It is a "customer's eye view" of goods and services, influencing decisions to buy and use them. Further, we have found that value defined in this way is directly related to customer satisfaction.

Note how this concept of value plays out in the migration of banking customers from "face-to-face" teller banking to automatic teller machines to home banking by telephone or computer. For most customers who have begun this migration, every element of the value equation changes as they move through each stage.

Automatic teller machines provide results comparable to those available from face-to-face relationships with human tellers. The range of transactions possible with the machine may not always be as great as those available from a teller, but all frequently used services are possible, including, of course, the dispensing of money. For many customers, particularly those anxious about transacting personal business in English, the machine programmed to "speak" many languages can actually provide better process quality than a human teller. The same can be said for "control freaks" concerned about the accuracy of transactions made by human tellers. Until recently, when several banks began charging for transactions by human tellers, the "price" of consumer banking by human and automatic tellers has been the same. But the twenty-four-hour availability and greater number of locations of the machines greatly lower acquisition costs incurred by customers using automatic teller machines. Many customers would actually be willing to pay more for this form of service than for face-to-face service even though it is more economical for banks than transactions by human tellers.

Going one step further, from automatic teller machines to home banking by phone, the relationships become more complex. Results available through the latter are not as great as by machine; the customer can't obtain cash through his telephone. Nevertheless, speedier transaction time represents enhanced process quality for many customers. In addition, phone banking is low cost, primarily because of greatly reduced acquisition costs for the customer, who saves gas, time, and anxiety in the comfort of his home.

When home banking is extended to the computer, "results" are once again enhanced. In addition to the convenience of in-home banking, the consumer using a computer enjoys added services, such as financial software that enables her to keep a running budget of expenditures and other financial records, all while paying bills. For some customers, an incremental value has once again been achieved over even phone banking.

It is important to note that value enhancement in this fashion in banking has been accompanied by dramatic reductions in costs per transaction to banks themselves. John Reed, CEO of Citibank, estimated for us several years ago that the costs of serving a customer totally by credit card and automatic teller machine were twenty-five times lower than through a Citibank branch.[14] If the relationships could be maintained by phone and computer, costs would be only 25 percent of those incurred by credit card. Of course, individual customer preferences and the limitations of each of these service delivery systems has made it necessary for Citibank to continue to offer all three.

Given the favorable economics of this "migration" to banks, they might well foster it by providing incentives, including free services and equipment, to consumers willing to take part in it. Instead, to date banks have tended to create disincentives for people to use human tellers by, in some cases, imposing user fees on them.

Quality as One Element of Value

The service profit chain and value equation it comprises helped us put into perspective much of the work on service quality. To the extent that it has focused largely on the elements of service *process* quality while ignoring results, it is essentially one of four elements of the value equation. In fact, in many cases it may be much less important to customers than results they obtain, regardless of process quality. In other cases, price and other acquisition costs may be more important than process quality in determining value for customers, their satisfaction, and their loyalty.

Price

Value is not equated with low prices. Goods and services of high value may carry high or low prices. In fact, customer needs are so different that they are often willing to pay greatly differing prices for a given service, depending on its importance at a given time and place. Because price is only one element of value, it can be influenced as well by the ease of accessing a service. That is, by making a service easier to acquire, it can be made less sensitive to price, thus enhancing margins and profits.

Results, Costs, Price, Value, and Profit

We said earlier that results for customers, an important element of value, is leveraged over cost to a service provider by means of the way in which an operating strategy is structured. It's not coincidental that those organizations testing every new product or service idea against the criterion of whether or not it creates results (and potentially value) for the targeted customer are able to maintain operating focus and outstanding profits. As David Glass, CEO of value-conscious Wal-Mart Stores, points out, one of his most important jobs is insuring that everyone in the organization acts as an "agent for the customer," whether negotiating with suppliers or thanking customers for their business as they leave Wal-Mart Stores.[15]

The resulting leverage of value (to customers) over costs (to a service provider) creates potential for profit. How much of that profit is realized depends on the level at which the service is priced in an effort to calibrate the value that a customer will attach to the service. Price and cost in turn are the determinants of profit to be realized from the business by the service provider. Thus, "leverage" is achieved in the strategic service vision by designing an operating strategy to produce maximum results as well as process quality for customers in relation to costs to the service provider. This leverage provides a "window" in which to price the service and make it more or less costly for the customer to access, essentially passing on some potential profit to the customer in the form of lower price or reduced acquisition costs.

Relationship to Service Profit Chain

Service profit chain management provides the means for implementing a strategic service vision. The two concepts are complementary, as suggested in Figure 14–2 on page 254. Both reflect an important objective of achieving market, operating, and human resource focus around a service concept that delivers results that customers desire.

FIGURE 1–3
Growth in Stock Share Prices, 1986–1995, Service Profit Chain vs. Comparison Firms, Compared with Growth in the Standard & Poor's 500 Common Stock Index

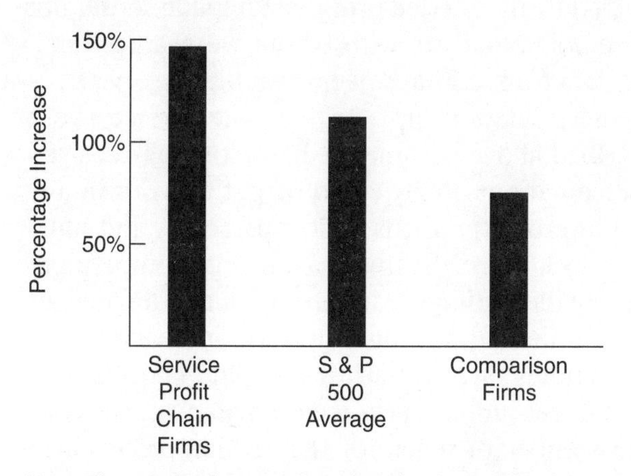

Note: The sample of companies included in the sample of those cited as showing evidence of service profit chain management was limited to publicly listed companies or parent companies of divisions cited in the discussion for whom reasonable matching comparisons could be found. The sample is comprised of MCI Communications; Southwest Airlines Co.; Wal-Mart Stores; WMX Technologies; Sears, Roebuck; Banc One; Citicorp; American Express; PepsiCo; and Intuit Inc. The comparison group comprised AT&T Corp.; AMR Corporation; Kmart Corp.; Browning-Ferris Industries; Dayton Hudson Corporation; NationsBank; The Chase Manhattan Corporation; Merrill Lynch & Co., Inc.; The Coca-Cola Company; and Microsoft Corp. Indices for these two groups of companies were calculated as the increase in the average price, adjusted for splits, of an unweighted marketbasket of shares for the group between 1986 and 1995. The index for the Standard & Poor's 500 stocks is, by contrast, calculated on the basis of a weighting reflecting the relative market value of each company in the composite. The increase in the average value of the index between 1986 and 1995 was used to approximate the method used for our samples. All data was adjusted for the fact that the stock of Intuit Inc. was only issued publicly in 1993.

WHAT DIFFERENCES DOES IT MAKE?

What difference does service profit chain management make? A lot. Between 1986 and 1995, the common stock prices of organizations from which we have drawn examples for this book increased 147%, nearly twice as fast as those for a group of companies representing their closest competitors (including well-known companies such as Microsoft Corporation, NationsBank, and the Coca-Cola Company), as shown in Figure 1–3. By contrast, the share prices of stocks included in Standard & Poor's 500 index increased only 110 percent during this same period.

While it is impossible to know exactly how much of the remarkable competitive advantage implied by the data in Figure 1–3 can be attributed to service profit chain management, we suspect it is a defining factor. But we'll let you be the judge as we explain in more detail the implications of service profit chain management for these organizations.

SPREADING THE WORD

The relationships described by the service profit chain made sense, not only to us but also to senior managers with whom we shared them. Cursory examination of data from perhaps twenty multiunit service organizations confirmed these relationships. In fact, the service profit chain relationships described above became the basis for well-received consulting and other presentations. They could be put to work in any organization desiring to improve the focus of its operations and marketing effort, positioning itself more effectively against its competition.

But as we began to apply the findings from our work and dig deeper into the data files of companies supporting our work, increasingly we found cases in which the findings were puzzling and didn't correspond to our expectations. Worse yet, under certain circumstances, we concluded that advice consistent with tenets of the service profit chain might, in some circumstances, be just plain wrong. This led us to explore our assumptions and expectations further. In the process, we have been able to develop more powerful guidelines for managers applying this philosophy.

As a result, this book is intended to relate what we know now about the service profit chain. It addresses the questions of when and where to apply what we have found, at least to the degree we are able to know at this stage of our work.

Before getting into its shortcomings and possible applications, it is first important to set forth in greater detail the service profit chain and some of the data on which it is based.

2

Capitalizing on the Service Profit Chain

Customers don't buy products or services. They buy results. The quality of the processes for delivering results, including the attitude of those in direct contact with customers, is important. But no amount of congeniality or empathy on the part of an auto dealer's service manager will substitute in the customer's mind for the failure to repair her automobile.

Outstanding organizations have to be managed for results. They don't create products or services, they deliver results. Their managers define their businesses and their missions in terms of results, not products or services.

For what kinds of results do service leaders manage? Our examinations of literally dozens of outstanding (as well as those we think of as merely good) service organizations, including those maintained by manufacturing firms, have convinced us that a small number of such results can provide strong direction in implementing effective strategies and achieving outstanding performance. They include financial measures such as profit and growth. But more important are those dimensions that are most critical to the achievement of financial success. At the heart of these is the value of services delivered to customers that leads to customer satisfaction and loyalty, two other critical kinds of results. And value is achieved primarily through frontline employees who are satisfied, loyal, and productive, in part because of the high degree of capability they possess to deliver results to customers. Combining these measures yields what we call the service profit chain, shown in Figure 2–1.[1]

Organizations that understand and manage according to the service profit chain, whether intuitively or by fact, achieve remarkable results. But they manage as well by a number of other carefully coordinated principles and practices that distinguish them from their competition. Two of our purposes in this book are to document by fact the accomplishments of these firms as well as capture a feel for the ways they achieve high marks on each dimension of the service profit chain. Like the game of chess, which can be played on several skill levels, service profit chain concepts can be accepted and utilized in a superficial way or in a more studied, careful manner. In the interest of full disclosure, we'll share more recent findings and experiences that suggest situations in which the common TV disclaimer "Don't try this at home" applies, situations in which service profit chain concepts have to be interpreted carefully and adapted for use.

THE SERVICE PROFIT CHAIN

Figure 2–1 shows the direct links we have measured and documented between profit and growth: customer satisfaction and loyalty; the value of services and goods delivered to customers; employee satisfaction, loyalty, and productivity; and what we term "capability" that employees have to deliver results to customers in every outstanding service organization we have observed. While the strength of various of these links in the chain may differ from one organization to the next, the pattern is undeniably significant.

As an illustration, let's follow the accomplishments of two organizations through the service profit chain as we take a look at each link to see how the chain functions as a whole. The first is Southwest Airlines, the only consistently profitable major U.S. airline whose managers instinctively practice profit chain management.[2] The second is American Express's travel business, whose leadership more recently has adopted measures and precepts implied by the service profit chain in remaking its business through conscious, coordinated management action.[3]

Managing for Results at Southwest Airlines and American Express

The customers that Southwest Airlines, the most consistently successful of all major U.S. airlines, seeks are the "road warriors," frequent

FIGURE 2–1
The Service Profit Chain

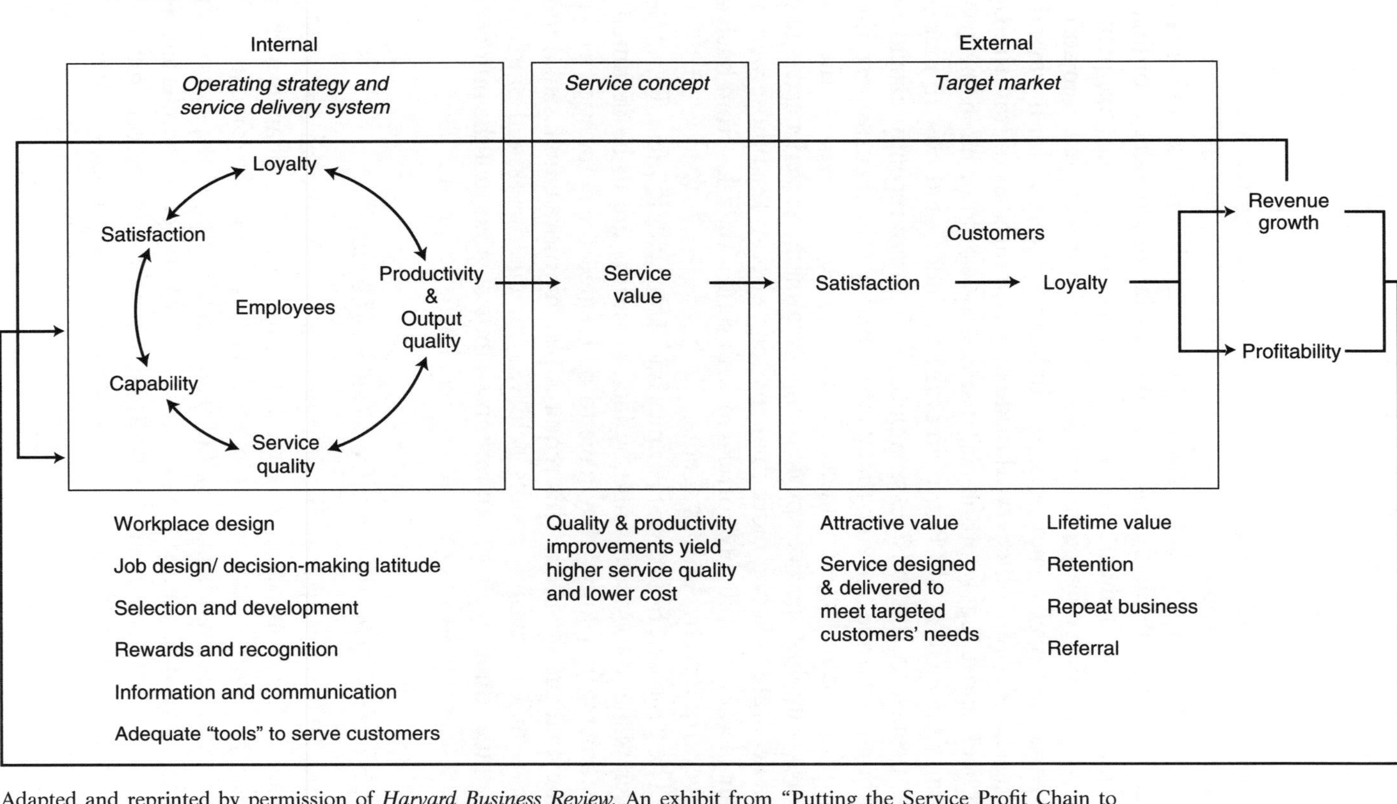

Adapted and reprinted by permission of *Harvard Business Review.* An exhibit from "Putting the Service Profit Chain to Work," by James L. Heskett, Thomas O. Jones, Gary W. Loveman, W. Earl Sasser, Jr., and Leonard A. Schlesinger, March-April 1994, p. 166.

business travelers over relatively short distances. They want dependable, frequent service at a reasonable price. How do Southwest's associates know this? They substitute "feel," daily knowledge obtained by being close to the customer and frequent opportunities to involve customers in their business, for more formal marketing research. But they make sure they know.

One of the most challenging of American Express's businesses is travel services. While the company has made literally billions of dollars from its traveler's check and credit card businesses, it has, like many of its competitors, enjoyed much less success in the highly competitive, low-margin travel agency business. In fact, if it weren't for the fact that American Express offices worldwide deliver a number of travel-related services, most highly profitable, it probably wouldn't be in the travel agency business at all. But in an effort to understand how to increase the profits of this business, American Express recently established through extensive research that its most highly valued customers, those associated with large commercial travel accounts served by the company, want fast service, professional treatment, experienced agents, and accurate ticketing more than anything else. At least those were the four factors most highly correlated with return on sales from business travel arranged by AmEx's agents.

The people at Southwest Airlines and American Express Travel Services manage for results and by fact. If results are to be delivered to customers, they know they have to be created for employees as well. They manage for both. This requires placing more emphasis on measuring and rewarding results achieved for customers and employees (outputs) than on effort (inputs). It sounds obvious, but the number of firms failing to follow this simple guideline is surprising.

Profit and Growth Are Linked to Customer Loyalty

In the 1970s, a major study of Profit Impact of Market Share (PIMS), based on the examination of data from hundreds of companies in many industries, concluded, among other things, that one of the most important determinants of profitability was market share.[4] It provided one more piece of evidence that led to a rash of mergers, purchases, and sales of companies in the 1980s as managers rushed to become number one or two in their respective industries. Organizations unable to attain such high relative shares of market were often labeled "dogs" and given up for lost. This apparently did not occur to the founders and managers at Southwest Airlines. Founded to fly its first flight in 1971, Southwest has never ranked higher than seventh largest in its industry. It has just been the most consistently profitable.

This and other apparent exceptions to the "market share = profit" principle led to close observations of a number of service industries first reported by Reichheld and Sasser.[5] As a result, they concluded that customer loyalty is a more important determinant of profit than market share in a wide range of industries. They estimated, for example, that a five percentage point increase in customer loyalty could produce profit increases of from 25 percent to 85 percent in the service industries they studied, as shown in Figure 2–2. As a result, they concluded that *quality* of market share, measured in terms of customer loyalty, deserves as much attention as *quantity* of share.

That's why the management of Southwest Airlines strives to build the highest levels of customer loyalty in the industry, even though airlines have limited means of measuring loyalty (for example, share of an airline passenger's ticket budget) other than through their frequent flyer programs. At Southwest, building loyalty means insuring that

FIGURE 2–2
Profit Increases Resulting from Five-Percentage-Point Increases in Customer Loyalty, Selected Service Industries

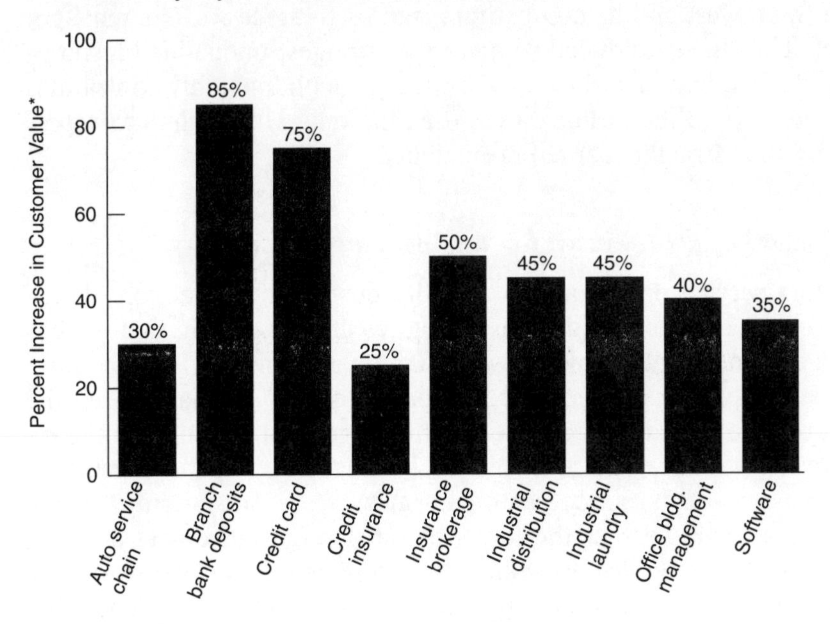

*Calculated by comparing the net present values of the profit streams for the average customer life of current defection rates with the net present values of the profit streams for the average customer life at five-percentage-point lower defection rates.

Adapted and reprinted by permission of *Harvard Business Review.* An exhibit from "Zero Defections: Quality Comes to Services" by Frederick F. Reichheld and W. Earl Sasser, Jr., September-October 1990, p. 110.

passengers give the airline at least three chances to prove that what it provides—dependable, frequent service over relatively short routes with no need to fly through a hub, delivered by friendly employees at low fares—is more important than what it does not provide. What it does not provide that airline passengers often expect are assigned seats (although Southwest's planes are not oversold), meals en route, and baggage interchange and connecting flights with other airlines. Given Southwest's primary target market, business travelers with responsibilities for visiting regional sites frequently, the service has been designed to provide those things they value highest. As Colleen Barrett, Executive Vice President at Southwest, puts it, "Once customers fly on us three times they're hooked."[6]

How does Southwest's management know that its customers are loyal? Through the most effective frequent flyer program in the industry? No. Through a data base of passengers' flying habits and patterns unavailable to any other airline? No. Instead, the Airline maintains a "feel" for its customers' loyalty through a continual effort to encourage its frontline employees to keep in touch with customers' travel needs. Our conversations with literally hundreds of people who have flown with Southwest and its competitors lead us to agree with its management. They have produced some of the strongest unqualified testimonials that we have heard for any service. This undoubtedly contributes in large part to the airline's record as the only U.S. airline to report twenty-four straight years of profitability.

Customer Loyalty Is Linked to Customer Satisfaction

Leading service organizations quantify customer satisfaction. These measures have often yielded surprising results, suggesting that there is not a constant relationship between customer satisfaction and loyalty.

Of all the links in the service profit chain, this one has proven the least reliable, based on recent research. Short-term measures of the relationship have been disrupted by such things as competitive price reductions that may entice customers away from outstanding service providers, regardless of the levels of satisfaction customers say that they have with a service. Reichheld has expressed the suspicion that the things that satisfy customers may not always be the same things that engender loyalty to a service organization providing them.[7] More about this in the next chapter.

It would be hard to convince the management of Southwest Airlines that customer loyalty is not linked to their satisfaction levels, although specific measures have not been developed by the Airline. At American Express Travel Services, an effort has been made to link customer satisfaction directly with office profitability. And the results have been quite remarkable.

Given its knowledge of customer preferences—fast, accurate ticketing carried out by professional, experienced agents—AmEx's management has established the degree to which customer satisfaction is influenced by these factors. Further, it has determined that those offices that deliver the fastest, most accurate ticketing are also among the most profitable, as shown in Figure 2–3. Here we see that the top 10 percent of AmEx's travel offices in terms of return on sales consistently outperform the bottom 10 percent on these two service dimensions. In fact, over all of its offices, it found a .51 (high) correlation between speed of ticketing and return on sales. And although the relationship was less significant at high levels of accuracy, for most offices there was a .65 (even higher) correlation between accuracy of ticketing and office return on sales.

It makes sense. Why shouldn't offices that ticket quickly and accurately be more profitable than those that don't? High speed and quality should be linked directly with profitability. But few organizations have calibrated the linkage as carefully as AmEx.

Customer Satisfaction Is Linked to Service Value

Customers today are strongly value-oriented. They seek results and service process quality that far exceeds the price and acquisition costs they incur for a service. At Southwest Airlines, customer perceptions of value are very high, even though the airline does not offer all of the amenities provided by its competition. Southwest's management knows that high levels of customer satisfaction result from Southwest's frequent departures, on-time service, friendly employees, and very low fares because its major marketing research unit—its more than 24,000 employees—is in daily contact with customers and reports its findings back to management.

In addition, the Federal Aviation Administration's performance measures show that Southwest, of all the major airlines, regularly achieves the highest level of on-time arrivals and the lowest number of customer service complaints per thousand passengers, as shown for 1995 in Figure 2–4. Southwest managed to achieve the best performance on both of these measures in addition to fewest lost baggage claims per thousand passengers (a "Triple Crown," in Southwest parlance) in four of the first five years in which the data was compiled and reported by the Federal Aviation Agency. No other major airline had succeeded in doing this once, even over a month's period of time, while Southwest had done it in twenty-nine different months by mid-1996.

FIGURE 2–3
Relationships Between Customer Satisfaction and Office Profitability, American Express Travel Services

Comparison of Top and Bottom 10% of American Express' Business Travel Offices, Ranked by Return on Sales, 1995

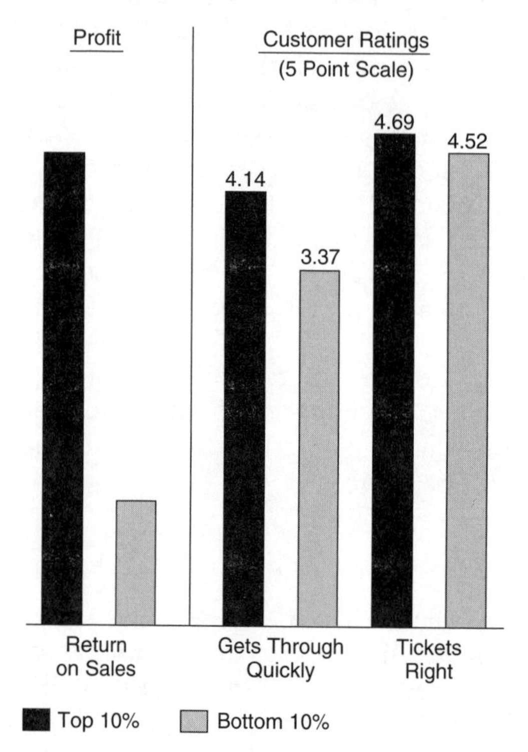

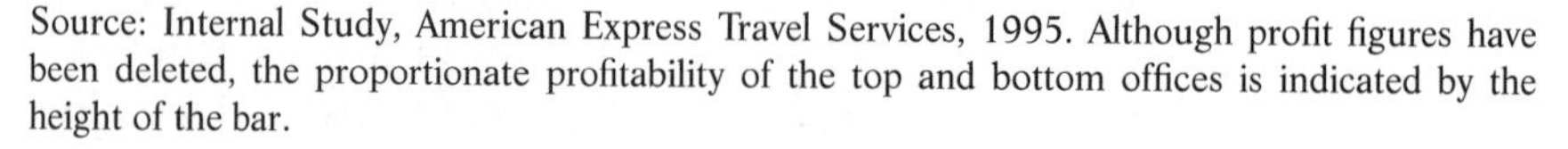
Source: Internal Study, American Express Travel Services, 1995. Although profit figures have been deleted, the proportionate profitability of the top and bottom offices is indicated by the height of the bar.

One might expect that Southwest traded potential profits for such high performance levels. Instead, its after-tax profits in relation to revenues were by far the highest of any major U.S. airline in the five-year period between 1990 and 1995.

When combined with Southwest's low fares per seat-mile, the indicators suggest a very high level of value for those passengers in need of these service features, primarily frequent, short-haul business travelers.

Southwest's value equation was seriously challenged in mid-1994 when two major airline reservations systems ceased providing information regarding its flights to travel agents because Southwest did not utilize the systems for making reservations, thereby yielding no revenue to the systems' sponsoring airlines. This made it more difficult for

FIGURE 2–4
Rankings of Eight Largest U.S. Airlines for Revenue, Profit, On-Time Arrival, and Customer Service Complaints, 1995

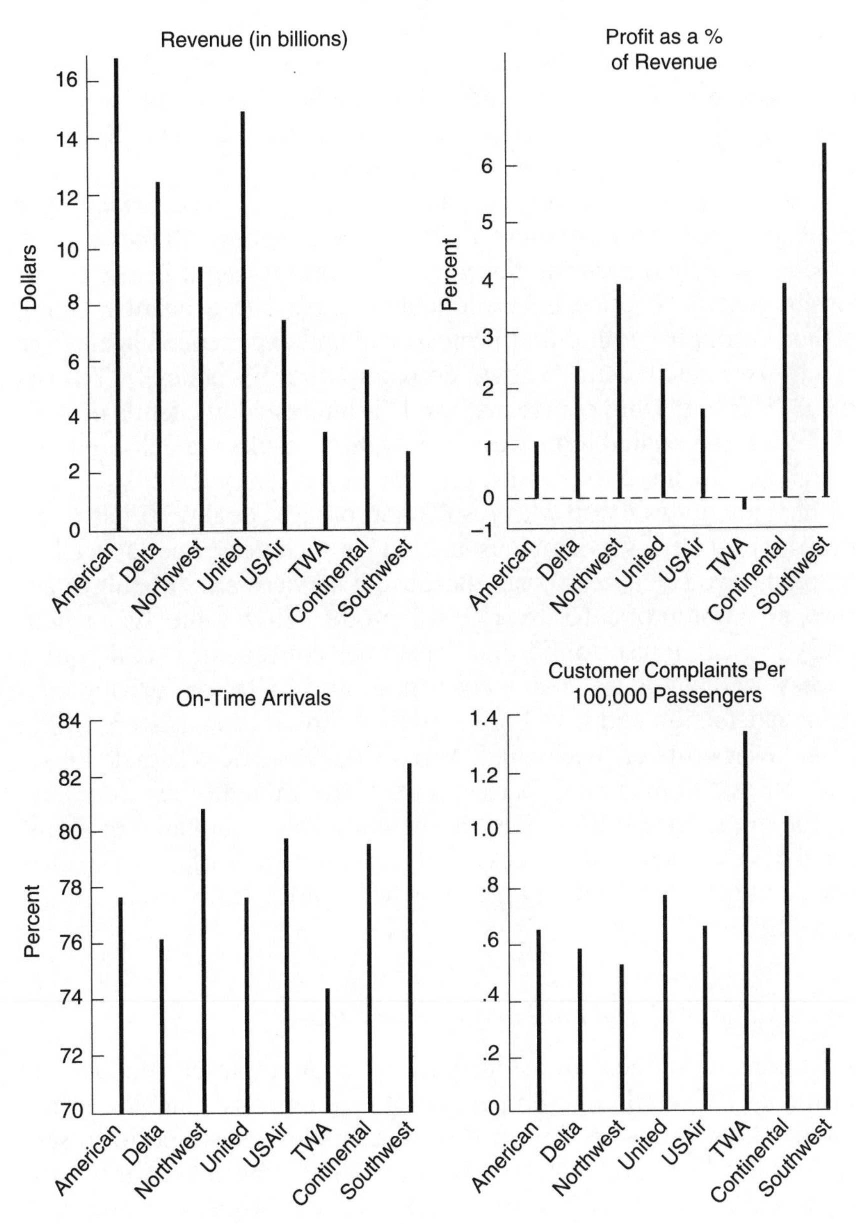

passengers to obtain tickets. It required that Southwest's management act quickly to introduce a ticketless service whereby passengers needed only to charge their reservations to their credit cards, obtain ticket confirmation numbers from the Airline, present them along with some identification at the gate, and board their flights. Competitors raised serious questions about whether airline customers would comply with the new procedure. Within days, Southwest's ticket volume was up 15 percent. Recently, several other airlines have adopted the procedure. Ticketless flying apparently has added to the value delivered by Southwest and some of its competitors. How did Southwest and its people know that it would work? Not by extensive formal research but by being in touch with its customers on a daily basis.

Value at AmEx Travel Services, as at Southwest, is a combination of results produced for customers as well as the way in which they are delivered. Quick and accurate ticketing is important. But it is just as important that it be done by professional, experienced agents. Going further, AmEx has found that professional and experienced agents are closely associated with "knows company (travel) policy," "returns calls," "is friendly and courteous," and "is interested in client's needs." All of these are related to process quality, how results are delivered. Although no substitute for results, they can be very important.

But value doesn't stop with results and process quality. It has to do with the cost of a service to its user. This includes price, as well as something we call access costs. Because if services are difficult to acquire, no amount of cut-rate price will produce high value. As a result, AmEx's research also found that "customer convenience" and "quick process" actually outranked "gets best airfare" as factors driving customer satisfaction and travel office profitability. Its clients were telling it that lower costs of "accessing" AmEx's travel services actually offset whatever additional prices its clients may have thought they were paying for the service. Of course, the winning value combination comprised good results, high process quality, reasonable air fares and other costs, and low costs of doing business with AmEx Travel (in accessing the service).

Service Value Is Linked to Employee Productivity

At Southwest Airlines, an astonishing story of employee productivity occurs daily. Even though 86 percent of the company's employees are unionized, positions are designed so that employees can perform several jobs if called upon to do so. Thus, pilots have been known to handle baggage for late departures. This kind of flexibility, along with schedules, routes, and company practices—such as open seating and the use of simple, color-coded, reusable boarding passes—enables Southwest to board many more passengers per employee than any other major U.S. airline. In addition, Southwest deplanes and reloads two-thirds of its flights in twenty minutes or less (as opposed to an industry average of forty minutes or more), giving it greater utilization of its aircraft. Because of resulting greater aircraft availability and short-haul routes that don't require long layovers for flight crews, Southwest has roughly 40 percent more pilot utilization than its major competitors. Its pilots fly on average seventy hours per month versus fifty hours at other airlines.

These practices help account for the data in Figure 2–5, indicating that in 1995, Southwest served 50 percent more passengers per employee than the second-ranking major airline on this measurement.

A recently completed analysis of nine selected city operations of Southwest, United, Continental, and American Airlines showed that, even after adjusting Southwest's data to account for the relative simplicity of its operations, it turned its planes around nearly twice as fast as the average of the other airlines while employing less than half the employees (per 1,000 passengers) as the average of the other airlines.[8] These factors help explain how the company can charge fares from 60 percent to 70 percent lower than existing fares in markets it enters, thus placing it in competition with the automobile rather than other airlines, and still achieve substantial profits.

In the Travel Services division of American Express, productivity is defined in terms valued by customers, the speed and accuracy with which tickets are prepared. This recognizes the fact that quality of service need not be "traded off" for high productivity; they most often go hand in hand.

FIGURE 2–5
Passengers per Employee, Eight Largest U.S. Airlines, 1995

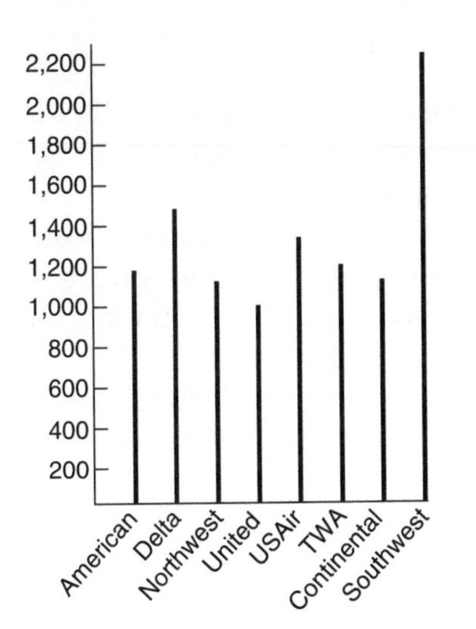

Employee Productivity Is Linked to Loyalty

Traditional measures of the losses incurred by employee turnover concentrate only on the cost of recruiting, hiring, and training replacements. But in most service jobs, an even greater cost of turnover is loss of productivity and decreased customer satisfaction. One recent study of automobile dealers' sales personnel concluded that the average monthly cost of replacing a sales representative who had five to eight years of experience with an employee who had less than one year of experience was as much as $36,000 in sales.[9] Even this number is relatively insignificant when compared to the costs of losing a valued broker at a securities firm. Conservatively estimated, it takes nearly five years for a securities broker to rebuild relationships with customers that can return $1 million per year in commissions to the brokerage house—a cumulative loss of at least $2.5 million in commissions.

It should be no surprise that Southwest Airlines, recently named one of the ten best places to work in the United States,[10] experiences the highest rate of employee retention in the airline industry. At some of its operating locations, turnover rates are less than 5 percent per year. This enables Southwest employees to get to know valued customers as well as carry out their jobs more productively with assurance and expertise.

Realizing that knowledgeable agents sensitive to the needs of individual customers are developed over time, not born, American Express's Travel Services division is placing particular emphasis on extending the average length of time that frontline agents spend with the organization.

Employee Loyalty Is Linked to Employee Satisfaction

In one 1991 study of a property and casualty insurance company's employees, it was found that 30 percent of all dissatisfied employees registered an intention to leave the company, a potential turnover rate three times higher than that for satisfied employees.[11] Given the costs resulting from loss of productivity, this organization could probably justify spending a substantial amount of effort and money to improve satisfaction.

Employee satisfaction levels at Southwest Airlines are high and carefully cultivated by management. Many organizations characterize themselves as big families. Few achieve it. At Southwest, more than half of its employees work together off the job in charitable activities. Judging from the pictures that cover the walls at headquarters, they party together off the job to an unusually high degree as well. And more than 800, nearly 6 percent of the workforce, are even married to each other. The results are unusually high levels of both employee satisfaction and loyalty. But to what is employee satisfaction linked?

Employee Satisfaction Is Linked to Internal Quality of Work Life

What we call the internal quality of a working environment contributes most to employee satisfaction. Internal quality is measured by the feelings that employees have toward their jobs, colleagues, and companies. In general, what do frontline service employees value most on the job? There is increasing evidence that it is their ability and authority to achieve results for customers, something we call capability.

At Southwest, only if frontline employees feel uncomfortable about possible individual initiatives on behalf of customers are they are asked to check with a supervisor. Otherwise, they are expected to act and perhaps tell the supervisor later. This leads to incredible acts of service for customers. As we will see later, one important reason this policy works at Southwest is that all employees with more than one year of service are actual owners of the company through its profit-sharing plan. Thus their "comfort level" is linked directly to their judgment about the possible impact on profitability of individual service initiatives on behalf of customers.

When American Express measured employees' attitudes toward various aspects of their jobs in high-performing and low-performing travel offices, it found direct relationships between what employees said about such things as physical surroundings, the safety of the workplace, and "the way things get done" and office profitability, as shown in Figure 2–6.

Internal quality is also characterized by the attitudes that employees have toward one another and the way they serve each other inside the company. This has led to a number of efforts to help employees identify their "customers" inside the company, find out what their internal customers need in relation to the services and service levels they are actually being supplied, and initiating corrective actions where necessary to improve service.

At Southwest, teamwork is stressed in the entry-level training through exercises like the Crocodile River exercise, in which employees have to cooperate in teams in order to get all of their members across an imaginary "river" without anyone falling off a carefully constructed bridge. The spirit is maintained through a wide range of on-the-job practices, from the extensive recognition of employee birthdays and anniversaries to a company-wide custom of helping each other out when needed regardless of job description.

FIGURE 2–6
Relationship between Measures of Employee Satisfaction and Office Profitability, American Express Travel Services

Comparison of Top and Bottom 10% of American Express Business Travel Offices, Ranked by Return on Sales

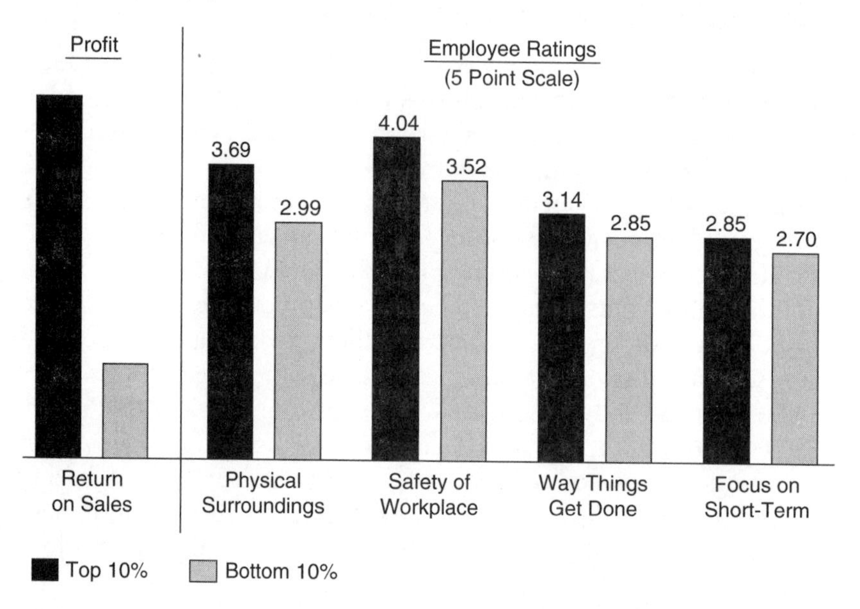

Source: Internal study, American Express Travel Services, 1995. Although profit figures have been deleted, relative profit is indicated by the height of the bars.

COMPREHENSIVELY RELATING LINKS IN THE CHAIN

A number of organizations are beginning to measure relationships between individual links in the service profit chain. We have listed several of those with which we are most familiar, along with the relationships observed in each, in Figure 2–7. For example, Banc One's operating divisions demonstrate a direct relationship between customer loyalty, measured by the "depth" of a relationship, the number of banking services that a customer utilizes, and profitability. This has led the bank to take action to encourage existing customers to further extend the number of the bank's services that they utilize. Waste Management has discovered recently that its operating divisions with the highest customer satisfaction measures also ranked highest on employee satisfaction and were 65 percent more profitable than divisions with the lowest customer and employee satisfaction scores.[12] And the management of Chick-Fil-A, a chain of restaurants operating in the Southeastern United States, determined several years ago that 78 percent of its

FIGURE 2–7
Documented Relationships between Elements of the Service Profit Chain, Selected Firms

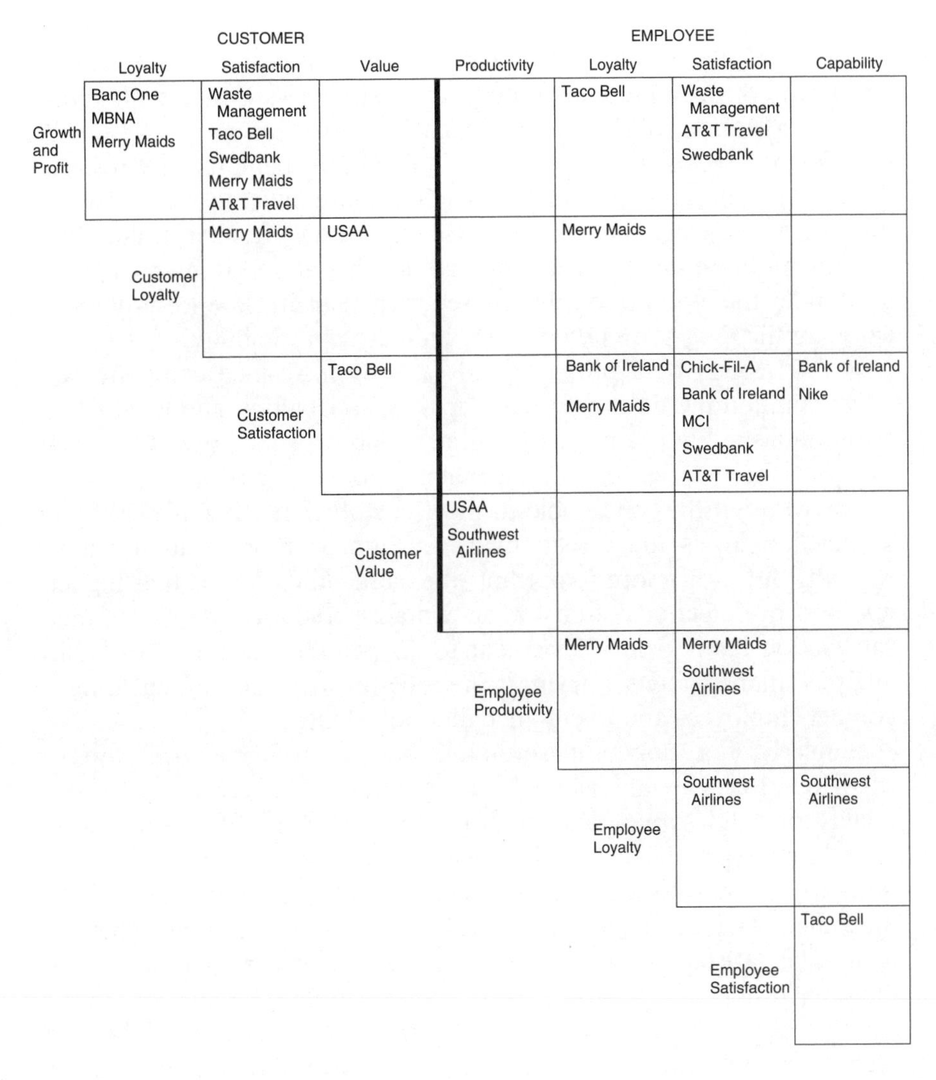

restaurants with customer satisfaction higher than the chain average also had team member (employee) satisfaction higher than the chain average.[13]

While the firms noted in Figure 2–7 are at the forefront of this effort, as yet only a few firms have related the links in truly comprehensive ways. Those who have done so have discovered several particularly strong and significant relationships between: (1) customer loyalty and company growth and profitability, (2) employee and customer satisfaction, and (3) employee satisfaction and capability. They are beginning to lead to comprehensive strategies for achieving lasting competitive advantage.

For example, a recent study of the operating divisions of a Western European Money Center Bank yielded the data in Figure 2–8. It shows strong and direct relationships between customer satisfaction and employee perceptions of their service capability, their job satisfaction, and their intent to remain on the job.[14] As a result, the bank has taken steps to develop continuing measures of each of these indicators and reward managers who can achieve improvements not only in profitability, but also in employee satisfaction, employee loyalty, and customer satisfaction under the assumption that these latter measures are leading indicators of the long-term potential for increased profitability.

A 1991 study by a property and casualty insurance company not only identified the links between employee satisfaction and loyalty but also established that a primary source of job satisfaction was the service workers' perceptions of their ability to meet customer needs.[15] Those who felt they were able to meet customer needs registered job satisfaction levels more than twice as high as those who felt they weren't. But even more important, the same study found that higher numbers of defections of customer-contact personnel drove customer satisfaction levels from 75 percent to 55 percent. As a result of this analysis, management is trying to reduce turnover among customer-contact employees and to enhance their job skills.

Similarly, in a study of its seven telephone customer service centers, MCI found clear relationships between employees' perceptions of the quality of MCI service and employee satisfaction.[16] The study also linked employee satisfaction directly to customer satisfaction and intentions to continue to use MCI services. Identifying these relationships motivated MCI's management to probe deeper and determine what affected job satisfaction at the service centers. The factors they uncovered, in order of importance, were satisfaction with the job itself, training, pay, advancement fairness, treatment with respect and dignity, teamwork, and the company's interest in employees' well-being. Armed with this information, MCI's management began examining its policies concerning those items valued most by employees at its service centers. And it has incorporated information about its service capabilities into training and communication efforts as well as television advertising.

Few organizations have made a more comprehensive effort to measure relationships in the service profit chain and fashion a strategy around them than the fast food company Taco Bell, a subsidiary of PepsiCo.[17] Taco Bell's management tracks sales daily by unit, market

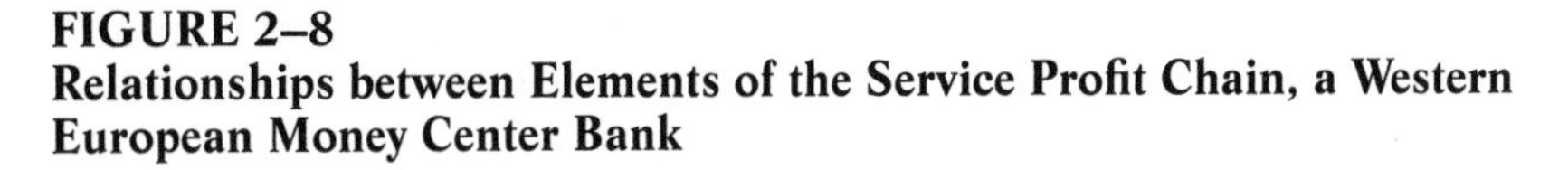

FIGURE 2–8
Relationships between Elements of the Service Profit Chain, a Western European Money Center Bank

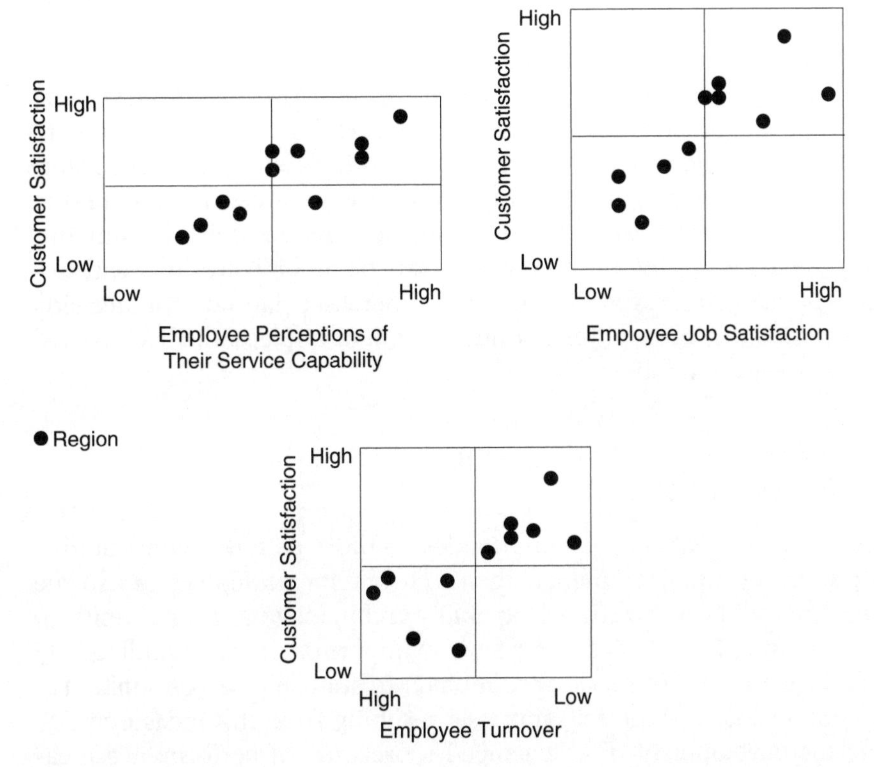

Source: Reported in Jeffrey J. Zornitsky, "Frontline Customer Capability: Measuring and Managing Customer Capability for Competitive Advantage," presented at a meeting of The Conference Board, February 14, 1995.

manager, zone, and country. By integrating this information with the results of exit interviews that Taco Bell conducts with 800,000 customers annually, management has found that stores in the top quadrant of customer satisfaction ratings outperform the other stores on all measures. As a result, Taco Bell has linked some of the compensation of restaurant general managers in company-owned stores to customer satisfaction, realizing a subsequent increase in both customer satisfaction ratings and profits.

However, Taco Bell's efforts haven't stopped there. By examining employee turnover records for individual restaurants, its management discovered that the 20 percent of the stores with the lowest turnover rates enjoyed double the sales and 55 percent higher profits than the 20 percent of restaurants with the highest employee turnover rates. As a result of this self-examination, Taco Bell has instituted financial and other incentives in order to reverse the "cycle of failure" that is associated with poor employee selection, subpar training, low pay, and high turnover.[18]

In addition, Taco Bell monitors internal quality through a network of 800 telephone numbers created to answer employees' questions, field their complaints, remedy situations, and alert top-level management to potential trouble spots. It also conducts periodic employee roundtable meetings, interviews, and a comprehensive companywide survey every two years in order to measure satisfaction. As a result of all of this work, Taco Bell's focus on employee satisfaction involves a new selection process, improved skill building, increased latitude for decision making on the job, and further automation of unpleasant "back room" food preparation jobs.

IMPLICATIONS OF THE SERVICE PROFIT CHAIN FOR MANAGEMENT

The service profit chain itself provides no more than the barest outline for a prescription for management. How then do managers use the chain to build organizational capability and manage operating units on a continuing basis? It requires several important steps, including: (1) the measurement of service profit chain relationships across units, (2) communication of the self-appraisal resulting from this measurement, (3) the development of a "balanced scorecard" of performance measures, (4) the design of efforts to help managers improve service profit chain performance, (5) the development of recognition and rewards tied to established measures, (6) widespread communication of service profit chain results at the operating unit level, and (7) the active encouragement of internal "best practice" information exchange.

Measuring across Operating Units

Many service organizations are distinguished by the large number of operating units central to their businesses. The data shown in Figure 2–8 is typical of the kind of data that can be plotted for multiunit operations. It is deceptively simple in appearance. But it requires an organized effort to reach definitions that provide measures that are credible to the managers who will be using them.

For example, customer loyalty can be measured in terms of the percentage of customers purchasing from an organization from one year or one month to the next, depending on the purchase cycle for the service in question. Or it can be measured in terms of the amount of purchases that each customer makes from the organization. Or for some businesses, particularly banking, it can be measured in terms of the number of services or products purchased from the organization. For example, at Banc One, the seventh largest banking organization in the United States, with a return on assets that typically is about twice the national average, customer loyalty is measured in terms of "depth of relationship," the number of available related financial services, such as checking, lending, and safe deposit, actually used by customers.

Consistency is at least as important as the actual questions asked of customers. Some of Banc One's operating units formerly conducted their own customer satisfaction surveys. Today the surveys have been centralized, made mandatory, and are administered by mail on a quarterly basis to around 125,000 customers. When combined with periodic measurement, the surveys provide highly relevant trend information that informs the managerial decision-making process.

Employee loyalty is a straightforward piece of information to compile. But it requires sorting out voluntary from involuntary employee departures under the assumption that the latter is a primary measure of hiring errors while the former denotes the relative attractiveness of jobs, including compensation, offered by two competing employers. Both are important pieces of information for evaluating the work of a manager at the operating unit level.

Employee satisfaction is usually obtained through direct periodic surveys. Again, because factors contributing to satisfaction may not be good indicators of employee loyalty, and because employees are not likely to provide reliable information about their intentions to stay on the job, it is important to measure sources of satisfaction to enable management to develop predictors of employee loyalty.

Communicating Results of the Self-Appraisal

Once service profit chain relationships are established for operating units, plots such as those shown in Figure 2–8 can be widely distributed among operating managers in order to provide credibility for the measures, their relationships, and the importance of establishing performance measures based on their continued monitoring.

Developing a "Balanced Scorecard"

Robert Kaplan and David Norton argue, based on their research, that performance measurement on strictly financial outcomes places too much emphasis on outcomes of past decisions and fails to identify and reward outcomes that contribute to future financial performance.[19]

They recommend, instead, a "balanced scorecard" that measures such nonfinancial outcomes as human resource effectiveness, innovation, and customer satisfaction or loyalty as well as financial outcomes.

The service profit chain represents an example of a "balanced scorecard" for a service organization, although it has to be adjusted to fit the needs of each industry and organization.

In order to insure high credibility for the scorecard, it is important that operating managers be involved in its development. At Banc One, for example, an effort is being made to establish the credibility for various measures of customer loyalty to be factored eventually into the organization's widely known Management Information and Control System (MICS), a comprehensive set of financial measures by which the managers of more than seventy banking organizations operated by Banc One are compared monthly.[20] It is a process that required more than a year of testing and validation.

Designing Efforts to Enhance Performance

Once a balanced scorecard of measures is agreed upon, initiatives to help managers improve performance on each can appropriately begin. This may involve a substantial amount of training centered around the data itself as well as ways of affecting outcomes. It may involve improved human resource management, the redesign of processes, reorganization, the development of new technologies, or the implementation of new policies, all of which are the subject of much of the rest of this book.

Tying Recognition and Rewards to Measures

Incentives tied to these measures are being increasingly implemented, but only after many other stages in the process of implementing initiatives on the basis of the service profit chain are accomplished. In some organizations, managers have been given the option of informing senior management when they are ready to be rewarded in this manner. This helps insure "buy in" from operating managers at the appropriate time.

Communicating Results

Service profit chain outcomes for individual operating units may or may not be disseminated to all units, depending on the culture of the organization. Increasingly, though, an open style of management being adopted by many organizations argues for it. For example, at Banc One, the monthly measures from the Management Information and Control System (MICS) are distributed for all operating managers to all other managers. This provides the basis for a system of comparing results that the bank's management calls "Compare and Share." It triggers an internal "best practice" exchange that results from the full acceptance of the system by those whose performances are being measured.

Encouraging Internal "Best Practice" Exchanges

According to John B. McCoy, CEO of Banc One, he rarely has to phone an operating unit manager (one of more than seventy individual subsidiary bank presidents) to inquire about subpar performance, as indicated on MICS measures. After one or two such calls that go something like "I don't know how to tell you to run your bank, but you might want to check with so-and-so, whose numbers seem to indicate that her bank is doing pretty well on [a particular measure]," operating managers get the idea that they should initiate their own call before the CEO rings them up.[21]

As a result, Banc One purposely budgets relatively high travel and communication costs to encourage operating unit heads to talk frequently to discuss ways of improving their performances. It's this process of continuous improvement through internal "best practice" comparisons that utilizes the full competitive advantage of a large organization with multiple operating sites.

QUESTIONS FOR MANAGEMENT

What we know and believe about the service profit chain is one thing. How they apply to a specific situation, business, or organization is another. With this in mind, it is important to consider the following questions:

1. To what extent do the relationships embodied in the service profit chain make intuitive sense for your business?
2. How many of the links in the chain does your firm already measure?
3. Is the resulting information used to mobilize management action? If so, how? If not, why?
4. How will you either begin to measure or coordinate those measures already being collected differently than in the past, given the potential positive impact on profit and growth to be obtained from effective service profit chain management?

GETTING ON WITH THE JOB: AN IMPORTANT CAVEAT

Soon after sketching out the elements of the service profit chain several years ago,[22] we were first attracted to the fragments of experience that suggested that the concept was not only intuitively acceptable but could be substantiated by fact derived from practice. Since then we have set about to explore its applicability more extensively. In the process, we have come to understand how complex relationships in the chain really are and how they can be misapplied.

As a result, this book is not just about ways of achieving outstanding performance on output measures that count, those highlighted in the service profit chain. It poses and seeks to address what we know about questions such as: For which customers, employees, and processes is service profit chain management most useful? How is it achieved under various conditions? And what challenges await those who attempt to develop the measures of output so important to the management by fact implied by service profit chain management?

One thing our explorations have demonstrated is that outstanding service organizations don't spend much time setting profit goals or obsessing about market share, the management mantra of the '70s and '80s. Instead, they focus on the things that drive profitability as well as things that drive the things that drive profitability. They start with customer loyalty and work their way back into the profit chain through customer satisfaction; service value; and employee productivity, loyalty, satisfaction, and capability.

Relating all the links in the service profit chain, or even just those most important for a particular organization, may seem to be a tall order. But profitability depends on measuring and managing for just a few central results. One of the most important of these is what we call the value equation, a "customer's eye" view of a service that determines its long-run profit potential. We turn to it next.

3

Managing by the Customer Value Equation

What happened to you the last time that you or an acquaintance had a minor collision with another automobile that resulted in a bent fender but no injuries? If your experience was like some of ours, you had to get information from the driver of the other automobile so that both of you could initiate a process involving your respective auto casualty insurance companies. Upon contacting your insurance agent, you may have been informed that you would have to obtain two or three estimates of the cost to repair the damage. After getting approval to proceed with repairs, you then probably had to take your car to the garage, arranging your own transportation back home or to work. If you were fortunate, the work was done properly when you returned to the auto body shop to pick up your auto. If you were one of the unfortunate many, a final resolution of the problem may have required several visits to the auto body shop. In total, you may have spent several days and endured a certain amount of anguish in resolving the situation. And for that, you actually paid the insurance company an annual premium for your policy, even though the value of your time spent resolving the issue was greater than the amount of cost incurred by the insurance company in repairing your car. In terms of service value delivered by the insurance company, the insurance company should have paid you to carry its insurance policy.

In fact, the entire casualty insurance industry has designed its services over the years to provide little value to policyholders for all but catastrophic loss claims. That's why organizations like USAA (United Services Automobile Association), a company serving military officers and their families (called "members"), elicits such universally enthusiastic claims of outstanding service from its members by literally changing every element of the customer value equation. What do we mean by the customer value equation?

THE CUSTOMER VALUE EQUATION

The value equation, viewed from the perspective of the customer, very simply is:

$$\text{Value} = \frac{\text{Results Produced for the Customer} + \text{Process Quality}}{\text{Price to the Customer} + \text{Costs of Acquiring the Service}}$$

Results Produced for Customers

As we emphasized earlier, customers buy results, not products or services. Anyone who disputes this should ask how much people enjoy going to their local service station to fill up the gas tank on their automobile. If there were any way to avoid it, most people would. They regard it as a necessary evil. But the result, convenient transportation, is worth the annoyance. The desired result for the casualty insurance policyholder is restoration of an auto or other possession to its original condition with as little effort and cost as possible. The value attached to results, of course, varies with the size of the service task and its importance for the customer.

Process Quality

The way in which a service is delivered is often as important as results delivered to the recipient. For example, several studies have shown that up to 80 percent of all medical malpractice legal suits involve no negligence associated with adverse patient experiences. In one study, more than half the claims didn't even involve patient injury or adverse effects. One explanation for this wide gap between patient perception and fact is that the patient or loved ones are somehow angered by the way in which the medical service is delivered, whether or nor the outcome is injurious.[1]

While most of us don't care how a manufactured product is made, we are aware of process quality that we can observe in the purchase of a service. According to work by Parasuraman, Zeithaml, and Berry, five universal dimensions of service process quality can be identified.[2] They are:

1. Dependability (Did the service provider do what was promised?)
2. Responsiveness (Was the service provided in a timely manner?)
3. Authority (Did the service provider elicit a feeling of confidence in the customer during the service delivery process?)
4. Empathy (Was the service provider able to take the customer's point of view?)
5. Tangible evidence (Was evidence left that the service was indeed performed?)

Other research has established that customers' views of service process quality depend primarily on the relationship between what was actually delivered (and in what manner) in relation to what was expected by the customer.[3] This has the following relatively profound implications for service providers. It suggests that:

1. Service quality is relative, not absolute.
2. It is determined by the customer, not by the service provider.
3. It varies from one customer to another.
4. Service quality can be enhanced both by meeting or exceeding customers' expectations or taking steps to control such expectations.

This knowledge has given rise to many continuous quality improvement initiatives in a wide range of service organizations. In some cases, they have been implemented at the risk of ignoring the importance of results to customers. The Florida Power & Light Company found this out when, in its quest for improved service process quality that led to its becoming the first non-Japanese company to win the coveted W. Edwards Deming prize for quality awarded each year by the Japanese government, the company's management neglected to plan for enough capacity to meet the peak summer season needs for power to run air-conditioning units in South Florida. As a result, its customers experienced unexpected brownouts during the summer following its winning of the prize. Process quality improvement efforts are no substitute for results.

Price and Acquisition Costs

Many customers and service providers measure their costs only in terms of price. But the costs of acquiring a service may, in some cases, outweigh price. Convenience costs something and it has a value to many customers. Marketing theorists for years have defined convenience in terms of such things as "place, time, and form utility." The value of convenience will vary among customers, requiring that a service provider remain sensitive to the needs of various customers.

Relationships between price and service acquisition (or access) costs have important implications for service providers. Providers finding ways to lower acquisition costs for customers often can charge higher prices for their services, particularly if they can convince customers of the value of such efforts.

Customer Value Equation Relationships

The customer value equation helps put into perspective each of its elements. For example, the rush to service process quality or continuous quality improvement initiatives that we have witnessed over the past decade is important. But these initiatives represent only one element in the value equation, an element that has to be evaluated in the context of results, price, and service access costs to the customer.

MANAGING BY THE CUSTOMER VALUE EQUATION: WHAT IT REQUIRES

All of this suggests that service value to most or all customers can be enhanced by increasing either results delivered or process quality, or both, while reducing either prices or service acquisition costs, or both. This often is more complex than it sounds. But it is a way of life in outstanding service organizations. Consider, for example, the way in which USAA has redesigned its accident claims process procedures to enhance customer value.

USAA

Policyholders maintain contact with USAA only by telephone, mail, or other media. The company has geared its systems to provide superior access through these means. At USAA, a call to the company's claims processing department at its San Antonio, Texas headquarters by a policyholder (called a member) experiencing an auto accident elicits a simple response and two alternatives for the member.[4] The member is given information about one or two of USAA's "service partners" in the vicinity of the member's community where the automobile might be repaired with all payments handled directly by USAA, including any costs of a replacement rental auto during the repair period. Such agreements between USAA and "service partners" often yield savings of perhaps two-thirds of the time otherwise required of a USAA policyholder. A second alternative offered to the member is the simple payment of a check of an agreed amount by USAA to the member, who then is free to have the auto repaired anywhere.

Consider the impact that these policies have on the value equation. Results are achieved by the policyholder in a timely manner. Given the control that USAA exerts over its "service partners," who are motivated to deliver good service because of the volume of business sent to them, the results experienced by policyholders often are better than they could obtain elsewhere.

USAA has concentrated a great deal of effort on the improvement of service process quality. Those processing claims calls often are capable of handling a claim without handing off the caller to a second person. They are supported by the latest technology that enables them to call up needed information quickly in order to make rapid recommendations and decisions. And they are selected on the basis of customer-friendly attitudes as well as their skills, and continually trained to improve both. As a result, USAA policyholders, who are able to transact their entire claim with one relatively painless telephone call, praise the company's service process quality.

Because of its legendary service to a so-called "affinity group" of military officers and their families in which word-of-mouth advertising is so important, USAA does not need to employ expensive sales agents. This enables it to achieve some of the lowest administrative costs in the industry while providing very low service acquisition costs. Instead of charging more for its services, which it could do, judging from the endorsements from its policyholders, USAA is actually able to charge up to 20 percent less than its competitors.

Thus, USAA has changed every element of the service value equation. In fact, the company is managed to deliver value, with managers asking repeatedly how an action will affect value for the customer. This single-minded concentration on value characterizes all great service organizations, but it doesn't have to result in the lowest prices, because value doesn't mean just price in the customer's mind. For example, British Airways, the airline that has been winning many kudos for its international service, does not seek to charge the lowest prices. But it does endeavor to provide high value for all of its customers, from economy to first class.

British Airways

At the time that Sir Colin Marshall became the chief executive of British Airways in 1983, the airline was the butt of scorn and an unusual bevy of jokes even from its English clientele. In its former incarnation as the combination of British European Airways and British Overseas Airlines Corporation, the airline had compiled a miserable record of service. Based on his previous experience with Avis, Hertz, and other service organizations, Marshall began to mobilize his organization to develop a spirit that communicated to its passengers that the people of British Airways cared about them and were doing something about their concerns.[5]

Given its relatively high costs, a low-price route to high value was not open to the airline. Instead, efforts had to be made to enhance the results provided to passengers, the quality with which they were served, and access of passengers to the airline's personnel before, during, and after their respective flights. This effort took on a number of dimensions, among them a massive retraining program, a reorganization of British Airways personnel into teams with expanded frontline latitude and responsibility, the redesign of processes, and a revamped information system to handle communications, including complaints, with BA customers.

The retraining program, "Putting People First," was carried out in several waves, each concentrating on a particular topic such as customer value, building customer loyalty, and service recovery. It resulted from a benchmarking effort in which British Airways personnel visited world-class performers of various processes such as order entry, complaint resolution, and even materials handling in a number of industries throughout the world.

As a result of both the benchmarking and retraining initiatives, frontline teams of employees were given the responsibility of working with internal consultants to rethink the way they carried out their responsibilities. Thus, teams of employees redesigned and implemented new check-in procedures for portions of the airline's major facility at Heathrow Airport outside London. Others rethought the baggage handling process. Still others spent time rethinking nearly everything that was done at the airline.

The objective was to do a better job of providing the results expected by passengers, especially those traveling at higher fares. Even though factors beyond the airline's control sometimes made it impossible to provide on-time arrival, the primary need of business travelers, efforts were made to, among other things, redesign boarding procedures to insure on-time departures, insure the availability of gates upon arrival, and manage expectations by keeping passengers informed of the status of flights at all times.

Further, surveys and focus group interviews were used to determine other service features that would add value to business travelers' experiences. Among these, for example, was the expressed need among business travelers for facilities for showering and changing after long-distance flights, especially night flights across the Atlantic. As a result, the airline constructed such facilities at its London Heathrow Terminal. These facilities contributed to the ultimate result for this segment of British Airways travelers, business success. Their value in the eyes of passengers far outweighed the cost to British Airways of providing them.

Service process quality improvement was the focus of both the reorganization into teams of British Airways employees and the extensive training that was provided to the entire organization. In these seminars, an effort was made to link the value of customer loyalty to the organization's profitability and the well-being of its employees. An emphasis was placed on the desirability, in terms of job satisfaction, of dealing with satisfied as opposed to dissatisfied passengers. And methods were introduced whereby employees might take steps to improve their interactions with customers, including keeping them informed, delivering on promises, acting with authority, taking the customer's point of view when possible, and actually providing some kind of tangible evidence of good service, including immediate recompense for bad service.

Employees staffing a new service called Careline were supported in their efforts to deal with passenger complaints and comments by a new information system called CARESS, which enabled them to recall, on demand and in one place, all of the correspondence with a single passenger that had been scanned into the system upon receipt. In addition to information, customer service representatives were given increased latitude to determine the expectations for restitution among passengers experiencing poor service and to respond to those expectations with on-the-spot "compensation" within liberal limits. Such limits were justified in view of the fact that dissatisfied customers were estimated to represent about 400 million pounds sterling (about $600 million at the time) in annual revenue. We'll examine this system of obtaining and addressing customer complaints in greater detail in Chapter 10.

The airline also took steps to improve avenues of access for passengers to its ticket agents, service representatives, cabin attendants, and others. Included in these efforts were additional phone lines, additional ticket agents for particularly busy airline sales offices, and more visible means of filing complaints, including even the testing of a video studio in which passengers could record comments upon deplaning from their flights arriving in London. The overall objective was to make the airline easier to deal with.

As a result of these and other efforts, nearly every operating statistic improved for the airline. Customer satisfaction levels increased. The proportion of employees handling customer complaints indicating high job satisfaction increased from the low teens to 69 percent. Revenues increased by 48 percent between fiscal years ending in 1992 and 1996, much faster than revenue increases for all European airlines. But most important, the market value of the airline nearly tripled during this time period. Clearly, "Putting People First" and many other related efforts proved to be an effective way to enhance the value equation for British Airways' passengers, even though the airline's fares actually increased, especially for its valued business-class passengers, during this period of time.

Requirements of Those Who Manage by the Customer Value Equation

Demands are exerted on those who manage by the customer value equation. It's these demands and efforts to meet them that result in service excellence. They begin with the imperative of understanding customer needs.

Understanding Customer Needs. Customer needs can be determined by more traditional forms of marketing research, asking customers. They can be determined by a careful reading of customer concerns, requiring that efforts be made to encourage customers to interact frequently with a service-providing organization. Or they can be determined by actually involving customers in the design of services and ways in which they are delivered.

At USAA, all three types of efforts are employed. But the company has a real advantage over many other organizations seeking to understand customer needs. Nearly every senior executive at USAA is a former military officer. Therefore, nearly all are USAA policyholders and members, and thus directly in tune with members' needs.

In order to determine passengers' needs, British Airways, on the other hand, has given primary emphasis to more traditional forms of marketing research, including both on-board surveys and small focus groups of passengers recruited for the purpose. Of equal importance has been a careful reading of the complaints that passengers are encouraged to register with the airline.

Determining Ways in Which Needs Influence Attitudes toward the Value Equation. A special set of needs characterizes nearly all of USAA's members. As military officers, they travel a great deal and are reassigned from one location to another periodically. As a result, they find it difficult to interact with their insurance company through traditional agents on a face-to-face basis. They find telephone access much more convenient and hardly less personal than interactions with a different agent (representing traditionally run insurance companies) with each successive move. Further, when moving on short notice under military orders, time is of the essence in rearranging insurance needs for many military officers. "Results" for them translates into the need for transactions with one phone call of limited length.

At British Airways, customer satisfaction levels have been correlated with perceptions of more detailed features of the airline's services in order to assess the impact of various elements of the value equation on overall customer satisfaction. Of perhaps even greater importance, the airline's customer service personnel carefully record the complaints registered by passengers along with potential root causes, providing a basis for establishing priorities for corrective action.

Establishing a Return on Value-enhancing Investments. Several efforts are underway to develop methods for determining how best to invest in service improvements that enhance the value equation. Much of this work is associated with service quality improvement. Recent research by Rust and others[6] has concentrated on methods for establishing returns, expressed in terms of increased profits resulting from reduced customer defections, on investments in various types of actions to enhance value. This involves collecting data from customers about levels of satisfaction, intent to repurchase a service, and specific ratings of various aspects of a service resulting from the management of identifiable processes. On the basis of this information, possible opportunities for service improvement are identified, providing the basis for a limited testing of the service improvement at an operating site. Given the impact of varying levels of expenditure and service improvement on customers' loyalty rates, a return on each level of investment can be calculated.

For example, data from passengers complaining to British Airways' Customer Relations group have been analyzed in combination with expressions of intent to fly again with British Airways to create a ranking of values associated with correcting various service problems, as shown in Figure 3–1. Thus, 11.5 percent of all complaints received had to do either with seat allocation or overbooking, a problem that led 37.5 percent of those complaining to indicate that they would not fly British Airways again. When extended to the entire group of about one-third of British Airways passengers expressing some kind of discontent, this produced an estimate of more than eight million pounds sterling in revenues that would be lost if the problem were not to be fixed. In all, the top ten complaints expressed by passengers represented a revenue opportunity of more than twenty-six million pounds sterling at the time of the study, as shown in Figure 3–1. Over time, as customer satisfaction levels rose, British Airways found that its cus-

FIGURE 3–1
Potential Revenue Enhancement from Correcting Service Problems, British Airways

The way our customers see it and what that means financially	% of Complainants Experiencing the Problem	And % of These Who Will Not Repurchase	REVENUE LOST
SEATING ALLOCATION/ OVERBOOKING Seat allocation	11.5%	37.5%	£8,187,750
OPERATIONAL DISRUPTIONS Delays	7.0	23.9	£3,172,105
BAGGAGE Baggage mishandled	4.0	29.8	£2,260,101
CATERING Food quality	3.4	33.0	£2,127,377
OPERATIONAL DISRUPTIONS Cancellations/Consolidation	4.2	24.4	£1,943,080
SEATING ALLOCATION/ OVERBOOKING Downgrading/Denied boarding	4.4	22.4	£1,868,755
CABIN ENVIRONMENT Smoking	3.1	31.0	£1,822,112
SALES EXPERIENCE Ticketing/Booking	3.7	24.4	£1,711,761
OPERATIONAL DISRUPTIONS Disruption services	3.7	23.7	£1,662,653
CATERING Food policy/Menu composition	2.7	28.9	£1,479,494
TOTAL/AVERAGE	**48.0%**	**29.0%**	**£26,224,187**

Norman Klein and W. Earl Sasser, Jr., British Airways: Using Information Systems to Better Serve the Customer, Case No. 395-065. Boston: Harvard Business School 1994, p. 15.

tomer relations staff members were actually awarding 8 percent less in monetary compensation to customers.

With this kind of information, proposals for improving offerings to passengers, the manner in which service is provided, and new ways of providing customer access to the company and its people can be calibrated in such a way that returns on investments can be estimated. As a result, BA research estimated that for every pound spent on customer retention efforts, the Airline was netting two pounds in revenue.

Developing Different Value Packages for Various Market Segments. Purchasers of insurance not only have different levels of tolerance for risk but also have very different accident experiences. Thus, insurers not only scale their rates on the basis of how accident-prone a policyholder might be (based on both demographic profile and personal experience), they also offer varying levels of "deductibles" that determine the amount of the total risk associated with any one accident to be shouldered by the policyholder. The greater the risk assumed by the policyholder, the lower the premium (price) for the policy. For those applicants with good safety records, it is almost always more beneficial for them to buy a package that allows them to assume higher levels of risk (through higher "deductibles").

Enlightened insurers like USAA train their service representatives to encourage policy applicants to buy the policy that is right for them, not the policy that represents the greatest margin to the company. Unlike competing insurers selling through brokers, USAA does not pay its representatives on the basis of how much or what kind of insurance they sell. As a result, service representatives can develop a great deal of empathy for policy applicants. Because these applicants are military officers or family members and generally have good safety records resulting from their character and training, USAA's service representatives often can help applicants save money on their premiums, further enhancing the value equation for them.

Another casualty insurer, the Progressive Corporation, became one of the most successful casualty insurers by pursuing a totally different strategy of providing a large array of so-called nonstandard insurance policies for high-risk applicants. The strategy was centered around providing insurance to people who owned and operated motorcycles or who had been arrested for drunken driving, people who often could not obtain insurance at any price from other insurers.[7]

Progressive's competitors for years had grouped all of these potential applicants into one or a very small number of "risk pools," groups of applicants with similar behavior patterns. As a result, some low-risk applicants were thrown together with high-risk applicants. Progressive's strategy was based on the careful analysis of the behavior of applicants in a large number of "risk pools," individuals with greatly different behavior patterns. As a result, it found that not all motorcycle owners or drivers previously cited for drunkenness represented high risks. For example, those with children under the age of twelve had distinctly lower accident rates than others. This enabled Progressive to provide insurance to some applicants thought by others to have high-risk profiles, applicants who could not get insurance elsewhere. Even though the rates charged by Progressive for this insurance were substantially above those for drivers posing average risks, the fact that insurance was available at any price created an attractive value package for policy applicants. Given actual behavior patterns that differed from those assumed from their profiles by other insurance providers, these applicants represented high-margin business for Progressive.

Although it is said that the real profits in the airline business are made on those who ride in the front of the plane, in either first or business class, other passengers help pay the vast overhead of an airline operation. Thus, the typical airline develops value packages for both business and pleasure travelers with greatly different needs.

Problems arise, however, when passengers have a chance to compare various value packages, typically while traveling in adjacent seats. Depending on such things as the availability of travel packages, the willingness and ability of passengers to reserve in advance, and the duration of trips, one passenger may be paying twice the fare of another in the same class. While this raises questions of fairness, even among experienced travelers, the key to such differences lies in the value packages designed for different needs. Often questions of fairness arise when two packages being compared have been designed improperly and do not reflect the combination of results, process quality, acquisition costs, and price associated with two sets of passenger needs.

Developing a Single-minded Emphasis on Value. The 1990s have been termed the decade when business competitors discovered value. This is often assumed incorrectly to be synonymous with a swing to low prices. And indeed many of the great success stories of recent years are centered around organizations offering low prices, organizations such as mass merchandiser Wal-Mart and Southwest Airlines. But there are just as many shoppers and travelers who will claim that the value they receive from Nordstrom, an upscale fashion department store, and American Airlines (charging substantially higher fares than Southwest Airlines between two points) is high as well.

The fact of the matter is that leadership of all four of these organizations devotes substantial attention to the value equation, making sure than any initiative undertaken by their organizations enhances value for the particular subset of customers that patronizes them. Thus, at Wal-Mart, value may represent a senior citizen greeting customers at the door along with everyday low prices. For the Nordstrom customer, it represents a grand piano being played in the foyer along with the most complete merchandise selections in town.

In fact, all organizations that have been successful in sustaining service breakthroughs over time have developed a widespread organizational capability for assessing proposed actions in the context of the customer value equation.

Ultimately Deciding Whether Value Can Be Provided at a Profit. The elements of the value equation may offer so little margin for error that they represent little opportunity for making a profit. In order to determine whether value can be delivered at a profit, it is necessary to tie the value equation to the strategic service vision.

LINKING THE STRATEGIC SERVICE VISION AND SERVICE PROFIT CHAIN

Earlier we pointed out that the primary objective in designing an operating strategy was the degree to which value to customers was leveraged over costs to the service provider. It's this "margin" between value and cost that represents a profit opportunity to the provider. Outstanding services are designed around operating strategies that enhance customer value while reducing operating costs. It can be done. We've seen it time after time. USAA once again illustrates this notion.

The "service partners" (estimators and auto repair shops) that USAA has organized to provide repair services in a dependable manner to the company's policyholders and at reasonable prices (costs) to USAA help the insurer leverage value over cost. Cost savings to USAA result in part from the fact that "service partners" do not require constant policing. Repair estimates and invoices can be handled quickly through standard procedures developed between the company and its partners. By striving to maintain relationships over time with these "partners," USAA enhances its services while controlling its costs.

At the same time, these "service partners" create value for policyholders by saving them time, speeding payment, getting the repairs done right, and being available at more locations than USAA could provide itself.

Carrying the concept of customer value further, USAA takes advantage of the fact that its clientele actually places a higher value on telephone access to the company than it does on face-to-face contact with company representatives. This has enabled the company to concentrate on making itself easy to reach and deal with by telephone and other media, media that all are less expensive than providing field sales and service representatives. For example, claims processing procedures have been redesigned to increase the probability that one phone conversation with one claims service representative will be enough to file a claim. This has actually resulted in increased productivity for claims service representatives. Thus, value is enhanced at lower cost to the company, further increasing the profit potential, or in the case of USAA, producing still higher "dividends" (effectively lower rates) to its "members," who under the mutual insurance form of organization actually own the company.

This example suggests that the value equation serves as the "conceptual link" between the strategic service vision and the service profit chain, as shown in Figure 3–2. It shows that marketing, operations, and human resource management are important elements of an operating strategy that leverages value to customers over costs. They are important determinants as well of the degree to which this effort is translated into profit for the service provider and true value for customers through decisions regarding the price charged for the service as

FIGURE 3–2
The Value Equation as "Conceptual Link" between the Strategic Service Vision and Service Profit Chain

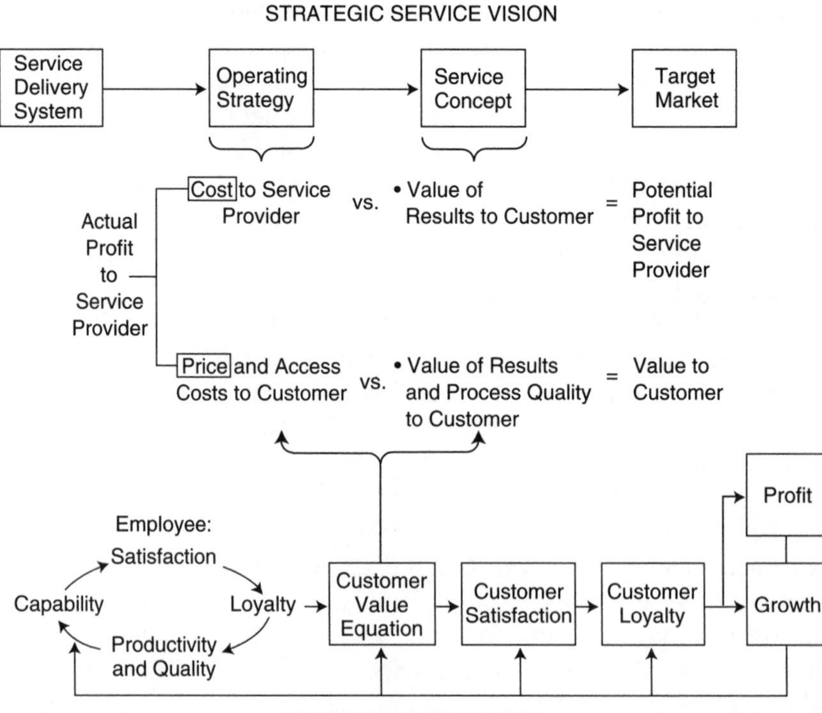

well as other components of the value equation. Because of decisions regarding results to be achieved, service process quality, and ease of access provided to the service, this need not be a zero sum game in which a $1 increase in price means $1 more profit for the service provider and $1 less for the customer. By working together, keeping in mind both strategic service vision and service profit chain concepts, both can increase profitability by expanding margin potential.

QUESTIONS FOR MANAGEMENT

Value is only one element in an operating formula for delivering breakthrough service on a sustained basis. It says little about the objectives for delivering value, although it might be assumed that the greater the value delivered to a customer, the greater the price that customer might be willing to pay, and the greater the potential margin between price and the cost of service provision. Our discussion raises several questions for management, including:

1. To what extent do your customers place emphasis on various aspects of the value equation? How do you know?
2. To what extent do needs, as reflected in the value equation, vary from one targeted customer segment to another? What's the evidence?
3. Have adequate mechanisms been put in place for tracking changing patterns of customer needs?
4. When proposals are made for new service features, are the costs weighed against the benefits, as suggested by what you know about your targeted customer groups?
5. When changes in price are contemplated, is the advisability of this action examined in the context of what targeted customers really want?
6. To what extent has customer-valued access to service been enhanced as an alternative to price reductions?

The experiences of USAA and British Airways illustrate the profit potential in matching customer needs with service offerings. Significant progress in this respect has been made by organizations that have focused their efforts on building relationships with loyal customers while shunning others. We turn next to this challenge.

Part II

Building Profit Chain Capability

4

Rethinking Marketing

Building Customer Loyalty

Intuit Corporation is a software designer and marketer whose growth in the early years was centered around a product, Quicken, designed as a user-friendly means to enable those not very familiar with computing to easily manage family finances, write checks, and perform other simple personal financial tasks with their personal computers.[1] Traditional marketing would have dictated that Intuit hire a sales force, begin a major advertising campaign, and generally plow as much money as possible into the introduction of its product. Instead, Scott Cook and Tom Proulx, Intuit's founders, concentrated on getting the product right by hiring software engineers interested in making things simple for users (not typical for the "breed") and having them conduct focus groups, observe potential customers using the product, and even follow those purchasing the software to their homes to observe them booting up the product and putting it to use. The result was software usable by even the greenest novice in as little as six minutes from the time the top was popped on an easy-to-open package (itself an innovation in the software business).

Then did Cook and Proulx haul out the heavy marketing guns? No. They next focused on a direct mail campaign in which potential users could request copies of the software, try it out, and decide whether or not to pay for it. This was much more effective than employing sales representatives. Very few satisfied customers failed to pay for the product sent them on approval. Even more important, they became salespeople by telling friends about their discovery.

Having begun the process of building demand for its product, Intuit then assembled an outstanding group of highly intelligent customer service representatives with empathy for customers and the ability to learn necessary service skills quickly, who could field phone calls from Intuit purchasers, providing them advice not only about the use of the software but also about related issues concerning personal finance. A decision was made early on to provide this service free for the life of the product, something for which other software producers at the time charged substantial fees.

Only then did Cook and Proulx give a nod to traditional marketing by hiring two sales representatives to call on software distributors to promote the product and elicit feedback. Working alongside thousands of satisfied Quicken users and "apostles" (Scott Cook's term), they proved to be quite sufficient as the company sales increased rapidly to $33 million per year by the end of the company's seventh full year of operations in 1990, primarily through invaluable word-of-mouth recommendations.

Of course, you might assume that software on which free lifetime service is provided would be very costly. You would be wrong. Quicken sells for prices ranging from $20 to $40.

How can the company make any money, you might ask? Surely it can't afford to make very many mistakes with a product that would elicit service calls, because the kind of expert and empathetic service Intuit provides is expensive. The key to understanding Intuit's success lies in its development of "new" marketing techniques typical of companies that have distanced themselves from competitors by concentrating on targeting profitable customers, realizing the full lifetime value of a customer, and managing customer loyalty in part through the development of effective listening posts.

DEFINING THE "NEW" MARKETING: ADDING THE THREE Rs TO THE FOUR Ps

Conventional marketing efforts centered around the four Ps of product, price, promotional activity, and "place" (distribution channels) have long influenced those responsible for the sale of consumer and industrial products, with the primary objective of building market share.

As we saw earlier, much of the rationale for this objective was provided by the Profit Impact of Market Share (PIMS) study, first initiated in 1972, that concluded that market share had an important direct association with profitability in the largely manufacturing enterprises for which data were collected and analyzed at that time.[2]

The resulting quest for market share has been built around philosophies such as "the customer is always right," strategies relying heavily on sales and advertising directed at broadly defined market segments, and a high degree of expertise assembled in a clearly defined function of the organization often having little to do with cross-functional activities such as customer service.

When Reichheld and Sasser tested the relationships between market share and profitability in a sample of service-producing organizations some years after the PIMS study, they found none.[3] In their search for other determinants of profitability, they discovered not only that service firms with higher levels of customer loyalty also enjoyed higher profitability in a given industry, but that loyal customers became more profitable over time. By definition, the most profitable year of a relationship with a customer was the last. This led them to focus on efforts to understand the lifetime value of a customer and the value of building customer loyalty by listening to their complaints, anticipating their defection, and understanding what motivated them to defect to competitors. It led them to emphasize that organizations seek out ways of not only retaining customers but encouraging them to buy related products and services and to provide referrals to friends of their good experiences with companies' products or services, essentially resulting in a strategy centered around the three Rs of retention, related sales, and referrals.

For these reasons, Reichheld and Sasser concluded that customer service was at least as important a function as sales in many marketing organizations. Their work provided a good deal of the basis for the service profit chain theory of management.

In short, service profit chain management is changing the face of marketing. Market share quality, defined primarily in terms of the share of loyal customers served, is becoming the primary goal instead of simply having the largest market share. To get it means abandoning the idea that customers are always right and embracing the idea that some customers are never right. It means marketing more by listening, often by providing outstanding customer service, as well as a heavy reliance on customer-to-customer referrals. It means less reliance on "telling" through costly sales and advertising. It means taking major cues for new products and services from customers, with the resulting product development process managed on a cross-functional basis. It means organizing in ways in which former marketing managers are barely distinguishable from their operating, manufacturing, and human resource counterparts. And it means taking full advantage of new electronic media that are replacing traditional channels of distribution and wreaking havoc with the four Ps.

This describes the terrain of the "new" marketing that Scott Cook, Tom Proulx, and their associates at Intuit were already practicing several years ago. It helps explain a success story built on the concept of the lifetime value of a customer.

ESTIMATING THE LIFETIME VALUE OF A CUSTOMER

The primary reason that Intuit could sell a product for $20 to $40 and expect to make money from it results from an understanding of the lifetime value of each purchaser of Quicken. The initial version of Quicken was only one of several products tied to the software. First, as with most software, updates are issued periodically to expand the capability of users. Given Intuit's close relationship with its customers through its customer service representatives, the stream of suggestions for product improvements at Intuit is so large that the company brings out an annual update of its product containing a hundred or more improvements, all for the price of the original version. But once "hooked," most Intuit users find that they can justify buying the annual update.

Using Quicken to write checks and pay bills requires special check blanks also sold by the company. In fact, the follow-on value of supplies is often much more substantial than the amount paid initially for the software. As an alternative, Intuit developed an electronic bill-paying process by linking itself to VISA. The use of this service yields Intuit a small fee for each transaction, thereby further increasing the flow of revenue.

But perhaps most important of all is what CEO Scott Cook refers to as Intuit's "apostles," those satisfied users who tell their friends and develop new users for Quicken. We said earlier that, when it reached $30 million in sales, the company had only two sales representatives; in fact, it had tens of thousands. They just weren't on the payroll.

Although Intuit has developed other software products since Quicken, including a small business version of the product called QuickBooks and various taxpayer aids such as Turbotax, its revenue and profit stream from Quicken alone has moved well beyond $100 million per year in revenue and perhaps $40 million in profit before tax through the exploitation of the three Rs of lifetime customer value, retention, related sales of old and new products, and referral.

Retention

Retention is the continuing, active relationship with a customer that yields a stream of revenue from the sale of the initial product or service. This stream of revenue becomes more and more profitable as existing customers become easier to serve with less need to spend "get acquainted" marketing effort on them.

Costs of serving existing customers decline as expectations are established and customers learn the service delivery process. This is particularly true for services in which customers participate in the process.

Retention cannot be taken for granted. Customer buying patterns may change little by little, even though customers don't bother to sever a relationship with a service supplier. This happened over time at MBNA, one of the largest credit card issuers (largely to clubs and other affinity groups) and service organizations in the United States.[4] In 1982, the company's President, Charles Cawley, assembled all of MBNA's employees to express his growing concerns about the service complaint letters he was receiving and a resolve that the company endeavor to keep every one of its cardholders going forward. Although he didn't have the data that Reichheld and Sasser would develop several years later, namely that a 5 percentage point increase in average customer retention of credit card customers (from, say, five to six years) would increase a credit card service company's profits by 75 percent, his intuition was correct.

MBNA launched several initiatives to extend customer loyalty. First and most simply and effectively, it called each cardholder who had stopped charging against the card. With one phone call, one in three cardholders immediately began using the card at or above the prelapse level.

In addition, the company started gathering feedback from defecting customers, using this information to correct service processes and develop new products. By 1990, MBNA's defection rate had fallen to one of the lowest in the industry, about half of the average for its competitors. As a result, in the eight-year period between 1982 and 1990, profits increased sixteen times and the company moved from thirty-eighth to fourth in its industry without making any acquisitions of credit card companies.

Various estimates place the cost to attract new customers at five or more times the cost to retain existing ones. And yet even today in many organizations practicing the "old" marketing, people are rewarded only for attracting new customers. This is a major factor differentiating "merely good" service organizations from those that are consolidating their service breakthroughs while building their leads in both growth and profitability over their competitors.

Related Sales of New Products and Services

It costs much less to sell new products and services to existing customers than to new customers. The explanation is clear. Sales to those you know and who know you require little marketing introduction, no new credit checks, and much less time. At Intuit, it doesn't even require a sales call. The company's follow-on sales to existing customers are achieved by direct mail or through dealers handling the company's software products.

It follows that margins on sales to existing customers should be higher, and they are. This is true even in cases where existing customers may negotiate lower prices on standard items in a supplier's line of products. At the same time, these same customers are often less price sensitive in purchasing new products. On balance, monetary margins increase from the overall relationship.[5]

In many manufacturing service organizations, keeping a customer on the books for service may yield a much greater amount of contribution over time than the initial sale itself. Thus, elevators for use in high-rise buildings are sold and installed at very little profit because of the competition to get "installations" on the books of the manufacturers' service organizations. It's in service that elevator manufacturers make their money.[6]

At Intuit, the company attempts to develop an extensive customer list through product warranties and its customer service organization, offering new products and services first to these customers in the knowledge that they will most readily purchase with the least effort and the fewest discounts on Intuit's part.

Intuit's growth is based significantly on the development of frequent updates of its basic products as well as new products and services. Owners of Quicken and other Intuit products are heavy buyers of periodic (roughly annual) software updates because they contain so many improvements. Most of these improvements result from suggestions obtained during the course of customer service calls.

Given the existence of a loyal customer base, there is a strong incentive to maximize its full potential by developing related products that appeal to it. More recently, Intuit has been among the first organizations to offer integrated processing of financial transactions by its software users utilizing the Internet. An owner of its software can combine files concerning check payments, the family budget, investments, and other financial records as well as make banking transactions and download information from credit card purchases for budgeting purposes and purchases. Its new "transaction-based" product and service line could eventually dwarf the software sales business that fostered the company's early growth. But the stream of revenue, which had reached $395 million by the end of fiscal 1995, all started with a $30 piece of software on which the company provided free lifetime customer service of outstanding quality.

Referrals

By far the greatest profit impact of efforts to retain customers and develop their satisfaction comes through the positive referrals they provide to potential customers. This is especially important for many industrial products and services as well consumer products for which potential customers have high levels of perceived risk that is best alleviated by asking a friend for advice. Of course, the reverse is true as well.

Data developed several years ago in a study for the U.S. Office of Consumer Affairs suggest that satisfied customers for consumer services in their survey were likely to tell five other people (whether or not they were potential customers). On the other hand, dissatisfied customers were likely to tell eleven other people.[7] While these figures vary greatly from one service to the next, it suggests the positive and negative leverage to be gained from developing either satisfied or dissatisfied customers, respectively.

Taken in total, the profit levels generated by customers from the three Rs over time can be conceptualized as shown in Figure 4–1. Actual data of a similar nature for several service industries are shown in Figure 4–2. It's clear from this data that relationships with customers don't turn profitable in some industries such as credit card servicing or life insurance for several years after the beginning of the relationship. Sales and bad debt costs in the first year account for much of this phenomenon in credit card servicing. In industries such as life insurance, where sales commissions on the entire contract are paid to the sales representative in the first year—creating inappropriate incentives for sales representatives to encourage policyholders to defect after several years, often before the company has a chance to profit from the relationship—this phenomenon represents a very large problem.

A customer may be worth $30 in revenue to Intuit from the initial sale of Quicken, but this increases to several hundred dollars or more in sales of the stream of follow-on products and services. Assuming that Quicken users, satisfied with both the results and the service quality that they experience, persuade just one new customer per year to become a regular user of the software, the lifetime value of an Intuit customer reaches truly substantial proportions, thousands of dollars, in the space of just a few years.

FIGURE 4–1
Why Customers Are More Profitable over Time

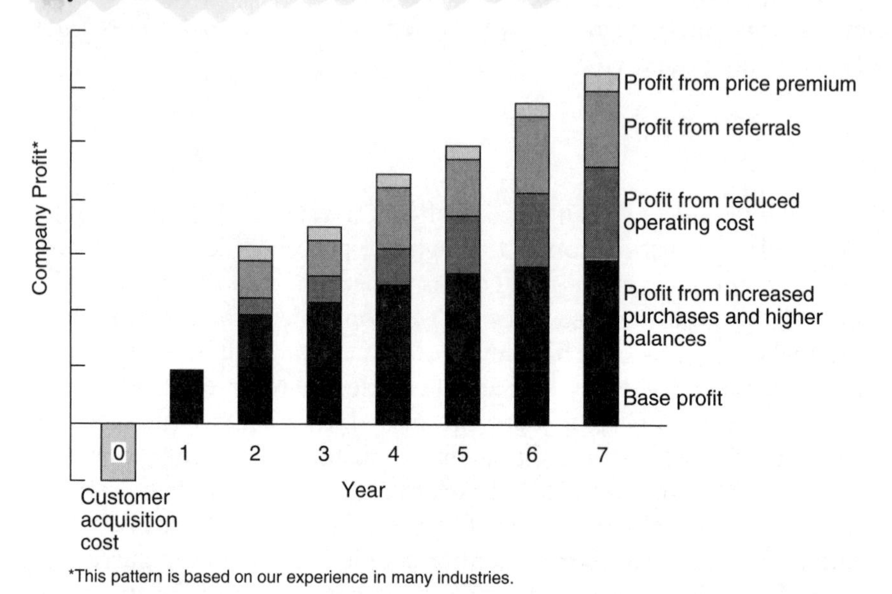

Reprinted by permission of *Harvard Business Review*. An exhibit from "Zero Defections: Quality Comes to Services" by Frederick F. Reichheld and W. Earl Sasser, Jr. (September–October 1990), p. 108.

FIGURE 4–2
Customer Profit Patterns over Time, Selected Service Industries

	Profit per Customer (in dollars) by Year of Relationship				
Industry	*1*	*2*	*3*	*4*	*5*
Credit Car Issuance and Servicing	(21)*	42	44	49	55
Industrial Laundry	144	166	192	222	256
Industrial Distribution	45	99	121	144	168
Auto Servicing	25	35	70	88	88

*Figures in parentheses denote losses.

Adapted and reprinted by permission of *Harvard Business Review*. An exhibit from "Zero Defections: Quality Comes to Services" by Frederick F. Reichheld and W. Earl Sasser, Jr. (September–October 1990), pp. 106–107.

MANAGING BY THE THREE Rs

Given data such as this, it might be concluded that losing a loyal customer is truly a tragedy in the new era of marketing. It has encouraged increasing efforts to both measure and communicate the lifetime value of customers to employees; identify, create, and enhance listening posts; create recognition and incentives for building customer loyalty; and utilize defections as learning opportunities. In general, it has placed a premium on listening to customers as well as marketing to them.

Measuring and Communicating the Lifetime Value of Customers

Some years ago, Phil Bressler, one of Domino's Pizza's most successful franchisees in the Baltimore area, calculated that the lifetime value of a loyal pizza buyer was about $4,000 in revenue, calculated on the basis of about fifty $8 pizzas purchased per year over an average ten-year period. Bressler then sought to impress all of his employees with this fact, encouraging them to think of customers in terms of $4,000, not $8 when making a delivery. This led to policies such as always trusting the customer's judgment about whether the delivery-time guarantee was met and recognizing crews who could prepare and deliver the most pizzas without customer complaint.[8]

Carl Sewell made the same calculation at his Dallas Cadillac dealership and found that the lifetime value of a loyal customer in terms of automobiles and service was $332,000.[9] He not only communicated this number of his employees, but also challenged them to come up with ideas to astound the company's customers. This led to a series of initiatives to achieve outstanding sales and service. Among other things, the floor of the service garage was painted a glossy white. Each time an auto was driven in for repair, the floor was dry-mopped. This communicated to customers visual evidence not only of the care that Sewell Cadillac took in servicing their autos, but also the respect the organization had for its employees, who responded with good service. In addition, customers were invited to meet and talk with the mechanics working on their autos, each of whom was given new uniforms and business cards and supplied with the latest technology. This helps explain why Sewell repeatedly is ranked among Cadillac's top five U.S. dealerships in terms of customer satisfaction.

A footnote to these two examples is in order. Neither included the value of referrals associated with satisfied customers. Factoring this in, the lifetime value figures calculated by either Phil Bressler or Carl Sewell could have been even more remarkable.

Identifying, Creating, and Enhancing Listening Posts

Most organizations have any number of potential listening posts. Foremost among them are the sales representatives found in any moderate-to large-size company. The problem is that most people in a position to listen are not given the time, tools, or incentives to do so. It is a significant distraction for a sales representative to take time to elicit, organize, and report customer comments in ways that can be helpful to product designers or manufacturing, quality improvement, or customer service teams. This is particularly true if the sales rep is neither recognized nor rewarded for doing so.

Customer service personnel are perhaps in a better position to collect data from customers and organize it into information for use by the organization. Often such personnel are in frequent telephone contact with customers with access to computer-generated information about their customers at their fingertips. Good ones can intuitively sense how close the organization is to losing a customer. But few are given computerized ways of easily organizing customer complaints and concerns into useable information. And few organizations follow Intuit's lead in placing some of their most capable people on the customer service front line.

Another problem associated with listening posts is that senior managers rarely, if ever, listen in. Listening (too little, along with spending too much of the time telling) in general is an increasing problem as executives rise in organizational ranks. To counter this trend, senior executives at MBNA are required to learn from customers. Each one spends four hours per month in a listening room monitoring customer calls, including some from customers who are canceling their cards. In terms of impact on their sensitivity to needs for service and product improvement, it is some of the most valuable time they spend each month on their jobs.

One of the most effective ways of creating listening posts is through the frequent-user programs created by many organizations based on the airline frequent-flyer model. This was part of the original competitive strategy of Staples, the office products discounter. Prior to opening business, Staples management had created the information-processing capability to support a member card system that enabled it to collect detailed information about customer purchase patterns. In return for access to special promotions and discounts, card holders provide information about themselves that can be combined with actual purchase information. This enables Staples to collect detailed information about buying habits, frequency of visits, average purchase amounts, and particular items purchased. Those customers found to be slowing or stopping their purchases are targeted for special promotions designed to renew their interest in Staples. All of this requires no additional effort on the part of frontline employees to collect valuable information that is lost daily in many other organizations.

One of the world's great listening organizations is the Ritz-Carlton chain of luxury hotels. In fact, listening is a central element of the hotel's effort not only to provide general excellence in hotel facilities and personnel ("Ladies and Gentlemen Serving Ladies and Gentlemen"), but also to create a system of listening whereby personnel can quietly meet the special needs of guests again and again with a manageable level of effort.[10] At the Ritz-Carlton, the staff is trained to listen for guest preferences, not always stated in the form of direct inquiries. A preference can be for something as incidental as a certain brand of bottled water with a meal or a down pillow on the bed. When a guest preference becomes known, it is noted on a Guest Preference Form by any frontline service person. Guest preferences are then entered into a computerized file called the Guest History at each hotel. Each night the file is downloaded into the chain data base, so that a guest staying at two different Ritz-Carlton hotels will be sure to have preferences honored at both. Each morning, the list of reservations at a particular hotel is then used to query the file for guest preferences so that the staff can take whatever action is necessary to prepare for guest arrivals. This is in addition to such listening "tricks" as having attendants at the front door collect names of arriving guests from baggage tags so that the names can be passed on immediately to the front desk for use by other hotel personnel.

Guest complaints are "owned" by the hotel staff member who fields them. After the problem (always called an "opportunity" at the Ritz-Carlton) is solved, the complaint is noted on a Guest Incident Form and immediately entered into the data base for use that day to make other personnel in the hotel aware of the fact that the guest had an unfortunate incident leading to a complaint and might need special treatment or recognition.

The Ritz-Carlton approach to listening is instructive for several reasons. It is central to the hotel's strategy. The tremendous amount of word-of-mouth advertising it generates replaces a great deal of traditional marketing expenditure for the hotel chain. Just as important is the fact that the system is relatively simple and easy to use and is reliant on human input by staff members at all levels in the organization. Further, the information is made available rapidly to those who have a need for it. Thus everybody is involved in both collecting and using the data daily, reinforcing the importance of the data collection effort for those who might otherwise think it an extra burden.

As Horst Schulze, President of the Ritz-Carlton, puts it, ". . . Keep on listening to customers because they change. . . . And if you have 100% (satisfied customers) then you have to make sure that you listen and change—just in case they change their expectations, that you change with them."[11] It is perhaps not surprising that the Ritz-Carlton's efforts to do this earned it a Malcolm Baldrige National (U.S.) Quality Award in 1992.

Recognizing and Creating Incentives to Build Customer Loyalty

In many financial services, brokers or agents often are rewarded on the basis of the amount of business they attract to their companies or the dollar value of transactions they process for customers. This can lead to the practice of "churning" customers' accounts for brokerage fees rather than acting in the best interests of customers in ways that encourage them to remain loyal. As a result, many financial organizations are slowly changing such incentives.

For example, investment brokers (now called financial consultants) at Merrill Lynch, the world's largest brokerage organization, are rewarded not just on commissions generated but also on "assets under management." The latter are increased most effectively by helping loyal customers make money and keep it invested with the company.

At MBNA, incentives are tied to customer defection rates. The company has identified for each department the one or two things that contribute most to building customer loyalty. Each department is measured daily on how well it does on these one or two things, with the previous day's performance posted throughout the company. As Reichheld and Sasser describe the program: "Each day that the company hits 95% of these (departmental) performance targets, MBNA contributes money to a bonus pool. Managers use the pool to pay yearly bonuses of up to 20% of a person's salary. The president visits departments that fall short of their targets to find out where the problem lies (and what they are doing to correct it)."[12]

Utilizing Customer Defections as Learning Opportunities

A gold mine of information can be provided by customers leaving an organization, including how to get them back. That's why MBNA has created a customer-defection "swat" team staffed by some of the firm's best telemarketers. They are often successful in eliciting specific, useful information about how the organization could have better served defectors. And in fully half the cases, the "swat" team is able to induce defectors to remain with the company, often by merely recognizing their defection, but also by promising corrective action and making sure the organization follows through with improvements.

Although many reasons for defections are only problem symptoms such as inaccurate bills or long waiting lines, they can be traced to root causes. In this way, the potential returns on investment in various kinds of service improvements can be measured so that such investments are no longer based on management intuition.

POTENTIAL-BASED MARKETING

Perhaps the most difficult thing for marketing managers to recognize is that: (1) some customers are worth more than others and (2) efforts to attract and please all potential customers can badly damage bottom-line performance.

Several years ago, the Swedbank organization, Sweden's largest bank, formed from the merger of ten smaller banks at a time when the country's banking system was deregulated, encountered high levels of customer satisfaction but profitless performance. Upon examining customers' banking activities and comparing revenues and margins with costs, it found that fully 80 percent of its customers were unprofitable. They were most satisfied with the service they were receiving from the bank. On the other hand, the 20 percent of customers who were providing more than 100 percent of the bank's profits were nearly uniformly dissatisfied with the service they were receiving from the bank. As a result, the bank systematically set about investing nearly all new capital in improvements for profitable customers. It lost some customers in the process and saw its profits begin to climb. The departing customers were nearly all some of the most unprofitable. In the meantime, pleasantly surprised profit-producing customers began increasing their usage of the bank even more.[13]

This experience provides a simplified illustration of potential-based marketing. Systematic efforts to practice potential-based marketing are yielding important insights and significant results in other organizations. In part, it is based on building customer loyalty. It is closely related to concepts being advocated under the term *relationship marketing,* which advocates actions to seek long-term relationships with customers rather than merely carry out transactions with them.[14]

At its heart, potential-based marketing combines measures of loyalty with data describing potential levels of usage, similar to "heavy user" information that has been employed for years by marketers. Its goals are to increase shares of purchases by customers who either have the greatest need for a product or service or who tend to exhibit strong loyalty to a single supplier. Having identified the potential for both usage and loyalty, it seeks to (1) lengthen the relationships with these loyal customers, (2) extend the relationship through increased sales, and (3) increase the profitability on each sale opportunity. The general concept is illustrated in Figure 4–3. A recent initiative illustrates the impact of potential-based marketing on profit.[15]

FIGURE 4–3
The Relationship between Current and Full Potential Performance in a Customer Relationship

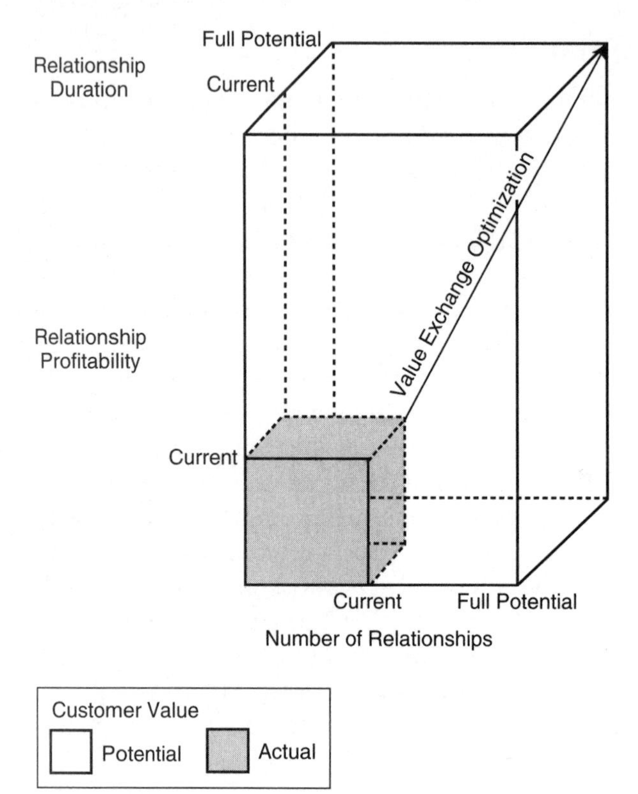

Source: Based on concepts set forth in Alan W. H. Grant and Leonard A. Schlesinger, "Realize Your Customers' Full Profit Potential," *Harvard Business Review,* September-October 1995, pp. 59–72.

In order to understand and quantify the gap between its actual sales and its full potential, Loblaw's, a leading Canadian grocery store chain, along with Alan Grant of Exchange Partners, a management consulting firm, analyzed the economics of the customer base of a typical store. Such a store operated in an area with about 15,000 households, generated annual revenues of $25 million, and realized an operating profit margin of 2 percent on sales.

Identifying Share of Loyal Customers

First, Loblaw's segmented the customer base surrounding the store into three categories: primary shoppers (those giving the store 80 percent or more of their grocery business), secondary shoppers (spending more than 10 percent but less than 50 percent of their total grocery budget at the store), and nonshoppers. The analysis showed that the store's primary and secondary shoppers represented less than one-half of the shoppers in the store's trading area.

Calculating Economic Impact of Customer Behavior Change

Loblaw's next calculated the impact on the store's profitability of favorable changes in the behavior of existing customers. Given the fixed cost structure of a grocery store, the contribution margin from each additional dollar spent by a customer can be 20 percent, not 2 percent, of sales. Thus, Loblaw's management found that even small improvements in any one of its many customer behaviors led to very significant profitability gains. Expanding the customer base by 2 percent with primary shoppers, for example, would increase the store's profitability by more than 45%. Converting just 200 secondary customers into primary customers would increase profitability by more than 20 percent. Selling one more produce item to every customer would increase profitability by more than 40 percent. Persuading every customer to substitute two store-brand items for two nationally branded items each time they visited the store would increase profitability by 55 percent. Obviously, generating several of these behaviors in combination would dramatically increase the profitability of the store's existing customer relationships.

Lengthening Customer Relationships

Finally, Loblaw's examined the average duration of its customer relationships. The research suggested an annual defection rate in excess of 20 percent, implying an expected duration of less than five years. Reducing this annual defection rate to 10 percent would increase the expected duration to ten years and more than double the lifetime value (measured in profitability) of the customer relationship.

Overall Impact of Potential-based Marketing

The analysis by Loblaw's management showed that each of these three key profit drivers independently represented a major opportunity for profit improvement. Multiplied together, however, even small improvements in all three areas would mean enormous increases in store profitability. For example, expanding the customer base by 2 percent with new primary customers *and* substituting two store brand items for two national brand items for each customer visit *and* reducing the customer defection rate by five percentage points would increase the future gross profits of a store by nearly 300 percent.

Implementing a Potential-based Marketing Effort

Loblaw's experience is typical. It had been paying attention to more traditional objectives, such as productivity, market share, and quality. As a result, it had overlooked the possibility of closing this full-potential gap by optimizing the value it delivered to customers. Its efforts to introduce potential-based marketing, like those of other organizations, required careful measurement of market segment potential, positioning of the company's offerings in relation to its competition and targeted customers' needs, investing in those features of its offerings that represented the greatest value to customers and profit potential to the company, and then delivering value by introducing new operational processes and supporting technologies as well as incentives for their successful use.

Measurement of Market Segment Potential. New data bases, software, and computing technologies have revolutionized the analysis of market potential. For example, thanks to advances in data base systems and mapping technology, grocery stores can now identify high-potential customers whom they are not serving and thus invest in ways designed to win their business. Customer identification cards and "membership" programs help track the quantity and type of transactions carried out at the checkout counter of a particular store. At the same time, grocers can record the license plates of cars parked in the parking lots of rival stores and feed the information into commercially available data bases that link license plates with street addresses, even right down to a portion of a specific block on a particular side of the street. As a result, grocers can devise offerings to win new customers almost on a street-by-street basis.

Positioning in Relation to Competition and Customers' Needs. Today's positioning requires a cross-functional process to identify customers' needs and make sure they are addressed. The objective of this effort is achieved when customers no longer pay for or receive benefits that they don't value.

The Union Pacific railroad has applied principles of potential-based marketing by creating cross-functional teams and making them responsible for designing service offerings for larger customers. These teams analyze the gap between actual and potential business for each customer as well as the economics of closing the gap. Furthermore, they have the authority to marshal rail cars, influence train schedules, change rates (prices), and reengineer transit times. The teams influence these variables as needed to maximize the long-term value of relationships with specific customers. While this is perhaps an extreme example of customization of product and service offerings, the same strategy is being practiced by mass marketers of consumer products and services through the use of improved data bases combined with consumer interviewing and the careful measurement of results from test offerings.

Managing Marketing Investments. Once markets are segmented and service offerings positioned against them, the next step is to decide how much and where to invest funds in support of marketing efforts. Since 1991, AT&T has transformed both the offerings it designs for residential prospects and the way it interacts with them.[16] Previously, the company spent hundreds of millions of dollars per year trying to attract new users, sending out millions of pieces of largely undifferentiated direct mail solicitations several times a year urging prospects to switch telephone service providers. Less than 5 percent of the time and money invested resulted in prospect conversion, a typical performance at the time.

Today AT&T managers supplement available market data with predictive models based on results of previous offerings and other data to determine which prospective segments and service offerings are likely to produce the greatest return on investment. It designs, through disciplined testing, offers that will entice attractive customers to AT&T for the least possible investment. As a result, the company now designs and delivers hundreds of tailored prospect offerings.

AT&T applies the same philosophy to efforts to retain customers. Cross-functional teams now preplan a series of up to seven phone and mail communications with varying messages and incentives. First, they send a defector a letter offering a basic incentive to switch back to AT&T. If the defector does not accept the offer, the company will call offering a larger incentive. If the former customer still does not accept, AT&T will ask a few basic questions about the service currently used, recording the new information and using it to tailor different value packages designed to overcome the barriers in each different customer subsegment. The return on investment of each offer is determined by carefully forecasting the economic potential of each relationship against the total cost of the investment strategy that is necessary to win the former customer back.

The impact of this effort on AT&T's operating performance has been profound. The company attracts seven times as many customers as it did in 1990. In 1994 alone, it saw a net gain of more than 1.2 million accounts while reducing the cost-per-acquisition by more than $3. Moreover, 50 percent of the dollars invested in attracting prospects now persuade prospective customers to initiate a relationship (vs. 5 percent in 1990).

Redesigning Processes, Investments, Incentives, and Organization. Efforts to realize full potential from relationships with customers in organizations like Loblaw's, the Union Pacific, and AT&T require the design and delivery of high-value packages. This may involve the redesign of processes, investments in people and technology, and the introduction of results-centered incentives, all matters to which we will devote more attention later in the book. The data to achieve these results are often available within the organization.

MINING CUSTOMER DATA TO ACHIEVE MASS CUSTOMIZATION

Forward-thinking organizations are building comprehensive information files that allow them to track, predict, and influence customer behavior. Several organizations we have visited earlier are engaged in the development of comprehensive "vertical" profiles, utilizing data from files gathered entirely from within the company, files that sometimes have existed for years but have never been integrated. Other efforts involve the development of customer files describing buying and other behavior associated with related product and service categories. We call them "horizontal" profiles. These concepts of customer data base development are diagrammed in Figure 4–4.

The objective of these efforts is to achieve what has been termed "mass customization," the ability to address customer segments of one, addressing each customer's needs individually.

Achieving Mass Customization on a "Vertical" Data Base

Having collected a great deal of information about its best customers through its guests' requests and complaints, all of which are captured in a vast guest history data base, the Ritz-Carlton hotel organization has created the potential for delivering customized service to literally tens of thousands of guests. It represents mass customization with a vengeance. It deals, however, only with consumer preferences in the purchase of hotel services, providing a sophisticated example of a "vertical" customer data base.

By combining the files containing information that it already knows

FIGURE 4–4
Vertical and Horizontal Customer Data Base Development

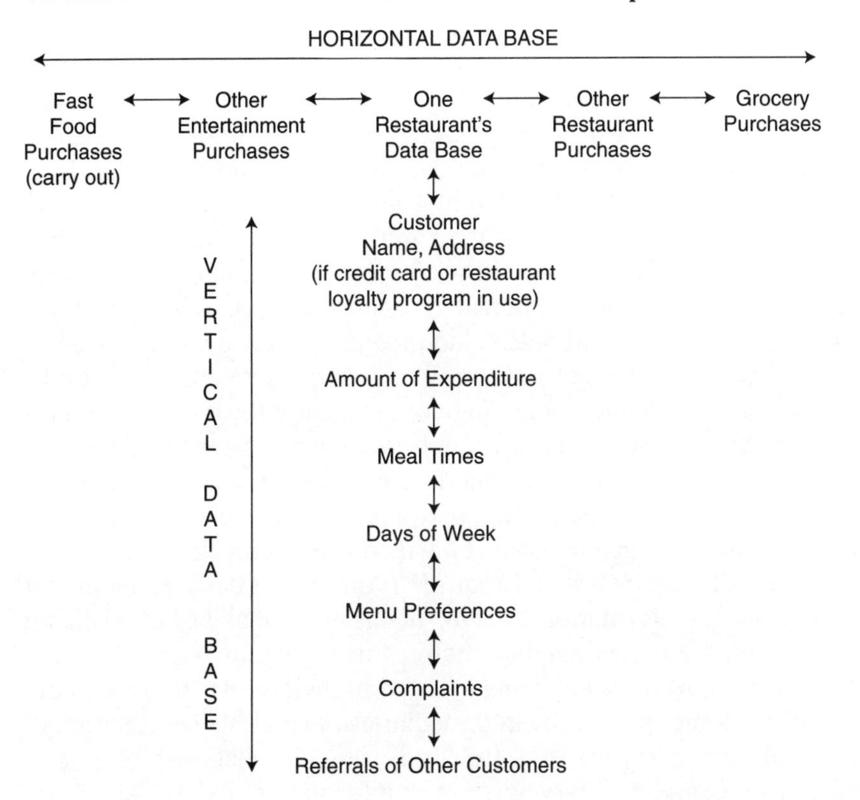

about travelers, British Airways is developing the capability to predict when and why customers will defect to other airlines, providing an opportunity to act in advance of such defections in ways designed to retain customers. USAA, offering financial services by mail, phone, and personal computer to tens of thousands of clients, collects information from them that enables it to know when events are likely to occur that encourage clients to think about insuring a family member, a home, or an automobile or investing in one of the mutual funds offered by the company. With the use of this information, the company can actually anticipate clients' needs.

Achieving Mass Customization on a "Horizontal" Data Base

Alternatively, organizations are linking their customer data bases with those of other organizations serving common customers. Here the long-term objective is to track customer behavior across product or service categories in order to better understand needs and design ways to meet them. The partnership between American Airlines and Citibank is a case in point. Citibank, through its VISA and other credit cards, has compiled comprehensive files of customer purchasing patterns that have largely gone untapped. Similarly, the American Airlines AAdvantage frequent-flyer program is a source of information about passenger travel patterns on American flights and, through awards of free travel miles for hotel and rental auto usage, several other purchases by travelers. By linking their initiatives to make available frequent flyer miles for every purchase by means of Citibank's VISA card, these two organizations immediately opened several new opportunities. Of course, new cardholders and greater use of Citibank's card has been an immediate benefit to the bank. As for American, it has stimulated travel on its flights, obtaining compensation for the utilization of largely excess capacity. But of much greater importance, it has obtained information about passengers' use of the services of American's competitors, which, when combined with the airline's existing data, provides a more complete profile on which new promotions and efforts to build loyalty can be based. Because of American's early development of the SABRE information system, it has the capability of realizing greater value from the data than many of its competitors.

Other organizations are being assisted in their efforts to build "horizontal" customer profiles by intermediaries or catalysts whose primary source of income results from the "brokering" of relationships among firms with complementary customer information needs. Air Miles Canada is an outstanding example of this trend. It has devised an ingenious way of making money in the short-run by arbitraging the excess capacity of airlines and the desires of consumers for air travel that can be obtained through their regular purchases of other things. At the same time, it is creating the potential for substantial long-term profits by building "horizontal" customer data bases that can be made available to its partners in the venture.[17]

Air Miles Canada, in its role as "information broker and clearing house" to other companies, has reached agreements, in effect, to purchase excess airline capacity and resell it to a number of other organizations for use as premiums for customer loyalty. The strategy involves a number of transactions, shown in Figure 4–5. First, Air Miles Canada has sold product and service retailers on the competitive advantages of offering free travel to customers based on their purchases. This requires that it sell its loyalty program to largely noncompeting organizations, ideally the Canadian leader in each of several "retail" industries. Clients have included Bank of Montreal, the Oshawa Food Group of supermarkets, Sears, and Shell Oil. After buying an inventory of Air Miles, each "retailer" then decides how many Air Miles to award to customers for each dollar of goods or services they purchase. Potential travelers then redeem their Air Miles from Air Miles Canada, which purchases the necessary tickets at a discount from airlines willing to sell "excess" capacity, pocketing the difference between miles sold to retailers and miles purchased from airlines. In addition, of course, Air Miles Canada profits from the "float," representing the difference between the number of Air Miles sold to retailers and those actually redeemed by prospective travelers. This has resulted in a business, founded in 1991, that is growing rapidly, largely through the use of other organizations' money. If the story ended here, it would describe a tidy little business. But the story doesn't end here.

In addition to trading in transportation and incentives, Air Miles Canada's agreements call for the merging and sharing of customer data bases compiled by its various clients. These resulting records, describing purchases of products and services ranging from groceries to apparel to appliances to travel by means of checking accounts, bank credit cards, and retailer credit cards, are perhaps the most extensive "horizontal" data bases of their kind anywhere. These data bases will only become more valuable, available for a fee for prudent use according to clearly established guidelines by Air Miles Canada's clients, suggesting that the more important payoff to Air Miles Canada and its clients may lie in the future.

ORGANIZATIONAL IMPLICATIONS OF THE NEW MARKETING

Common experiences of organizations implementing potential-based marketing and mass customization include the need to utilize information from several different cooperating organizations and functional departments, organize around cross-functional teams to put the infor-

FIGURE 4–5
Basic Elements of the Air Miles Canada Strategy*

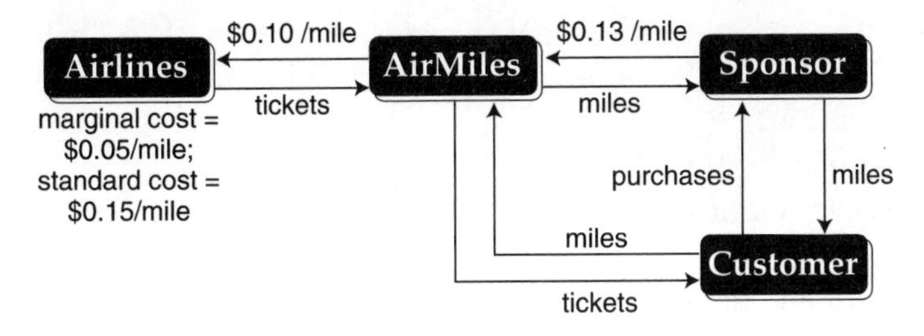

*Monetary amounts shown here are hypothetical.

mation to good use, and give such teams the latitude to commit the organization to service features attractive to a particular customer. This was the case, for example, at both the Union Pacific railroad and AT&T. It is reflected, too, in what happened at Intuit.

Intuit's highly-successful early efforts were achieved with an organization comprising essentially three functions: marketing research, product development, and customer service. Further, every effort was made to ensure that software engineers responsible for product development engaged in both marketing research and customer service activities and that other cross-functional initiatives were carried out.

Note the absence of sales and advertising as activities highlighted in the company. Note the absence of marketing, manufacturing, and personnel functions in this organization. In fact, note the absence of conventional organization functions. This speaks volumes about the impact of new business methods on the future of marketing management in a world where products and services have to be developed so rapidly in response to customer suggestions and purchases that there simply is not time to coordinate the activities of specialists associated with some part of the marketing effort or product development. What an organization may give up in specialized expertise it will gain in response time and accuracy, as measured by customer responses.

QUESTIONS FOR MANAGEMENT

The "new" potential-based marketing is centered around the importance of enhancing the lifetime value of a customer through retention, related sales, and positive referrals and efforts to listen for and respond to customer needs. It represents an important shift in thinking about marketing effort. It is anathema to some who find it difficult not to compete for the favor of all customers in seeking all the demand available for a given product or service.

It raises a number of questions for management, including:

1. What effort have you made to measure and communicate the lifetime value of a loyal customer?
2. To what extent are incentives being redesigned to seek a "balance" between attracting new and retaining old customers for your organization?
3. How are loyal customers defined?
4. What is known about the economics of serving your loyal versus nonloyal customers?
5. To what extent are initiatives to build customer satisfaction directed to loyal, profitable customers at the risk of alienating others?

6. What is the gap between actual and potential sales in your relationship with high-potential customers?
7. How is information from tests and other sources pooled across the organization to identify the potential return from various types of value offerings and marketing efforts?
8. To what extent are cross-functional efforts encouraged that break down traditional barriers within marketing and between marketing and other functions?

There is an important assumption underlying this philosophy. That is that once desirable customers are identified, they will be satisfied so completely through the value package that is created for and delivered to them that their loyalty and usage levels will be maximized. That requires achieving what we term total customer satisfaction, the topic to which we turn next.

5

Attaining Total Customer Satisfaction

Not Whether but When

In 1987, as part of a larger effort (called "Leadership Through Quality") to reverse Xerox's declining market share, CEO David Kearns, President Paul Allaire, and their management team decided that customer satisfaction should become the number one corporate priority, requiring greater care in measuring both customer satisfaction and loyalty. It was an effort that would not only prove instructive to Xerox's leadership, but also be of great value to a number of other firms attempting to link customers' satisfaction to their loyalty and to their companies' profitability.

THE XEROX EXPERIENCE

The Xerox Leadership Through Quality initiative involved several stages, including leadership "buy-in," mission formulation, benchmarking, training, measurement, and reward and recognition. As any Xerox executive will tell you, the initiative is still ongoing. It doesn't have an end. And it represents such a large investment that the payout has to be very great. It results in large part from an interesting finding resulting from Xerox's measurement effort.[1]

In the mid-1980s, Xerox initiated customer satisfaction measurement, reasoning that it would learn what the possible return might be on its already large expenditures to improve the quality of the products and services provided by the company. With the long-term intent of linking measurements to rewards and recognition, Xerox elected to survey its customers in large numbers, frequently, and with period-to-period consistency. It decided that, allowing for a majority of nonreturns, a sample of 40,000 customers per month would give it sufficient numbers of returns to measure satisfaction not only on an overall level, but right down to individual sales and service districts.

After a period of experimentation, the form evolved to that shown in Figure 5–1 with three central questions, all "based on your (the user's or customer's) recent experience." They were: (1) How satisfied are you with Xerox? (2) Would you acquire another product from Xerox? and (3) Would you recommend Xerox to a business associate? It featured a five-point scale on which customers could register the degree of their satisfaction. An overall company goal was set to achieve 90 percent 4s and 5s on the scale by 1990 and 100 percent 4s and 5s by the end of 1993. Division offices would receive special recognition for attaining such high satisfaction scores.

At about this same time, a junior member of the Xerox management team decided to compare the repurchase intentions of those customers giving Xerox 4s and those giving it 5s on the satisfaction survey. What he found was eye-opening. Customers giving Xerox 5s were six times more likely to repurchase Xerox equipment than those giving the company only 4s.

Many things changed as a result of the finding that the Xerox satisfaction-loyalty relationship was not "straight line," but highly bowed, similar to that shown in Figure 5–2. It was quickly concluded that 4s were relatively meaningless, given the company's objectives. Henceforth, only those organizations winning 5s from customers would be recognized. The overall goal was changed to one of 100 percent 5s by the end of 1996. Relatively large amounts of money could be spent to achieve this goal.

Years after Xerox first launched its initiative to attain total customer satisfaction, questions are still being raised about the links between customer satisfaction, customer loyalty, and profits. Data have been produced questioning the linkages. Only recently have we begun to understand the true nature of these linkages with data that point up the critical need to do just what Xerox's management concluded, achieve total customer satisfaction.

FIGURE 5–1
Xerox Customer Satisfaction Survey Form

This questionnaire should be completed by the individual who makes decisions about the acquisition of ______________________________. Please focus on your experiences in the product areas mentioned as you complete the questionnaire.

SECTION I: GENERAL SATISFACTION

	Very Satisfied	Somewhat Satisfied	Neither Satisfied Nor Dissatisfied	Somewhat Dissatisfied	Very Dissatisfied
1. Based on your recent experience, how satisfied are you with Xerox?	☐	☐	☐	☐	☐

	Definitely	Probably	Might or Might Not	Probably Not	Definitely Not
2. Based on your recent experience, would you acquire another product from Xerox?	☐	☐	☐	☐	☐
3. Based on your recent experience, would you recommend Xerox to a business associate?	☐	☐	☐	☐	☐

	Very Satisfied	Somewhat Satisfied	Neither Satisfied Nor Dissatisfied	Somewhat Dissatisfied	Very Dissatisfied
4. How satisfied are you overall with the quality of:					
a) Your Xerox product(s)	☐	☐	☐	☐	☐
b) Sales Support you receive	☐	☐	☐	☐	☐
c) Technical Service you receive	☐	☐	☐	☐	☐
d) Administrative Support you receive	☐	☐	☐	☐	☐
e) Handling of Inquiries	☐	☐	☐	☐	☐
f) Supplies support you receive	☐	☐	☐	☐	☐
g) XeroxUser Training	☐	☐	☐	☐	☐
h) Xerox Supplied Documentation	☐	☐	☐	☐	☐
Please complete 4i and 4j only if you are the decision maker for systems products (printers, workstations, personal computers and wordprocessors)					
i) Your Xerox supplied software	☐	☐	☐	☐	☐
j) Xerox Systems Analyst Support	☐	☐	☐	☐	☐
k) Telephone Hotline Support	☐	☐	☐	☐	☐

SECTION II: SALES SUPPORT

	Very Satisfied	Somewhat Satisfied	Neither Satisfied Nor Dissatisfied	Somewhat Dissatisfied	Very Dissatisfied	Not Applicable
5. How satisfied are you with Xerox Sales Representatives with regard to:						
a) Timeliness of response to your inquiries	☐	☐	☐	☐	☐	☐
b) Frequency of contact to review your needs	☐	☐	☐	☐	☐	☐
c) Frequency of contact to provide information about new Xerox products and services	☐	☐	☐	☐	☐	☐
d) Product knowledge	☐	☐	☐	☐	☐	☐
e) Application knowledge	☐	☐	☐	☐	☐	☐
f) Understanding of your business needs	☐	☐	☐	☐	☐	☐
g) Accuracy in explaining terms/conditions	☐	☐	☐	☐	☐	☐
h) Ability to resolve problems	☐	☐	☐	☐	☐	☐
i) Professionalism	☐	☐	☐	☐	☐	☐

SECTION III: CUSTOMER SUPPORT

6. What was the purpose of your most recent call to Xerox? ☐ Inquiry ☐ Problem ☐ Haven't called, can't answer (skip to question 10)

FIGURE 5–1 *(Continued)*

7. How long ago did you make this call? ☐ less than 3 months ☐ 3 - 6 months ☐ 6 -12 months ☐ Greater than 12 months

8. What Xerox function did you contact? ☐ Sales ☐ Service ☐ Billing ☐ Collection ☐ Supplies ☐ Telephone Hotline Support ☐ Systems Analyst ☐ Customer Relations Group

9. How satisfied are you with the support you received:	Very Satisfied	Somewhat Satisfied	Neither Satisfied Nor Dissatisfied	Somewhat Dissatisfied	Very Dissatisfied
a) Ability to get to the right person(s) quickly	☐	☐	☐	☐	☐
b) Attitude of Xerox personnel who assisted you	☐	☐	☐	☐	☐
c) Ability to provide a solution	☐	☐	☐	☐	☐
d) Time required to provide a solution	☐	☐	☐	☐	☐
e) Effectiveness of the solution	☐	☐	☐	☐	☐
f) Overall satisfaction with support received	☐	☐	☐	☐	☐

10. What specific things can we do to increase your satisfaction with Xerox, our products and our services?
Thank you for your feedback!

Melvyn A. J. Menezes and Jon Serbin, Xerox Corporation: The Customer Satisfaction Program, Case No. 591-055. Boston: Harvard Business School, 1991, pp. 19–20.

FIGURE 5–2
Relationship between Customer Satisfaction and Loyalty (intention to repurchase), Competitive Industries

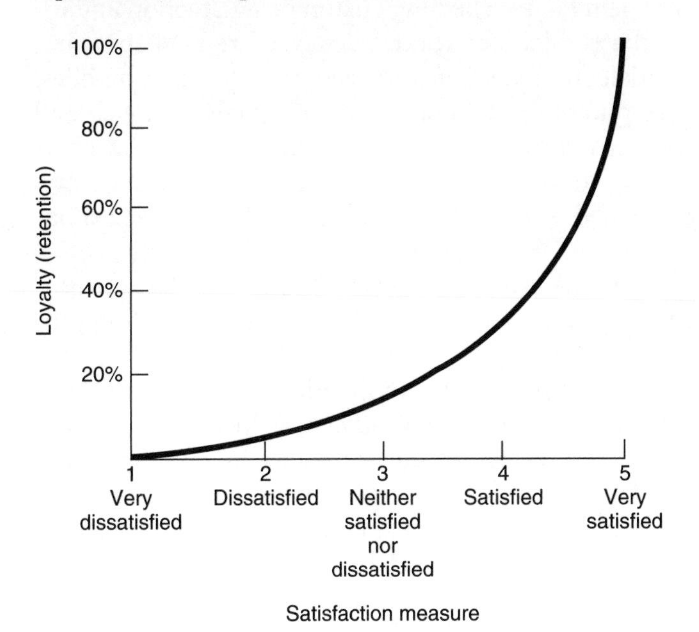

THE TOTAL CUSTOMER SATISFACTION IMPERATIVE

There are those who say that it is neither possible nor a sensible investment to try to attain total customer satisfaction. They are probably second cousins to those who said that "zero defects" in manufacturing was an impossible goal and an unwise quest. As Tom Jones and Earl Sasser point out, this lore probably underlies common management assumptions that: (1) it is sufficient to satisfy a customer, (2) the investment required to create completely satisfied out of merely satisfied customers is rarely worth it, and (3) efforts to improve satisfaction should concentrate on customers in an organization's lowest satisfaction categories. The data they developed in five industries bring these assumptions seriously into question for companies in many industries.[2]

Relationship of Customer Satisfaction and Loyalty

In recent years, several studies have concluded that customer satisfaction and loyalty do not always vary directly, that there are a number of factors that may interfere with the relationship between the two measures. One study found that 90 percent of defecting customers reported that they had been satisfied. The authors of the study concluded that "satisfaction scores provide useful early warning of problems, but . . . satisfied customers do not systematically buy more than . . . unsatisfied ones."[3]

Jones and Sasser, using data reflecting customer satisfaction and intent to repurchase the service or product, analyzed relationships between customer satisfaction and customer loyalty for automobiles, personal computers purchased by businesses, hospitals, airlines, and local telephone services. From this data they constructed the chart shown in Figure 5–3, showing different "curves" for each industry. The relationships yielded some interesting conclusions. First, situations in which customers have a number of alternatives, relatively low costs of switching from one product or service to another, few government regulations limiting competition, and few loyalty-promotion programs produce satisfaction-loyalty curves similar to that for the automobile industry in Figure 5–3. As competition or alternative products or services are reduced or "switching costs" (for example from one doctor to another) are raised, the curve may begin more and more to resemble that for local telephone services in Figure 5–3. Customers in this latter situation may become more and more "captive." They exhibit what Jones and Sasser term a "false loyalty," one that may result in the immediate loss of customer loyalty with the introduction of competition and the reduction of switching costs.

This work has led Jones and Sasser to characterize customers and their loyalty in four main groups, as shown in Figure 5–3. "Apostles" are those who are not only loyal but are so satisfied that they recommend the service to others. "Mercenaries" are those who may switch service suppliers to obtain a lower price, for example, even though they may have high satisfaction. "Hostages" are highly dissatisfied but have few or no alternatives. "Terrorists" have alternatives and use them, and they utilize every opportunity to convert others by expressing their dissatisfaction with their previous service supplier.

Relationships in Figure 5–3 help explain why customers giving Xerox a 5 on customer satisfaction were six times more likely to repurchase a Xerox product or service. Xerox has severe competition, from both Far East imports in lower-volume copiers and U.S. competitors in higher-volume copiers. It can afford to invest large amounts of money to attain satisfaction ratings of 5 from customers currently only giving it a 4.

The phenomenon also occurs in services. John Larson, a vice president of Opinion Research Corporation, found in his study of retail bank depositors that completely satisfied customers were 42 percent more likely to be loyal than merely satisfied customers.[4]

There are logical explanations, not well supported by research, for the wide gulf between the loyalty of customers registering a 4 and 5, respectively, on the satisfaction scale. Many may not want to experience

FIGURE 5–3
How the Competitive Environment Affects the Satisfaction-Loyalty Relationship

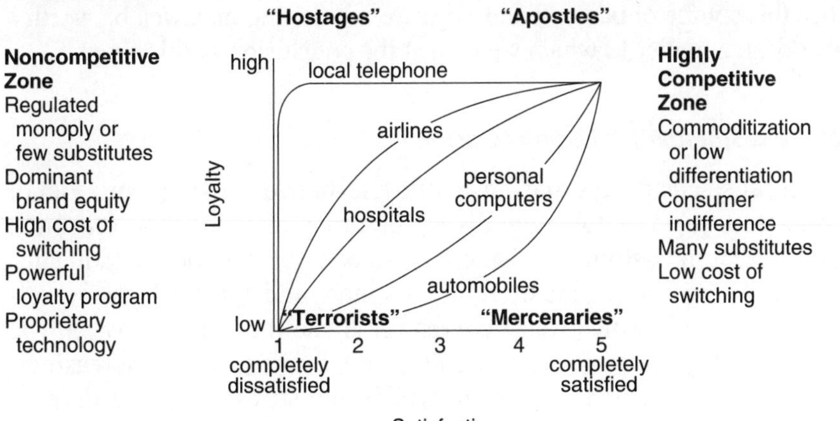

Note: Words in quotation marks have been added by the authors to describe customers exhibiting varying degrees of satisfaction and loyalty.

Adapted and reprinted by permission of the *Harvard Business Review.* An exhibit from "Why Satisfied Customers Defect," by Thomas O. Jones and W. Earl Sasser, Jr., November-December 1995, p. 91.

the possible displeasure or penalization of a long-time service or product provider by registering low ratings. On the other hand, a sense of values prevents them from lightly rating such providers at the level of 5 when they clearly deserve something less. As a result, they elect the "courtesy 4," a nearly meaningless evaluation under the circumstances.

Relationship of Customer Satisfaction and Profitability

Measurements of the impact of customer satisfaction on loyalty and profitability also suggest strategies for investing in customer satisfaction improvements for the greatest amount of profit improvement. For example, their findings led Jones and Sasser to conclude that the three most important groups on the satisfaction-loyalty curve are what we might call "apostles," "near-apostles," and "terrorists," shown in Figure 5–4 as those giving an organization 5s, 4s, and 1s, respectively, on a five-point customer satisfaction scale. As we saw earlier, apostles are those who not only are satisfied but regularly tell others about a product or service, becoming an extension of the sales force. They can be an invaluable resource. For this reason, it is often a wise use of effort and money to convert "near-apostles" to "apostles" on the scale. By the same token, however, it may be a poor investment of resources to concentrate on raising the satisfaction level of customers not already registering 4s on a five-point scale, with one exception. The exception is the "terrorist," who not only expresses extreme dissatisfaction with a product or service, but also tells others, often many others according to those who have studied the phenomenon.[5] To silence this source of bad will and negative advertising may well be worth a great deal, a matter to which we turn at the conclusion of this chapter.

Total Satisfaction for Captive Customers

Just because customers may have little alternative to using a product or service today, no matter how dissatisfied they may be, is no reason to fail to invest in customer satisfaction. As competition increases in such previously protected industries as hospitals and local telephone services, the satisfaction-loyalty curves for those industries may shift to look more like those for automobiles and copiers. In an increasingly global and competitive market in which industries are being deregulated and privatized, there is a general trend toward the development of competition. Those who recognize and prepare for it by cementing the loyalty of captive customers in advance, as AT&T attempted to do just prior to and during the early days of the deregulation of the long-distance telephone business, may be able to retain a high proportion (in AT&T's case, roughly 90 percent of the market) of such customers.

FIGURE 5–4
"Apostles" and "Terrorists" on the Satisfaction-Loyalty Curve

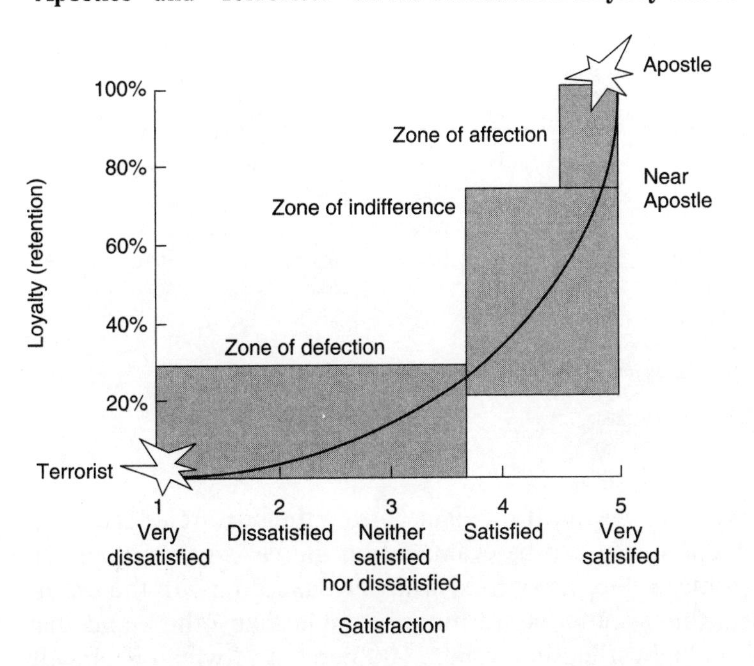

THE IMPORTANCE OF FOCUS

Organizations that have not identified the customers they are targeting have a special handicap in achieving total customer satisfaction. They too often attempt to please everyone, creating too many "merely satisfied" customers and too few "apostles" in the very core of the customer base in which they should be investing. Further, customer satisfaction measures too often are averaged across segments and not related to other measures that could provide insights into profitable strategies.

The Tyranny of Averages

All customers count equally only in organizations that haven't identified and established customer segments to be targeted, measured satisfaction levels, and tracked the share of potential sales that the organization actually is gaining from them.

Consider the example shown in Figure 5–5 for a hypothetical company enjoying an "above average" customer satisfaction rating of 3.5 on a scale from 1 (low) to 5 (high). If all that is known about customer satisfaction is what is inside the dotted-line box in Figure 5–5, managers have little basis for knowing how to act in building satisfaction

FIGURE 5–5
Data Needed to Interpret and Understand Average Customer Satisfaction Ratings

Customer Satisfaction Rating*	Proportion of Customers	Degree of Loyalty to (Share of Purchases from)			Estimated Lifetime Value of Purchases		
		High	Medium	Low	High	Medium	Low
5	10%	70%	30%	0%	20%	60%	20%
4	50%	20%	60%	20%	20%	50%	30%
3	25%	0%	80%	20%	20%	50%	30%
2	10%	0%	50%	50%	15%	45%	40%
1	5%	0%	0%	100%	15%	45%	40%
3.5	100%						

[dashed box] = Extent of typical data regarding customer satisfaction

* 5 = highest rating, 1 = lowest rating.

and profitability. However, if the data outside the box are added, customer satisfaction data can be evaluated on the basis of the potential lifetime customer values associated with various ratings. In the example, it appears that some 5s are more valuable than others and that those with the highest lifetime value (100 percent of which is already being realized by the company) may be well worth the investment required to retain them. However, the best potential return on investment could possibly result from an effort to move "high lifetime value" customers currently rating the company as above-average (4 on the five-point scale) to a level of total customer satisfaction (5s on the same scale). We'll return to these questions later in the chapter.

Satisfying Targeted Segments

Southwest Airlines seeks to target "road warriors" traveling a territory by automobile. The British Airways trans-Atlantic Concorde service, on the other hand, targets high-status executives and others who place high values on time and prestige. At the MTV (music television) cable channel now broadcasting on a nearly global basis, the target is 18- to 24-year-olds. Each of these organizations pays special attention to those in their target segments, often discounting the views of others.

The Ultimate Source of Focus: Affinity Groups

Because they often band together out of a common sense of purpose or a common background, members of affinity groups afford organizations attractive targets in which there is an opportunity to achieve total customer satisfaction. As a result it is very difficult to find a USAA casualty insurance policyholder who is not an "apostle" of the service. They are all military officers, with a strong common sense of purpose and somewhat similar psychographic characteristics (way of life, views on issues, values, etc.). USAA designs its products and services confident that it can completely satisfy a large proportion of the customers in its target group. Others don't count.

This helps explain why some of the most successful providers of insurance, credit card services, and travel services are focusing their efforts on large organizations comprising people with similar interests and, in some cases, backgrounds. One of the largest of these organizations, the American Association of Retired Persons (AARP), has developed a wide range of services for its members, all over the age of 50, most of which it contracts to other providers. Its "label" on a product or service provides both access to a "franchise" and a source of focus that are difficult to match.

MEASURING CUSTOMER SATISFACTION AND LOYALTY

Customer satisfaction and loyalty can be tracked by means of "listening posts" such as customer surveys, feedback volunteered by customers, formal marketing research, reports filed by frontline service personnel, and actual customer involvement in certain affairs of organizations serving them.

Customer Surveys

Surveys of the kind shown in Figure 5–1 can be especially effective. They are constructed simply and administered frequently and consistently. We are often asked about survey methods by managers who have gone to great pains to construct lengthy satisfaction questionnaires. But consistency and frequency are often more important than the actual content of the questionnaire, especially if it is simple and contains one or more requests for overall satisfaction levels. A complex questionnaire administered infrequently simply does not provide the data necessary to establish trends needed to provide ongoing feedback to various units of a service organization that can be factored into decisions regarding efforts to improve satisfaction.

Just as customer expressions of satisfaction have limited meaning if they fall in the middle of a range of values, so customer expressions of loyalty, such as intent to repurchase a product or service, have to be read with caution. Customers tend to overstate their intent to repurchase in relation to what they actually do sometime later. However, organizations able to build a data base of such information over time have found that the amount of such overstatement is somewhat constant. As a result, they are able to deflate the data to reach reasonably accurate estimates of future buying behavior, assuming that nothing happens in the meantime to discourage repurchase. At Xerox, for example, the company has compiled reliable ways of interpreting responses to the question, "Would you acquire another product from Xerox?"

Customer Feedback

This source of information results from complaints and comments volunteered by customers, often to higher levels of management in a service organization. It is hard to evaluate, as to both level and trend, because it is offered in an almost random manner in a variety of forms. Worse yet, because many customer complaints to top management result from "escalation" of a problem up through the service-providing organization by responses such as "I'll have to clear that with my boss," they are obtained long after the time when meaningful response is possible.

Much unfavorable comment is "lost" or "bottled up" in lower levels of the organization out of the fear that it will result in penalties or poor evaluations by top management. It is nevertheless important to encourage such feedback and to take measures to collect as much of it as possible, because it can provide the trigger for service recovery efforts that are so essential to the achievement of total customer satisfaction.

Organizations serious about factoring direct customer feedback into decision making reward both customers and employees for surfacing complaints as soon as possible after they occur. They studiously avoid criticizing or penalizing employees for doing so, although such complaints may lead to the eventual retraining of some employees.

Marketing Research

Where possible, questions concerning customer satisfaction and loyalty can be "piggybacked" on marketing research designed to learn other things about customers. Rarely is the research designed specifically for these purposes. Tom Jones and Earl Sasser have suggested that this can be particularly effective at the time a customer is added to or subtracted from an organization's customer list.

New customers can be queried about their motives for switching to a provider's services, whether or not they were aided in their decision by a referral from an existing customer, or had other reasons for making their selection.

Every effort should be made to contact defectors to learn both the reasons for their defection and the competitor to whom they are defecting. Obtaining accurate information from defectors requires skilled interviewing at a time of stress for both parties and may require objective third-party assistance. Defectors often will give "easy" responses for their defection, such as obtaining a more favorable price from a competitor, when in fact the real reasons for their action are unfavorable service experiences. When in-depth interviewing reveals real reasons for defections, the machinery for service recovery can be initiated. It is often the last chance for obtaining valuable information and possibly saving a customer.

Feedback from Frontline Personnel

Frontline service providers are in the best position both to elicit feedback from customers and do something about it. While many organizations elicit feedback from the front line, all but a handful are unsuccessful in obtaining much of value. Why? They don't make feedback easy and painless to provide, reward employees who provide it, or devise ways of organizing such data into information appropriate for use in management decision making.

At Marriott's Fairfield Inns, for example, customers can register their satisfaction with the friendliness of employees, the cleanliness of their rooms, and the overall value they obtained during their stay on a touchscreen computer system called Scorecard. The resulting data are used both to track unit performance and to reward employees.

As we saw in the last chapter, the Ritz-Carlton hotel chain, in contrast, relies more heavily on Guest Preference and Guest Incident forms prepared manually by employees. But employees are recognized and paid above-market rates for doing this well along with other aspects of their jobs. This type of data collection can be used to personalize feedback about customers from the front line, helping to insure that customized service based on information in the forms can be recreated to a guest's satisfaction.

Complementarity of Methods

Each of the methods for obtaining inputs regarding customer satisfaction and loyalty yields data of somewhat different reliability and character. When taken in total, they can provide a rich and reliable base of information for management. But it requires that all such data eventually reach a common point in the organization whose responsibility it is to track and interpret such data, converting it into information and disseminating it to the right places.

ADDRESSING CUSTOMER SATISFACTION AT THE LIMITS: APOSTLES AND TERRORISTS

Customers usually tell others only about extraordinary experiences, both good and bad. But in total, only a small proportion ever voice their feelings to the service provider. We know, for example, that in most services, less than a third of dissatisfied customers ever complain to the service provider. The complaints of some are "lost" in the channels of communication. Others just quietly take their business elsewhere or take it upon themselves to tell friends and others about their unsatisfactory experiences. Those who tell others about positive experiences are what we call "apostles." They are a subset of those, for example, who regularly give an organization top ratings on customer satisfaction. Dissatisfied customers who don't quietly take their business elsewhere, but take others with them through their criticism, are "terrorists." Again, they are only a portion of those giving an organization the lowest ratings on customer satisfaction, and they can have an extremely negative impact on performance. Because of their importance, some part of every customer satisfaction improvement effort should be dedicated to addressing the special opportunities posed by these two groups.

The Economics of the Extremes

Consider, for example, the analysis of our hypothetical data base for the service clients of an office machine manufacturer shown in Figure 5–6. Here, the components of those giving the organization 5s and 1s on its customer satisfaction survey have been broken out to identify the subset of each that regularly provide word-of-mouth comments, both positive and negative, to others.

When average economics are estimated and calculated for an actual or potential group of customers, misleading results are obtained. By identifying and estimating lifetime (or, more typically, annual) values for apostles and terrorists, typically high returns on efforts to preserve and increase the numbers of apostles and reduce the numbers of terrorists are isolated.

Figure 5–6 presents data for eight levels of customer satisfaction, ranging from apostles (5+) to terrorists (1-), and including noncustomers (0). The actual number of customers falling into each category is associated with the potential and actual lifetime revenue flow for each, with the difference between the two being an important measure of loyalty. This provides the basis for estimating the potential both for doubling loyalty and for increasing customer satisfaction by one level

FIGURE 5–6
Targeted Investing to Maximize Returns from Improved Customer Satisfaction and Loyalty

Customer Satisfaction Level	*No. of Customers in the Market*	*Individual Potential Lifetime Value × Loyalty**	*Individual Actual Lifetime Value × Loyalty†*	*Potential from Doubling Individual Loyalty‡*	*Potential from Increasing Individual Satisfaction§*	*Total Revenue Increase from Increasing Satisfaction by One Level, 10% of Customers (Millions)‖*	*Contribution on Increased Revenue (Millions)#*	*Investment Required Over Customers' Lifetimes (Millions)*	*Return On Investment (Non-discounted)*
5+ (Apostles)	2,000	$480,000	$450,000	$30,000	$300,000	$60	$12	$4	300%
5	4,000	160,000	150,000	10,000	300,000	$120	$24	$8	300%
4	12,000	160,000	50,000	50,000	100,000	$120	$24	$24	100%
3	8,000	160,000	30,000	30,000	20,000	$16	$3.2	$16	20%
2	8,000	160,000	20,000	20,000	10,000	$8	$1.6	$16	10%
1	4,000	160,000	10,000	10,000	10,000	$4	$.8	$8	10%
1– (Terrorists)	2,000	–360,000	–360,000	0	370,000	$74	$14.8	$4	360%
0	60,000	160,000	0	0	0–480,000††	$270††	$54	$120–600**	9–45%
Total	100,000								

*These amounts are calculated by multiplying potential annual purchases over the estimated lifetime of the customers in each satisfaction category, with the amount credited to "5+" assuming revenue streams from customers to whom the "apostles" have recommended the service and the amount shown for "1–" customers based on estimates of potential customers discouraged from purchasing the product by "terrorists."
†These amounts are estimated on the basis of the share of each customer's total purchases realized.
‡Potential for "5+" and "5" is limited by the currently high share of total purchases realized by the firm.
§These figures are based on the assumption that satisfaction is increased by one level. In the case of "5+" customers, the amount reflects the value of maintaining "5+" vs. "5" status for apostles.
‖Column 2 multiplied by column 6 multiplied by 10%.
#Calculated at the rate of 20% of the revenue figures shown in column 7.
**Investment is assumed to be $2,000 over the lifetime of an existing customer, with one to five times as much investment required to attract a new customer.
††The figure of $270 million is based on a lifetime value of $45,000 per customer, the weighted average for all of the current customers.

for each customer. By multiplying the estimates for each customer by the number of customers in each category, the total revenue increase to be realized by increasing by one level the satisfaction of 10 percent of customers in each category is shown in column 7 of Figure 5–6. Twenty percent of this figure is shown as the incremental contribution of this amount of increase in revenue flow. When compared with the estimated investment needed to raise customer satisfaction by one level or, in the case of noncustomers, to convert them to customers with a value equivalent to the average for existing customers, returns on investment associated with each group of customers can be estimated.

While the data in Figure 5–6 are hypothetical and will vary from industry to industry, overall they reflect what we are beginning to find in situations we have observed—namely, that the best returns on investment are at the extremes of customer satisfaction.

Neutralizing Terrorists. First, the highest return results from neutralizing terrorists, because they have such a high potential negative value to the firm. Ways of doing this may require little more than recognizing their dissatisfaction, apologizing, and making special efforts to address their concerns, actions discussed in Chapter 10. Often, this will result in at least an acknowledgment that an organization is "trying," even if the terrorist continues to criticize it in front of friends and potential referrals.

Terrorists represent a complex challenge, because many of them will have ceased using the service, assuming they aren't "captives" for reasons described earlier. Failing to prevent their emergence in the first place, tracking terrorists may require special attention to complaints, assuming that some do complain to the service provider before taking their "cases" elsewhere.

One frightening relationship in our example is that one terrorist, with a negative lifetime revenue stream of $360,000, can neutralize the positive returns from more than five other customers (at a weighted average value of $67,000 each). This further underlines the importance of insuring that the number of terrorists is minimized.

Preserving and Creating Apostles. The next highest returns on "investments" outlined in Figure 5–6 result from either preserving existing apostles or creating new ones from among those already experiencing total customer satisfaction.

Rather than take apostles for granted, their individual identification can provide the basis for customized efforts to make sure that they continue to tell others about their successful experiences. Recognizing apostles and thanking them for their business may be all that is necessary to maintain their loyalty and enthusiasm for the organization. But their value clearly suggests that extraordinary efforts may be warranted to do this.

We are perhaps least certain about the assumptions associated with creating apostles from among those already experiencing total customer satisfaction. Whether or not a customer tells someone else about an extraordinary service experience may well have more to do with the psychological makeup and social behavior of the customer than with the actual experience. If this is true, the creation of apostles may be beyond the capability of an organization once it has achieved the total satisfaction level. If so, investments to create apostles may have a lower return than we have assumed. Clearly, we need to understand more about this phenomenon.

Investing to Achieve Total Customer Satisfaction. In our example, investments to increase customer satisfaction levels from 4 to 5 on a five-point scale rank third in priority, but carry a very high rate of return of 100 percent. The monetary potential from this investment is very large, however, because of the larger numbers of customers typically found in the "4" category. Further, some of those customers may become apostles with their elevation to the ranks of the 5s, thus increasing returns on such investments.

The data in our example illustrate several other typical relationships.

Minimizing Investments in Low-Satisfaction Customers. Our example suggests little incentive for trying to raise the loyalty levels of customers registering 1, 2, or 3 on a five-point satisfaction scale. The gains from raising them one level on the scale are low. And the investment of effort and cost required to increase satisfaction levels more significantly may well be too high, especially when compared with other opportunities discussed above.

Questions might be raised about investing enough in thoroughly dissatisfied customers (1s on the scale) to prevent them from becoming terrorists. But again, terrorists may be "born," not made. That is, if their psychological makeup and social behaviors are responsible for their status, organizations may be better advised to invest in satisfying terrorists rather than preventing all dissatisfied customers from complaining about their treatment by the organization in public.

Investing in Existing versus New Customers

The investment opportunities described above all eclipse those associated with converting noncustomers as a group to customers. We have assumed costs per individual to do this to be five times those required to improve customer satisfaction and retain customer loyalty. This reflects the generally held belief, supported by some data, that it costs five times as much to attract a new customer as it does to retain an existing one. It raises required investments to unattractive levels in comparison with other opportunities.

However, lest we fall victim to the tyranny of averages, it should be pointed out that noncustomers exhibit the same wide ranges of potential as customers. This suggests the need to segment the noncustomer group in search of those with the greatest potential to create improved returns on investment in increased customer satisfaction.

Creating Terrorists as a By-Product of Focus

The achievement of marketing and operating focus can breed terrorists when those for whom a service was not designed somehow end up in the user group. One illustration of this is the increasing number of "home pages" on the Internet being created by disgruntled patrons of some of the most outstanding service organizations in the country. One of these is Southwest Airlines.

Who converses electronically on these "home pages"? In Southwest's case, sometimes it is a regular patron with high expectations who may be truly disappointed. Often, however, it is an "uninitiated" Southwest flyer who may expect a meal, luggage interchange, or nonstop, long-distance flights. This is not the kind of patron for whom the service was designed. The more highly targeted the service, the greater the likelihood that these kinds of reactions will be generated despite all efforts to accurately communicate the dimensions of the service, including what to expect and what not to expect.

Increasingly, service providers may find it useful to regularly monitor public channels of communication such as the Internet to identify individual terrorists whose concerns might be addressed in customized ways. Our earlier analysis suggests that the returns from this activity may far outweigh the costs.

MEANWHILE, BACK AT XEROX

By 1989, Xerox was regularly measuring customer satisfaction and loyalty, tracking it to the unit sales or service level, and contemplating the possible development of incentive pay systems based on the satisfaction measures. In spite of the fact that the company had not yet approached the level of total customer satisfaction, Xerox's measurement efforts, among others, earned the company the Malcolm Baldridge National Quality Award in that year. Xerox's award, presented to then-Chairman David Kearns by President Bush, merely represented one more sign of progress toward the ultimate goal, a goal that would require additional efforts over an extended period of time, efforts that will be described in further detail later.

QUESTIONS FOR MANAGEMENT

The size of the payoff resulting from tracking and relating customer satisfaction and loyalty may warrant actions suggested by the following questions:

1. Has your organization developed a definition of customer loyalty and a way of measuring it?
2. Does your organization measure customer satisfaction, customer loyalty, and relationships between the two?
3. Are a variety of complementary measures used to construct a well-rounded picture of customer satisfaction and loyalty?
4. Is there one location in the organization where all such measures are collected and analyzed, with the results communicated to other entities?
5. Is an effort made to differentiate totally satisfied customers from those registering merely above-average levels of satisfaction?
6. Are rewards and recognition limited only to those employees achieving total customer satisfaction?
7. Are investments in customer satisfaction prioritized by payoffs to be gained from such improvements?
8. Is the same kind of estimated return-on-investment calculated for investments in customer satisfaction as for other capital investments?

UNDERSTANDING DETERMINANTS OF CUSTOMER SATISFACTION

The economics of increased customer satisfaction can be dramatic in their impact on the profit realized by an organization, providing a strong rationale for understanding the influences on customer satisfaction. One of the strongest and best-documented of these is employee satisfaction. For this reason, we next turn our attention to the relationship between customer and employee satisfaction.

6

Managing the Customer-Employee "Satisfaction Mirror"

Stories about outrageously good service leading to high customer satisfaction and almost fanatic loyalty among shoppers at Nordstrom, the fashion department store chain, are legion. They include Nordstrom employee efforts to change tires or warm up customers' cars for them on the parking lot, take goods that Nordstrom doesn't even sell in exchange for other merchandise, and even shop for and deliver bizarre items on short notice to customers. Most are probably exaggerated through the retelling process. Some may never have happened. But enough of them are true that these stories have become more important to Nordstrom than the relatively modest advertising in which the company invests.

THE SERVICE ENCOUNTER

These stories characterize what academics have come to call service encounters between customers and service providers.[1] These service encounters are at the heart of the profit chain for many services. And they distinguish most services from manufacturing processes.

When the Nordstrom salesperson in the shoe department not only shows a customer the most extensive collection of women's shoes offered by any department store, but also accompanies the customer through the dress and other departments to find the elements of the perfect fashion ensemble, something special happens. The resulting customer satisfaction contributes to employee satisfaction with the job. And it produces yet more Nordstrom stories to be told and retold to others.

It doesn't take many of these kinds of service encounters to encourage the development of a relationship, either with Nordstrom or with the individual salesperson. Nordstrom does whatever it can to encourage these relationships, most importantly rewarding results by paying salespeople a substantial commission on sales as opposed to a salary dangerously close to minimum wages. As a result, successful Nordstrom salespeople are among the highest paid anywhere in retailing.

Literally, customer satisfaction produces a "mirror" effect in Nordstrom's employees, further enhancing the potential for future customer satisfaction.

EVIDENCE OF THE "SATISFACTION MIRROR"

Customer and employee satisfaction measures in multiunit service operations typically track closely with one another. But in fact, the cause-and-effect relationship between them is not clear. The management of Nordstrom clearly believes that the goal of complete customer satisfaction is achieved through satisfied employees. That's why it not only pays its customer contact personnel well in a manner that rewards long-term sales success achieved through customer satisfaction, but also provides an attractive selling environment, often including a pianist playing soft music, plush carpets, and well-appointed and well-located stores. It backs this up with complete merchandise assortments, all but guaranteeing that customers will find something they will want to purchase. And it establishes a liberal return policy that enables employees to consistently help resolve customers' problems with little fanfare.[2]

Nordstrom employees with whom we have spoken have repeatedly cited their positive interactions with customers, as well as their freedom in exercising judgment in their relationships with customers, as important elements of the quality of their working environment. This provides incentives for continued efforts to satisfy Nordstrom customers, continuing the "satisfaction mirror" effect that has no beginning and end.

Among the first to document the "satisfaction mirror" were Benjamin Schneider and David Bowen. In a study reported in 1985, they established close links between customer and employee satisfaction levels in the branches of a banking organization.[3] In a replication of the study eight years later, they concluded that "the degree to which employees believe their work is facilitated [an expression of satisfaction] yields the most consistent information about customer satisfaction."[4]

This effect has been found at every multiunit service organization for which we have data. A sample of relationships between customer and employee satisfaction in several well-known companies is shown in Figure 6–1.

FIGURE 6–1
Relationships between Customer and Employee Satisfaction, Selected Organizations, 1990–1995*

Organization	*Business*	*Type of Employee*	*Finding*
MCI Communications	Telephone communication	Service center employees	Significant relationship between employee satisfaction, customer satisfaction, and customer intentions to continue to use services†‡
Chick-Fil-A	Food Service	Restaurant employees	78% of restaurants with above-average customer satisfaction have above-average employee satisfaction†
Western European Money Center Bank	Banking	Bank branch employees	Significant relationship between employee satisfaction and customer satisfaction†‡
Major U.S. Travel Service	Travel service	Branch office employees	Significant relationship between employee satisfaction and customer satisfaction†‡
Merry Maids Subsidiary of The Service-Master Company	Cleaning services	Providers of cleaning services	1% increase in employee satisfaction = .5% increase in employee commitment = .22% increase in customer satisfaction†
Rank Xerox	Office machines	Service center employees	Significant relationship between employee satisfaction and customer satisfaction†‡

*Data for each organization was collected at various points in time during the period 1990 to 1995.

†Based on data collected internally by the organization.

‡In each case where it is used, the word "significant" is used to indicate a correlation at the 99% level between employee satisfaction and customer satisfaction.

In all cases where data allow statistical analysis, the relationships are statistically significant. Other cases where data analysis was less precise nevertheless support the same conclusion. These and other experiences have led us to conclude that, in the absence of data regarding either customer or employee satisfaction, one can be predicted from the other. Show us an operating unit with higher employee satisfaction than another and we can predict with a high degree of reliability that its customers will also be more satisfied.

WHY THE SATISFACTION MIRROR OCCURS

Rocket science is not required to explain the satisfaction mirror. The "mirror" probably occurs in its simplest form in the restaurant where waitpersons enthusiastic about their jobs not only communicate their enthusiasm to customers but also go out of their way to make customers' dining experiences pleasant. Customer satisfaction is expressed through both comments and often a larger-than-normal tip, reinforcing the relationship and increasing the waitperson's enthusiasm for the next customer encounter.

More often, the process comprises a number of intricately linked factors, several of which are shown in Figure 6–2. Once consistently

FIGURE 6–2
The Satisfaction "Mirror"

More Repeat Purchases ← → More Familiarity with Customer Needs and Ways of Meeting Them

Stronger Tendency to Complain about Service Errors ← → Greater Opportunity for Recovery from Errors

Higher Customer Satisfaction ← → Higher Employee Satisfaction

Lower Costs ← → Higher Productivity

Better Results ← → Improved Quality of Service

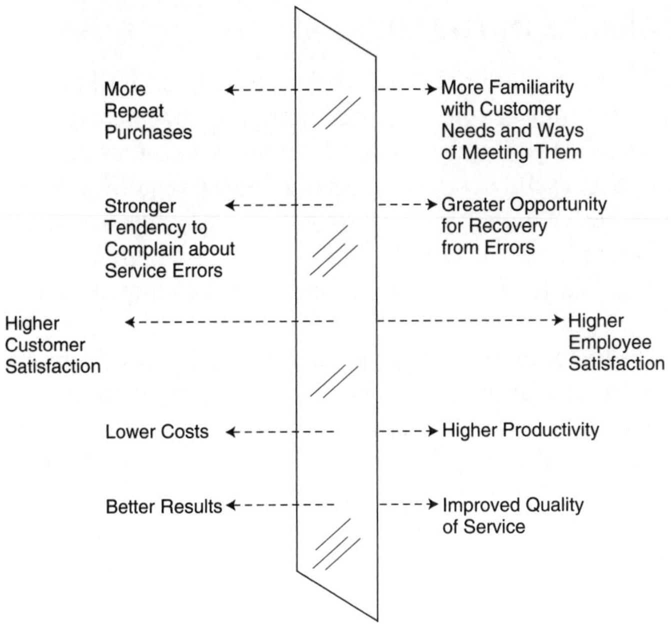

positive service encounters lead to a level of satisfaction that promotes employee loyalty, the possibilities for leveraging both work effectiveness and customer satisfaction become significant. Employees stay on the job long enough not only to begin to learn the requirements of the job and how to perform it well, but also to get to know customers and their specific interests and needs. It is at this point that what was merely a series of service encounters becomes a customer-employee relationship in which both customer and employee become more tolerant of each other in the case of a possible error or misunderstanding.

This is particularly true of services that are consumed frequently. One of the most successful store managers several years ago at Au Bon Pain, the chain of French bakery cafés, understood the phenomenon very well. In a business typically employing people forty hours per week, Gary Aronson hired only people who were willing to work fifty to sixty hours per week, paying them 10 to 20 hours of overtime. In addition to increasing the amount he was able to pay people, thereby increasing the quality of restaurant personnel he was able to hire, he understood that customers, many of whom frequented his restaurant on a daily basis, wanted to see the same faces on the job. Counterpersons literally could remember the orders of a hundred or more of their regular customers. The satisfaction mirrored in the faces of Aronson's customers, coupled with his other policies, undoubtedly contributed to the lowest turnover rate among the employees of any of Au Bon Pain's stores at that time.

PREVENTING CRACKS IN THE MIRROR

Gary Aronson's strategy would not have worked if he had hired people who didn't want to put in overtime, were not motivated by positive customer feedback, or didn't particularly like to interact with other people.

In a sense then, successful service encounters and a resulting interactive relationship begin with hiring the right people. In Aronson's case, these were individuals with limited educations but high levels of motivation and a desire to accumulate income for self-improvement and other uses.

Relationships are fostered by appropriate incentives for good service to customers, incentives that may be tied to customer satisfaction. Appropriate training and recognition help as well.

Central to the satisfaction mirror are efforts to attract the "right" customers, those who will respond favorably to good service and willingly enter into the kind of relationship that can lead to continued business, lower costs, and higher profits that naturally result from high levels of customer loyalty.

Lower costs and higher profits enable the Gary Aronsons of the world to enhance returns to employees, thereby differentiating themselves from other employers and building a basis for competitive advantage.

FROM SERVICE ENCOUNTER TO RELATIONSHIP

Successful service encounters occur for a variety of reasons. But unless they can be replicated consistently, they do not lead to the kind of relationship that induces customers to feel like "owners" of the service.

Factors Creating the Successful Service Encounter

We have emphasized the human element in the successful service encounter. It is an important element of service quality, as perceived by customers. However, it is necessary to keep in mind that a service encounter is only as successful as the results it produces for the customer and the profit produced for the service provider, along with other elements of the customer value equation discussed earlier. The importance of the human element contributed by the service provider varies greatly, depending on the nature of the encounter.

For example, several types of service encounters are described in Figure 6–3. They range from face-to-face without technological intermediation to machine-to-machine, with the latter characterizing many business-to-business service encounters.

Face-to-Face. Face-to-face encounters can provide a high degree of "human touch" that is reassuring for services involving high levels of perceived risk. These types of encounters are especially important to those who have not been raised on and taught to trust computers and information technology. They include teller banking for middle-aged and older clients, airline counter ticket sales for inexperienced travelers experiencing a certain amount of anxiety about their flights, personal broker services for investors not willing to perform their own research and transact their own purchases and sales of stocks and bonds, and contact with the mechanic for those who have some knowledge of automobile repair or who wish additional assurance that the person working on their auto is not a complete idiot.

The face-to-face encounter can be made more pleasant and ultimately successful by the right kind of surroundings (i.e., a banking office that looks inviting and substantial), information, and other technology that helps the service provider get the transaction right (whether it's a banking transaction or the repair of an automobile) in a reasonable period of time. As we will see later when we examine service quality, these are clas-

FIGURE 6–3
Factors Influencing the Success of Various Types of Service Encounters

Face-to-Face Encounters (with service visible to the customer)

Careful customer segmentation and selection
Frontline server selection emphasizing human skills
Easy access for customers
Pleasant, comfortable surroundings
Good support technology
Well-trained employees
Customer and employee loyalty
Timely, dependable service
Employees whose appearance and behavior engender trust

Face-to-Face Encounters (with service invisible to the customer)

All of the above plus:
  Tangible evidence that service is performed
  Bonding, guarantees, and warranties

Human-to-Machine

Easy-to-understand procedures
Easy-to-access technology
Verification of service performance
Fast response
Access to humans, if necessary
Information and transaction security
Fail-safe mechanisms and procedures

Machine-to-Machine

Efficient software
Compatibility of hardware and software
Tracking capability (for information, shipments, etc.)
Automatic verification procedures
A transaction record
Information and transaction security
Fail-safe mechanisms

sic components of most outstanding service encounters. But the importance of each will depend on the profile of customers being targeted for service, who they are and how they think and live.

Needs may be influenced by whether or not the service is performed in a way that is visible to the customer. Tangible evidence becomes especially important in these cases, whether it is presented in the form of a worn auto part that has been replaced during repair or the careful arrangement of toiletries during the cleaning of a hotel room. If perceived risk is an important element of the transaction, the bonding of servers, service guarantees, or product warranties may be needed.

Human-to-Machine. To an increasing extent, service encounters are mediated by some kind of technological device, most often hardware and software that process and communicate data and information. This has had greatest appeal to customers with higher degrees of self-confidence in making decisions and dealing with technology rather than other humans.

While the growth of either telephone or computerized banking was slow at first, these methods of banking have grown in recent years. Studies have shown that users tend to be among the younger groups utilizing banking services. Of course they must have access, in the case of computerized banking, to the necessary hardware, software, and communications media. But perhaps most important, it is this group that places the greatest value on time saved in the process and the greatest trust in the technology employed in these services.

Machine-to-Machine. The most common application of machine-to-machine service today is in the replenishment of retail and wholesale inventories by suppliers utilizing EDI, or electronic data interchange. The replenishment process is triggered by the customer's computer containing a model that specifies both levels at which inventories need to be reordered and the quantity of the order. A triggered order is transmitted directly to a supplier's computer, which can then check the supplier's inventories, order a shipment or place a back order for inadequate stocks, and notify the customer's computer of its actions. The process is particularly effective for relatively standard products ordered routinely in large quantities where little human judgment is required.

Achieving Consistency in Service Encounters

A series of service encounters between a provider and customer will lead to a productive and profitable relationship only if the provider is able to achieve consistently high quality in the encounter. In this case, superior service recovery, in the event mistakes are made, is of limited value, because if the service provider has to resort repeatedly to service recovery to deliver results expected by a customer, he will have failed to deliver the service with what has been termed "authority" by those studying excellence in service processes. In other words, customers' perceptions of possible risks will have been heightened. The most risk-averse, instead of applauding the server's recovery capabilities, will simply go elsewhere.

The achievement of consistency in the service provided is one of the most important factors in McDonald's success. While this organization may not produce the best hamburgers its customers have ever tasted, customers know that they will get what they expect in the form of the product delivered. Even though the food is prepared by relatively inexperienced, often young, servers, McDonald's has designed its technology and developed methods that insure that food will be prepared with an amazing degree of uniformity throughout the world. (Several of these methods involve the introduction of fail-safe devices, such as timers, bells, and automatic shutoff switches, devices that we will discuss in more detail in Chapter 9). Further, the food will be prepared and served in surroundings that are familiar and meet worldwide standards for cleanliness. The human interaction with customers is reduced to a minimum to allow the technology and other elements of the service encounter to deliver consistency while enabling counter personnel to concentrate on providing fast, accurate service.

Enlisting the Customer in Relationship Building

Initiatives that recognize the importance of the relationship mirror can be designed to enlist the customer to play a more active part in providing the kind of feedback that can create the mirror effect. One of the best examples of this that we have seen is American Airlines' "You're Someone Special" initiative that the airline has sponsored for several years. This involves distributing coupons to frequent flyers that can be filled out and "awarded" by customers to employees providing outstanding service or sent directly to company headquarters. The coupons are used as the basis for special recognition by the airline. This particularly clever initiative has given valued customers a vehicle for recognizing employees at the time and place a special service is provided, interacting with them in the process, and coming away feeling that they have participated in a process designed to enhance future services.

Consistent product and service delivery, created with the help of the customer or not, creates the *possibility* for a service relationship. Whether the relationship develops depends on other efforts and policies on the part of a service provider. Only through the further development of a relationship does the relationship "mirror" effect have a chance to develop.

ENGINEERING AN ORGANIZATION FOR CUSTOMER RELATIONSHIPS

The most common complaint of customers in a number of consumer and business-to-business services we have studied is the inability or unwillingness of service providers to maintain stability in their customer-contact employees. Even where employee turnover is low, rapidly growing organizations may unwittingly shuffle their best people from customer to customer both to accommodate growth and to provide personal promotions from low-reward customer assignments to high-reward assignments. While continuity in the employee base may appear satisfactory from the view of the service provider, it is nonexistent in the eyes of the customer. And of course, complaints about broken relationships with service providers only occur when the best servers are transferred.

This situation occurred, for example, during the days of the greatest growth of ServiceMaster's core business, that of providing cleaning and other support services to hospitals, schools, and industrial firms. It led directly to efforts by the organization to find a way of promoting frontline facility managers other than moving them away from valued relationships with existing customers.

Customer-server relationships may be valued so highly that customers may be willing to follow servers, even if they change employers. This is particularly true in services involving a high degree of personal service in which the server can contribute a great deal to the customer's health, wealth, or general well-being. Thus, patients follow doctors from one hospital affiliation to another. And investors follow brokers from one brokerage firm to another. This raises the stakes for service organizations wishing to facilitate customer relationships through valued employees, as shown in the service relationship triangle in Figure 6–4.

Developing the Service Relationship Triangle

The success of the customer-server relationship can help cement relationships between customers, servers, and the service firm. One recent study that we conducted in a banking organization found that employees with highly satisfactory relationships with customers and attitudes toward their jobs had significantly lower levels of job turnover. This in turn resulted in employees developing: (1) a greater understanding of the requirements of their jobs (i.e., learning by doing), (2) enhanced teamwork and coordination within and among departments of the service organization, (3) enhanced knowledge of the needs of their customers, (4) a greater appreciation of the value of a highly satisfied customer, and (5) a better understanding of and commitment to key corporate goals and objectives such as that of improving customer satisfaction. In a very real sense, a successful customer-server relationship in this firm was found to contribute to the other relationships in the triangle shown in Figure 6–4.

The service relationship triangle is so important that successful service firms spend a great deal of time and effort engineering their organizations

FIGURE 6–4
Factors Affecting the Strength of Relationships in the Service Relationship Triangle

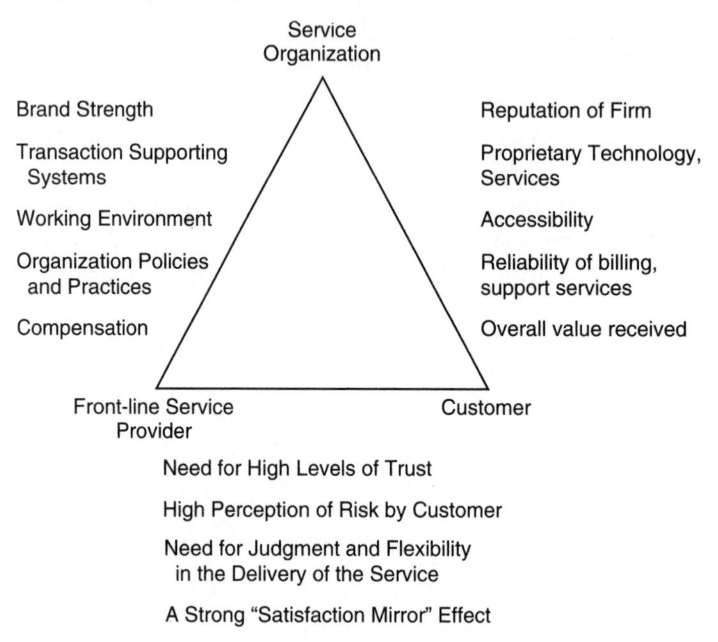

for effective customer relationships. It begins with the identification of the people most critical, in the eyes of a customer, to the relationship and then deciding how to organize these people for effective service delivery.

Identifying Relationship-Critical Jobs

Many jobs and the people who staff them are important to the delivery of outstanding service. But some are especially important in the eyes of a customer. It is important to determine who they are.

For example, in the commercial banking relationship, the bank officer in charge of lending often is the focal point of interaction between a business borrower and the bank. By the same token, in personal banking tellers may be important in relationships with relatively low-profit, high-cost, transaction-oriented individuals demanding personal service, but it is often those lending money for auto and other purchases who generate profits at the branch level. The irony is, of course, that banks for years concentrated on having highly capable tellers at their branches so that serious mistakes in handling money would not occur and relations could be maintained with individuals from the neighborhood. In the process, they often neglected paying adequate attention to the jobs and people who were actually generating the profit.

The clients of one well-known public accounting firm told us that memorable relationships were formed when their accounting firm delivered an idea or opinion that resulted in significant profit enhancement for them, not from the year-to-year delivery of mundane auditing or tax work. In this case, the message was: give particular attention to the hiring and development of a few individuals able to do creative work for the firm's clients, perhaps on a consulting basis when called in or referred by a regular audit team.

The point is that it is important to identify the jobs requiring outstanding people to staff the small number of jobs that are particularly critical to the maintenance of relationships once they develop.

Dedicated Servers or Not?

Without consideration to cost, customers for services with high transaction values (as in office equipment repair), high requirements for accuracy (as in a breakfast order), and high perceived financial, legal, or personal risk (nearly any professional service) prefer to deal consistently with the same person. Customers of brokerage services, for example, value both dedicated brokers and frequency of contact, according to one survey conducted several years ago by a leading brokerage firm. However, dedicated servers nearly always are a costly solution to the relationship challenge, primarily because a dedicated server can rarely have the kinds of specialized knowledge held by others in the organization, cannot inventory and allocate time effectively to various customers, and cannot provide round-the-clock service coverage demanded in some businesses. This has led to the organization of service delivery around teams of providers.

Service Teams or Not?

One Saab auto dealership in the Boston area known for outstanding customer service has organized its relationships with customers by team. Thus, individual customers are instructed to contact the Blue, Red, or Green Team rather than an individual in the service department. Our personal observation of this process from the customers' viewpoint suggests that customers really do perceive themselves as having a relationship in the service process, albeit with a team. Invariably, they tell us that their team "is the best," suggesting a curious kind of pride and loyalty to a largely unseen team. However, this organization gives the auto dealer an opportunity to schedule and allocate work within teams rather than for individuals, allowing it greater flexibility within the relationship. Also, contests can be devised to encourage teams to compete for customer satisfaction, further cementing the relationship.

This same motive led the Xerox Corporation to organize its vast field service corps into "work groups" comprising eight to ten field service engineers assigned on an individual basis to major accounts. Work groups take calls from members' assigned customers, organize and schedule their work, cover for members who are overloaded at a particular time, and discuss and solve common problems with the equipment or their service procedures. The work group form of organization has enabled Xerox to deliver higher levels of service, as measured by response time and reductions in callbacks (for machines not fixed the first time), as well as higher levels of customer satisfaction with the relationship at lower costs to Xerox.

In service jobs in which service providers are not interchangeable in the eyes of a customer or in which the proper motivation is difficult to instill through the vehicle of a team, organizations center their efforts around talented individuals who are encouraged to perform as individuals in interacting with "their" clientele. Thus, at Nordstrom, salespeople are little more than agents agreeing to appear on the premises of the store at regular hours. The store provides them with an unmatched selling environment, a great selection of merchandise, and the incentives to encourage them to act in their (and for the most part, the store's) best interests. This occasionally produces the charge of "sharking" or stealing one salesperson's customers by another.[5] But this is a small price to pay for the high level of customer service and satisfaction that the strategy produces. The strategy recognizes and capitalizes on the inherent nature of the retail department store sales process.

Nordstrom has recognized that perhaps the other most important job in the organization is that of the buyer, or merchandise manager. If outstanding selections of merchandise are to be maintained, merchandise managers have to buy the right things. As a result, Nordstrom not only requires merchandise managers to work part-time in the departments for which they buy alongside other sales personnel, it also ties their compensation to the sales success of the department. In this case, the company has formed a kind of cross-functional team to insure effective buying, once again recognizing the critical nature of the job and structuring a set of job requirements and incentives to encourage the most effective development of customer relationships at the retail sales level.

QUESTIONS FOR MANAGEMENT

The importance of the relationship mirror in most services naturally suggests several questions for managers interested in achieving improved service and profit:

1. How strong is the relationship between customer and employee satisfaction at the unit level in your firm? How do you know?
2. Does this relationship hold for all or a few of the job categories associated with the delivery of your service?
3. Given the identification of job categories critical to the relationship mirror, what are you doing to attract the "best" people to these jobs, with "best" defined by those attitudes and skills needed to carry out the job most effectively?
4. What are you doing to insure the consistency of the quality of the service encounters most critical to the performance of your service?
5. Once a relationship is established, what is being done to insure that the customer is made to feel as if the same server or servers are available to maintain the relationship over time?
6. Have you considered reorganizing, perhaps into teams, in order to insure the continuity of a service relationship that is simply not possible or feasible to achieve by assigning customers to individual servers?

In many services, satisfaction is mirrored in the faces of customers and the people who serve them, whether the encounter takes place on a face-to-face basis or not. But it's clear that this magical interaction doesn't occur without a great deal of preparation and thought. Outstanding service providers tell us that just any kind of preparation and thought will not do. Very often it is preparation and thought that produces the kind of job definition, management policies, supporting technologies, and rewards and recognition that customer-contact people describe with enthusiasm. We have come to call this package of things "capability." It is our next concern.

7

Building a Cycle of Capability

Alvin "Bugs" Burger intuitively has understood for years what one of us rediscovered several years ago in examining determinants of employee satisfaction. He built the largest independently owned extermination company in the United States, Bugs Burger Bug Killers, Inc., on the premise that if you take particular care in selecting and hiring employees on the basis of their attitudes rather than their skills, provide them with a wide range of training, supply them with the best materials and methods, give them a great deal of latitude in the way they perform their jobs under difficult-to-supervise circumstances, reward them for achieving an objective of completely eradicating bugs, take just as much care in the selection of customers, and insure customer feedback and learning through the application of an unconditional guarantee, a lot of money can be made in businesses that have poor reputations for results and a lack of customer orientation.[1]

In a sense, Bugs Burger two decades ago created a cycle of capability that the best frontline service workers, in a study in which one of us participated recently, cited as the most important determinant in their satisfaction.[2] But we're getting ahead of ourselves.

FRONTLINE FRUSTRATION

Our interest in what we have come to call capability was aroused several years ago by a study conducted by The Forum Corporation.[3] Based on a survey of 611 Fortune 500 executives in the United States, it found that while 92 percent of chief executive officers indicated that service quality was extremely important to the success of their businesses, the percentage declined at lower levels of management. Specifically, 87 percent of chief operating officers and 83 percent of division vice presidents agreed.

On the other hand, 51 percent of chief executive officers indicated that immediate financial results were important in their businesses. This compared with 69 percent of chief operating officers and 70 percent of division vice presidents. Clearly, perceptions of priorities were quite different at the second and third levels of management than at the top.

Following up on the findings of this study, we began interviewing employees at several levels of organizations whose leaders were proclaiming, in ads and annual reports, their intense desire to satisfy customers. What we found in most cases was that top management was communicating, through both ads to customers and speeches to employees, the impression that one of its primary goals was to deliver solutions to customer problems and needs. The messages to customers invariably were: "The customer is always right. We're here to solve your problems. This is a customer-driven organization."

At the same time, frontline service providers in these same companies told us that: "The customer is always right as long as it doesn't cut into the bottom line. Just try to solve customer problems and you run into one company policy or another that prevent you from doing it. What the customer is told is 180 degrees different from what we're allowed to do."

Although we didn't measure it at the time, it seemed to us that inability to deliver results to customers was the number one source of frustration to frontline service employees. This was confirmed by other studies focusing on relationships between management policies and employee satisfaction, especially those by John Parkington and Benjamin Schneider, Warren Bennis, and Peter Blau.[4] They have pieced together a link between top management behavior that "walks the talk" regarding efforts to enable employees to meet customers' needs, the satisfaction of employees, and, by extension, the satisfaction of customers. They also have identified relationships between employee dissatisfaction and frustration and managements that impose rules and procedures inhibiting frontline employees from serving customers.

In our experience, when this situation occurs, the most dissatisfied and frustrated of all are the best frontline employees. Our intuition was confirmed several years later when one of us undertook an examination of the data from an extensive study of employee satisfaction.

CAPABILITY DEFINED

The meaning of what we have come to call capability was provided for us by nearly 1,300 employees and more than 4,000 customers of a personal lines insurance company.[5] Their definition provides the basis for management action.

First, a strong "customer-employee satisfaction mirror" of the type described in Chapter 6 was found among the respondents to the study—so strong, in fact, that the researchers were motivated to identify the sources of employee satisfaction. Customers and employees alike evaluated the company's recent performance similarly on dimensions important to customers such as: (1) ease of doing business with the company, (2) the competence of service people, (3) the timeliness of the service, (4) service representatives' availability and concerns for customers, and (5) the interest displayed by service personnel in helping customers.

However, it was the investigation of the sources of employee satisfaction at this company that yielded the most interesting results. About two-thirds of employees' satisfaction levels were caused by just three factors: (1) the latitude given employees by their management to meet customers needs, (2) the authority given them to serve customers, and (3) possession of the knowledge and skills needed to serve customers. When combined with rewards for serving customers well, these factors in total accounted for over three-fourths of the job satisfaction experienced by these frontline service workers as shown in Figure 7–1. These factors comprise much of what we have come to call "capability."

The impact of capability on job satisfaction was identified even more clearly in this study. For every two-percentage-point increase in service capability, there was nearly a one-percentage-point increase in the percentage of frontline employees expressing their overall satisfaction with their jobs.

Based on the results of this study, it was concluded that "capability" is made up of several components, including: (1) the latitude to deliver results to customers, (2) a clear expression of limits within which frontline employees are permitted to act, (3) excellent training to perform the job, (4) well-engineered support systems, such as service facilities and information systems, and (5) recognition and rewards for doing jobs well, determined at least in part by the levels of customer satisfaction achieved.

FIGURE 7–1
Determinants of Frontline Employee Capability in a Personal Lines Insurance Company

Determinants	Explanatory Power*
Latitude is given to meet customer needs	36.6%
I have the authority to serve the customer	19.2
I have the knowledge and skills to serve the customer	12.9
Rewards are provided for serving the customer well	7.3
Customer satisfaction is a high priority with the director/manager	4.2
Production requirements are reasonably balanced with serving the customer	3.1
Supervision overall is satisfactory	2.8
Underwriting training is satisfactory	2.1
13 other determinants	11.8
Total	100.0%

*Each figure represents the proportion of the total *r* squared (correlation between the determinant and general feelings about capability to do the job) explained by each determinant.

Source: Leonard A. Schlesinger and Jeffrey Zornitsky, "Job Satisfaction, Service Capability, and Customer Satisfaction: An Examination of Linkages and Management Implications," *Human Resource Planning,* Volume 14, Number 2, pp. 141–49, at p. 145.

Based on our other experiences, there is one additional element to the capability formula, although this study didn't measure it. It has to do with selection. In other efforts we have undertaken, the best-performing employees appeared to care most about their capability and that of others around them. Further, "winning" employees seemed to value working with "winning" customers and other "winning" employees. With this in mind, it is logical to conclude that customer and employee selection methods and results are critical to the successful creation of a high-capability frontline service organization. We'll start there in constructing our cycle of capability.

HIRING FOR ATTITUDES FIRST, SKILLS SECOND

In visiting high-performing service organizations on several continents, we began to hear common themes in talking with their leadership. The first of these was an emphasis on hiring frontline service people with the right attitude, then training them for the skills needed in their jobs. In fact, this often meant not hiring people with experience in a particular job if it meant hiring from a competitor, something these organizations for the most part preferred not to do in order to avoid getting people with poor training or poor attitudes.

The leadership of Rosenbluth International, a fast-growing corporate travel agency with revenues in excess of $2 billion, has articulated this policy very well. According to CEO Hal Rosenbluth, "It's not technical skills we're looking for, it's nice people. We can train people to do anything technical, but we can't make them nice."[6] At Southwest Airlines, a similar policy prevails. As Herb Kelleher, the CEO, puts it, "Hiring starts off looking for people with a good attitude—that's what we're looking for—people who enjoy serving other people."[7]

The Bugs Burger Method

Bugs Burger set out to form a company capable of eliminating pests such as rodents and insects from infested restaurants or other premises that had proven difficult or impossible to serve by typical exterminators offering, in Burger's terms, "pest control" services. His service concept was that of a "pest elimination" service offered at a premium price, often four to six times that of his competition, to customers with severe and potentially costly pest problems. Typically, this included a prestigious list of restaurants and hotels that could not afford citations by local health departments for infested premises.

Because he performed the service himself in the early days of his fledgling firm, Burger knew what was required to do the job. As his business grew, he began to hire others with the same interests and motivation as he had, that is, to become members of a "bug-killing elite" competing in an industry with a questionable reputation in the minds of many customers. The hiring decision was particularly critical in view of the fact that many of his employees would have to operate somewhat independently, often in the middle of the night, in situations difficult to supervise.

In order to find the right people to become "service specialists," Burger developed a process over time that indeed began to yield a bug-killing elite. But it required more than just conducting the usual interviews. It required that he check out their references and their credit ratings, have them complete elaborate personality and aptitude tests, ask them to take polygraph (lie detector) and drug tests (where permitted by law), and even interview members of their families. The objective was to hire both perfectionists and individuals with reasonably stable lives who would be called on to work unusual hours, often late at night. According to Burger, "When we opened branches in Chicago and Detroit . . . we interviewed over 400 people before we found one applicant who met our standards." The cadre of people surviving this rigorous selection process shared many of the same characteristics, developed a strong sense of pride and camaraderie, and proved effective in interacting with clients and each other.

This great care in selecting people has proven effective for organizations ranging from the hotel business (Marriott and Ritz-Carlton) to oil field service (Schlumberger), from auto rental (Avis) to fast food service management (Taco Bell). In fact, in examining a sample of outstanding service providers, we began to notice a pattern in the techniques used for employee selection. An unusually high proportion of these organizations were employing nontraditional approaches to the task, in particular one relying on the matching of "life themes" important to job success with those exhibited by job applicants.

Selection by "Life Themes"

The "life themes" approach to selection involves eight basic steps: (1) identifying the star performers in the particular job to be filled, (2) interviewing those stars to find out what distinguishes them from less successful colleagues in order to create a life-themes model for the job, (3) scripting a questionnaire around the life-themes model and structuring it for telephone interviewers of prospective job candidates, (4) identifying the pool of job candidates, (5) conducting and taping interviews over the telephone, using trained interviewers, (6) transcribing the interviews for analysts trained to interpret them using "listen for's", (7) creating a life-themes profile for each job candidate, and (8) recommending which applicants to hire.[8]

Where it has been applied in organizations such as Motorola, Hyatt Hotels, the Fairfield Inn subsidiary of Marriott, the Taco Bell subsidiary of Pepsico, the ServiceMaster Company, Searle Pharmaceuticals, and even the Cleveland Cavaliers professional basketball team, results have yielded a group of employees that roughly reflects the demographic profile of the pool of applicants interviewed.

Organizations that have applied this approach successfully claim that the approach does not require face-to-face interviewing; in fact, they claim that face-to-face interviews introduce interviewer biases and reduce the reliability of results produced by the technique. Further, it is important to note that the "life themes" approach places little emphasis on technical skills and specific knowledge needed to perform a job. Its primary emphasis is on attitudes and values. It shouldn't be a surprise that the approach has been maligned by traditional personnel administrators, although the growing body of evidence about the effectiveness of this approach in hiring frontline service providers is becoming harder and harder to refute.

Substituting Self-Selection for Selection

One of the greatest sources of frontline employee turnover is a misunderstanding on the part of the new hire of what the job actually requires. This is particularly true in businesses where frontline jobs are demanding and not very glamorous. The cost of weeding out the most successful among a large group of new hires has become far too high to ignore the problem. That's why well-known organizations such as ISS, the Danish-based janitorial service with an international clientele, which hires tens of thousands of new employees annually, has pioneered efforts in Europe to help prospective employees select themselves into jobs at its recently established Job Centre in Copenhagen, serving the Danish operation.

Among many other things, this includes the mandatory viewing of a "job preview" video that conveys a strong impression of just how hard the work will be, including the early-morning starting times for those who might otherwise find it difficult to rise early. It is part of a process at ISS that actually encourages employees to opt out at any point that they feel uncomfortable. Those who survive are assumed to have selected themselves into the jobs being offered. This accounts in no small measure for the fact that ISS's employee retention rate in Denmark is five times higher than the industry average.[9]

Bugs Burger also recognized that the outstanding pay and benefits provided by his company could attract exterminators who might overlook the negative aspects of their work. As a result, he structured a training process that included an early exposure to the nature of the work to be done. After each on-the-job experience, trainees were encouraged to drop out if they had any doubts about their enthusiasm for becoming a member of the bug-killing elite.

Involving Customers in the Process

Southwest Airlines is not alone among the service organizations we have visited in involving customers in the task of selecting customer-contact personnel. But it has perhaps followed the practice longer by adding frequent flyers to its personnel panels selecting flight attendants and other ground personnel who come into frequent contact with Southwest's customers. As Southwest's manager in charge of the process, Rita Bailey, puts it, "Who else is better able to tell us what they want to see in people staffing our airplane cabins?"[10]

For those doubting the feasibility of this practice in other consumer or business-to-business services, we might add that we asked several of these frequent flyers why they took time off from work to assist Southwest Airlines in its work. The replies were enlightening. Several said it was both fun and educational. Others pointed out that it was a somewhat natural thing to do "for my airline," suggesting a degree of "customer ownership" to which any organization might aspire.

SERVING CUSTOMERS WHO QUALIFY

High-capability organizations we have observed rarely serve all customers who desire their products or services. Customers have to qualify for their service.

Bugs Burger Bug Killers (BBBK) required, for example, that customers, prior to entering into a service agreement with the firm, agree to prepare their premises for monthly servicing by Burger's people and, in some cases, agree to increase the frequency of cleanups, change trash-disposal procedures, or make BBBK-specified repairs. Part of the incentive for doing this was an unconditional service guarantee provided by BBBK that its clients and their customers would never see another pest on the client's premises. And part of the incentive was an intense desire for pest eradication. Potential customers refusing to allow BBBK to enter their premises, typically at night, for an initial cleanup did not qualify to do business with the company. As Burger put it, "If they don't want to follow the strict clean-up regimen we require, we don't want to do business with them."[11]

The careful matching of customers with company offerings helps insure a higher degree of success in longer-term relationships. It stacks the deck in favor of the successful delivery of results by frontline employees, employee satisfaction and loyalty, and customer satisfaction and retention.

DESIGNING TRAINING AS BOTH ENDS AND MEANS

Kenneth Wexner, former Chairman and CEO of the ServiceMaster Company, providing management services for housekeeping and other functions in hospitals and other institutions, often said that "we want to help people *be* something before we ask them to *do* something."[12] Pride and dignity are considered to be important elements of what ServiceMaster's managers bring to jobs that have received little recognition in society. And education is seen as an important way in which this is achieved. In addition to providing regular instruction to help employees perform their jobs better, ServiceMaster managers frequently arrange for training their charges in what might be termed life skills, including such things as basic as language.

USAA, the financial services supplier to military and other clients, boasts seventy-five classrooms and a curriculum of more than 200 courses at its corporate headquarters in San Antonio. Led by former military officers who understand the benefits of a wide-ranging education as a normal feature of a job, they have extended the concept to their company. As a result, many employees have obtained college degrees as a part of their employment, an accomplishment that positively affects the attitudes with which they approach customers in their everyday jobs and makes USAA one of the outstanding employers in the United States in the eyes of its employees.

At BBBK new hires experienced a five-month training program. It was carried out both in the classroom, with Bugs Burger often in front of the class, and on the job under the full-time instruction of a field manager. The company spent over $15,000, including salary and living expenses away from home, training each new employee. The training was designed both to develop technical skills and to improve the effectiveness with which BBBK employees could interact with customers.

Many outstanding service organizations view training as both an end and a means. The means may be to prepare employees to do their jobs better. The end in this case is an improvement in employee self-confidence, pride, and ability to cope with life.

PROVIDING LATITUDE AND LIMITS

Latitude and limits are our alternative to the most overused and least understood word in the English business lexicon today—one with eleven letters, beginning with "e", and containing the word "power," a word that Robert Simons maintains has led in some cases to poor control and even irresponsible behavior on the part of managers.[13]

Just as frontline employees repeatedly have told us they want enough latitude to be able to deliver results to customers, they also like to have the limits of their authority described. This description may at times be subtle and subjective, as in Southwest Airlines' instruction to frontline employees to "do whatever you feel comfortable doing for a customer." In this case the word "comfortable" describes the limit. This, however, may not be definite enough for other organizations and other jobs. That is why, for example, the Ritz-Carlton organization has set a dollar limit (albeit a high one) on the costs of things that employees can do to resolve customer "opportunities" (the word for complaints within the Ritz-Carlton organization).

The Traditional View

One view of employee latitude is described in Figure 7–2. It is that of a "box" within which an employee is free to operate. Actions that exceed the limits, such as at Southwest Airlines or the Ritz-Carlton, require the approval of a superior. This has the advantage of giving employees the latitude to carry out their missions while not subjecting the organization to the risks of unnecessarily large commitments to customers or others. Note that the objective of this approach is to enlarge the size of the "box" to the degree practicable, given the demands of a particular business.

The Nontraditional View

Bugs Burger, Au Bon Pain, and several other organizations have elected a nontraditional approach to the provision of job latitude, as shown diagrammatically in Figure 7–2. For example, under Au Bon Pain's Partner-Manager program, designed to "enfranchise" managers of its French bakery cafés, managers entered into contracts with the company in which they were allowed to keep half the incremental profits over an agreed-on amount. They were free to increase profits by any means at their disposal *provided* they met a set of nonnegotiable standards for such things as product availability, the appearance and cleanliness of the premises, the proper display of the brand, and several other requirements. Failure to pass inspection on these matters was

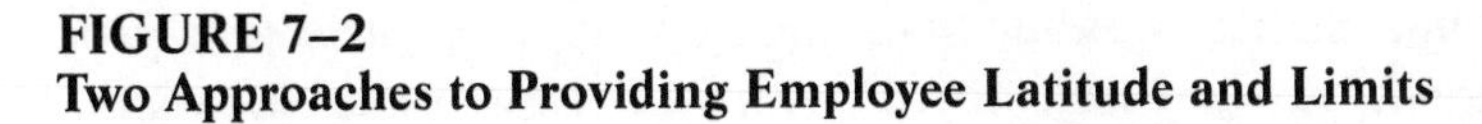

FIGURE 7–2
Two Approaches to Providing Employee Latitude and Limits

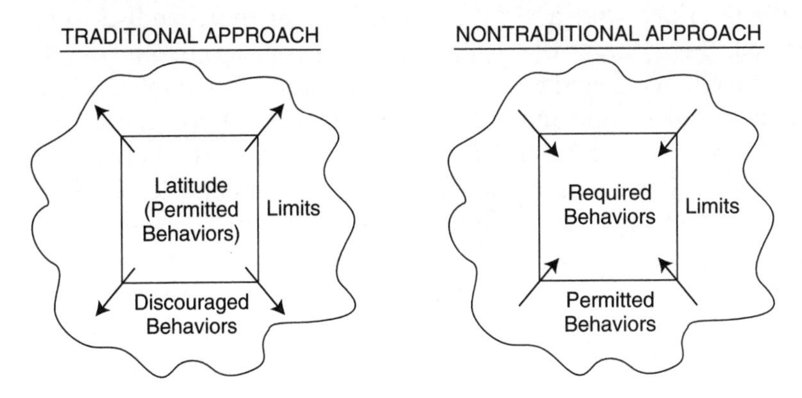

grounds for discontinuing the contract with individual store managers. As a result of this initiative, profits increased dramatically shortly after its introduction. Store managers increased profits by adding seats to their premises, initiating catering services, and seeking out institutional customers for their products as well as managing personnel and other aspects of the operation differently.

Similarly, employees at Bugs Burger, often working at odd hours without supervision, were given wide-ranging latitude concerning the methods they could use for cleaning and eliminating pests from client's premises. However, they were rewarded for such efforts only if they met required standards for appearance, dependability, and training.

In contrast to traditional approaches to the issue of latitude, the objective under this philosophy is to reduce the size of the "box" to the minimum needed to control quality and other features of a service. Such nontraditional approaches often are designed to encourage entrepreneurial behaviors in frontline employees. They assume that frontline employees know best how to perform their jobs, and that the potential costs of occasional risks incurred by such policies are well worth the benefits gained in terms of greater sales, service quality, and productivity.

Robert Simons has coined a term, boundary systems, to encompass issues of job latitude and limits. He believes, based on his research, that organizational belief systems, or shared values, combined with clear guidelines regarding appropriate and inappropriate behavior, are necessary to avoid surprises, prevent employees from straying from an agreed-on strategy, and even fostering innovation. We couldn't agree more.[14]

INVESTING IN SUPPORT SYSTEMS

USAA has spent more for customer-oriented state-of-the-art information systems than any other insurance company. Nordstrom provides its crack fashion salesforce with the best store locations, impressive interiors, and a complete selection of merchandise from which to sell. Bugs Burger Bug Killers for years concentrated on developing the best methods and materials for its exterminators. In addition, it tracks client satisfaction and guarantees its services. Recognition and reward are important elements of a strategy of outstanding customer service organizations such as Marriott's Fairfield Inn and Rosenbluth International's corporate travel service. And the senior management at Southwest Airlines, after giving a customer who persisted in outrageous conduct a second chance, notified affected employees that the passenger had been requested not to fly with Southwest again. In addition to personal development efforts discussed earlier, all of these constitute elements of support systems important to frontline service providers.

Information and Communication Technology

It's perfectly logical that USAA outspends other insurance companies for information and communication technology, because it is the lifeblood of a system of distribution in which the company's products are sold by direct mail, telephone, and word-of-mouth and backed up by customer service representatives who are limited to telephone contact with customers with inquiries, problems, and claims. But just as important, information system support is vital to enabling USAA's service representatives to deliver results to its customers. It is the core of a strategy that has resulted in some of the highest customer satisfaction and loyalty levels in the industry. And it accounts for the high level of job satisfaction among USAA's customer service representatives, job satisfaction that pervades the entire organization.

At times, such support systems represent a critical source of competitive advantage. For years, Schlumberger has invested much more than its competitors in technologies to detect and record geological structures critical to advising oil exploration companies what to expect when they drill. At the same time, it has collected the world's most complete data base about geological structures and the presence of oil. It supplies its technologies and data base to its field engineers, responsible for operating remote field facilities, each utilizing perhaps a million dollars or more worth of computing equipment. On the one hand, because of the impossibility of providing close supervision to its field engineers, Schlumberger must give them a great deal of latitude in operating their facilities. On the other hand, it supplies them with outstanding supporting technology and information, providing them with a means of differentiating their services from those of their competitors.

Facilities

Those who have studied the effectiveness of service encounters cite the influence of the surroundings in which transactions are carried out on both customer and employee satisfaction. Retailers such as Nordstrom are well aware of the favorable impact that facilities and merchandise selection can have on sales. And the ServiceMaster Company discovered some years ago that its extensive management education facilities and laboratories at its Downers Grove, Illinois corporate headquarters earned it a number of sales. In fact, at one point, 90 percent of all school superintendents and hospital board members who could be induced to visit the facility as part of the selling process eventually entered into contracts with ServiceMaster for cleaning and other support services.

Methods and Materials

In the same vein, BBBK insured that its field exterminators were supplied with the most effective exterminating materials available. Beyond that, however, continued study of the best methods for conducting an initial cleaning and for administering chemicals and other materials insured that BBBK's personnel achieved the results promised by the company, bug elimination rather than merely control. As a result, the company devoted more than twice as much of its revenues as the industry average to chemicals. And it encouraged its service specialists to devote four to six times as much time to a typical service call as BBBK's competitors.

Field Quality Control "Safety Nets"

Field inspections, mystery shoppers (involving company employees or hired consultants posing as customers), and customer satisfaction surveys constitute several of the methods by which outstanding service providers insure consistently high performance. At Taco Bell, these are called "safety nets."

BBBK utilized a full-time, two-person quality-control team headed by Burger's daughter, who traveled the country calling on customers and filing their own reports. In addition, district managers called clients a day or two after each service call to check on satisfaction.

Such practices, with the possible exception of mystery shoppers (which are considered by some to be prone to arbitrary appraisal without recourse), seem to appeal to the better frontline service providers. The reaction of one BBBK service specialist is typical of this attitude: "Yeah, it's pressure but it helps you keep up to your standards. Without it I guess we'd be just like any other company." As another specialist put it: "It gives us that little extra motivation."[15]

Service Guarantees

Yet another element of BBBK's support system was its unconditional service guarantee, which was designed to significantly penalize company earnings for consistent failure to achieve outstanding results. It stated that, in return for a client's submitting to and paying for a complete cleanout prior to the contract, Bugs Burger would, if a client were cited by a local health department: (1) pay any fine incurred by the client, (2) pay the client for all lost profits due to being shut down plus $5,000 in damages for lost reputation, and (3) provide the next six months of service free or pay for one year's service by another exterminator of the customer's choice. For customers of a client who might sight a pest, BBBK sent them letters of apology and coupons for free services.

Obviously, organizations employing service guarantees as rigorous as this one can't afford to honor very many of them without suffering punishing financial results. And the best don't have to. At BBBK, for example, claims averaged about $2,000 per month on a revenue base of more than $30 million per year.

You might ask how a guarantee constitutes part of a support system. In this instance, it was regarded as a way of controlling the quality of the company's service as well as providing information in addition to complaints that could serve as the basis for improved methods and results. Perhaps most important, the occurrence of a complaint was not used to penalize BBBK employees. Rather, it was seen as an opportunity to provide additional training to the service specialist and give him an opportunity to impress the client with the company's services and recovery capabilities.

In a very real way, Bugs Burger's service guarantee was a way of enlisting the help of its clients in maintaining outstanding results-oriented performance. We'll examine service guarantees in greater depth in Chapter 10.

Latitude to Fire Customers

A recurring theme in several of the high-performing organizations we have visited in recent years has been the latitude given frontline employees to fire customers.

At Rosenbluth Travel, for example, clients whose personnel are repeatedly rude to Rosenbluth employees have been asked to find another travel service. According to Hal Rosenbluth, company CEO, "Usually these are companies that mistreat their own people, so they mistreat ours over the phone. I think it's terrible to ask one of our associates to talk with someone who's rude to them every fifteen minutes."[16]

Herb Kelleher, CEO of Southwest Airlines, is even more outspoken when he says, "Something . . . that is entirely wrong . . . that has almost achieved a religiousity in America . . . [is] the customer is always right. That is a betrayal of your people. The customer is not *always* right. . . ."[17]

Where it exists—for example, at Carl Sewell's Cadillac dealership in Dallas—frontline authority to fire customers is accompanied by clearly defined processes, middle-management involvement, and a mutual understanding among managers and frontline employees that it is a "silver bullet" to be employed under only the most extreme circumstances in which the organization has failed to understand how to meet the needs of a particularly troublesome, unruly, or rude customer.

The assumption underlying support systems utilized by leading service organizations is that employees who survive rigorous selection and training can be trusted to perform in their and their employers' best interests and deserve all of the support that can be provided to them. In Bugs Burger's words: "What I say is, 'I really care about you. I'll go to bat for you.' I also tell my people that I expect them to make mistakes. If you don't communicate this attitude—if you tell people they're no good—you'll have uptight, unhappy people, and you'll live by distrust."[18]

PROVIDING CONSISTENT REWARD AND RECOGNITION

None of the innovative practices described above work unless incentives, rewards, and recognition are designed to motivate frontline employees in ways required by other policies. For example, it is irresponsible to provide such employees with wide-ranging latitude if there is little incentive for them to use it responsibly. In a word, the incentives and rewards must encourage them to take "ownership" of customers' problems and, figuratively speaking, the business. That is why Au Bon Pain's management devised a way of making store managers feel as if they were franchisees without having to invest any of their own money (hence the term "enfranchisement," used by the company) by cutting them in for a significant share of their stores' profits over a negotiated target.

The founders of the Outback Steakhouse chain of restaurants provide an example that characterizes the compensation patterns we have found in a number of high-capability service organizations.[19] In an effort to create a modest business that would support their golfing habits, these entrepreneurs instead developed a strategy that within seven years of the opening of their first restaurant would result in a chain realizing more than $500 million in annual revenue. At Outback, the restaurant management compensation program is an important element in a strategy that also features an attractive casual "life style" dining format, the highest-quality meal ingredients, a dinner-only service schedule (a product of what one competitor attributes to its founders interests' in golf) with carefully paced food preparation (and consumption) that allows restaurants to be operated with one shift of employees serving only three tables, working reasonable hours, "turning over" their tables in an hour, and each serving more than 200 customers per week who provide more than $350 in tips on food alone. Managers earn a base salary of $45,000, slightly less than several of Outback's competitors. But in addition, Outback offers its managers the opportunity to invest $25,000 in their restaurants in return for a five-year contract in which they receive 10 percent of the cash flow (earnings before taxes, interest, depreciation, and amortization, calculated monthly). The results, although they cannot all be attributed to its unit management compensation practices, have been remarkable. An average Outback restaurant recently was realizing $3.2 million in annual sales (substantially more than its closest competitor offering both lunch and dinner), spending more for food and less for occupancy (with restaurants not located in high-rent locations catering to the business lunch crowd) as a proportion of revenue than its competition, and generating a very high cash flow of $736,000 (23 percent of sales), worth $73,600 per year to Outback's manager-investors. In total, Outback's managers' average incomes were nearly twice that of its closest competitors, with about 65 percent of total income from incentives as opposed to no more than 20 percent for Outback's major competitors. In addition, each manager receives roughly 4,000 shares of options in the company's stock that vest over the five-year period. Of special note, however, is that Outback's intense utilization of labor means that even though its employees earn much more than its competitors, its labor costs as a proportion of revenues are much less. In other words, high wages and salaries do not have to equate to high labor costs.

Of equal interest are other results that this strategy has produced for the Outback Steakhouse chain. First, the high levels of compensation have enabled it to attract the best managers in the business. Second, the five-year contract has enabled the chain to lower its turnover rates for managers to about 5 percent in a sector of the restaurant industry in which 30 percent to 40 percent turnover is typical. Third, this has kept managers in the same locations, where they can develop a local clientele, longer. This insures greater continuity in restaurant frontline ranks as well. And, given the quality of its unit management, Outback has been able to operate with only one level of management between more than 400 restaurant managers and the chain's founders. It helps explain why the chain of more than 200 restaurants achieved revenues of more than $500 million in the seventh year after its founding while yielding a 52 percent return on its owners' investment.

The attitude of Outback's founders reflect the pattern of support for frontline service providers that we have found in many other high-capability organizations. As one of them, Tim Gannon, has put it, "(We) have all worked as cooks and waiters and bartenders. We know what it's like to have the right equipment and the right space to produce the food. We believe that if you treat employees as if you were one of them and give them the right environment, they will blow you away with their performance."[20]

At BBBK, field service specialists received market-level wages and full benefits plus 20 percent of all monthly gross billings on their individual routes in excess of $5,100. Upon the failure of a customer to renew a contract through no fault of the specialist, the company reimbursed the specialist for the lost business until a new client could be found that provided comparable gross billings. Again, the results are not surprising. In total, BBBK's personnel strategy yielded the company turnover rates among service specialists as low as 3 percent per year in an industry typically experiencing 60 percent turnover rates.

FITTING THE ELEMENTS TOGETHER

No one of the ideas or policies described in this chapter can be introduced in a vacuum without examining all other elements of what we have come to call a cycle of capability, shown in Figure 7–3. The cycle of capability in Figure 7–3 represents a point of view, that frontline employees should be given as much latitude to perform their jobs as possible and supported with other elements of the cycle accordingly. While whatever is done has to be consistent with the nature of the business and the frontline jobs it requires as well as the nature of middle man-

FIGURE 7–3
The Cycle of Capability

agement available to provide the leadership for such policies, there nevertheless is room for a wide range of strategies in any industry.

For example, organizations may elect to deliver high value to customers by employing technology and methods that actually restrict frontline employee latitude. To a degree, this is what McDonald's has done to achieve consistently high quality in the products produced by its frontline employees. The McDonald's "system" has little room for frontline employee latitude, extensive and expensive training of counter employees, careful selection, and rewards tied to performance. It does what it does very well (even though employees often seem to be confounded by our requests for nonstandard service).

Taco Bell, on the other hand, elected to move from a McDonald's-style strategy to that of a higher-capability frontline organization several years ago. Its success since that time has been at least as great as McDonald's. (We'll return to the Taco Bell experience in Chapter 12.) The point is that both high- and low-capability initiatives can work and work very well. But only if they are designed to be internally consistent and reflective of a broader strategy and set of customer needs.

QUESTIONS FOR MANAGEMENT

Questions associated with elements of the cycle of capability are posed in Figure 7–4. But the paramount question to be asked by management is:

1. How much capability should we develop on the front line? Answers to this question depend on those to a number of other questions, including: (1) How important is personal service (as opposed to that delivered by other means) to customers? (2) What kinds of risks are perceived by customers in purchasing the product-service package? (3) To what degree must services be customized at the point or time of purchase? (4) How important is the absolute consistency with which the product-service package is produced and delivered? (5) How important is the development of new ideas and methods by frontline employees? and (6) To what degree can frontline employees actually influence the amount of business generated?

Our discussion suggests several other questions worthy of review from time to time. Among them are:

2. When was the last time the strategy for frontline employee capability was reviewed for internal consistency and the degree to which it supported the overall strategy of the firm?
3. Is the organization devoting enough time and effort to the selection of new associates?

4. Can greater use be made of self-selection or nontraditional selection techniques?
5. Are customer-contact employees being selected primarily on the basis of attitudes and secondarily on the basis of skills?
6. To what degree are customers involved in achieving various elements of a high-capability strategy, for example, in the selection of important customer-contact frontline employees?
7. Does training reflect both the needs of the frontline job and the needs of the individual required to fill it in order to achieve competitive advantage with both customers and potential employees?
8. Do frontline service personnel have the degree of latitude necessary to deliver on the promises made by management to both customers and the organization?
9. Have all possible forms of support for frontline servers been reviewed in the context of questions concerning the degree of latitude that is appropriate for them in their jobs?
10. Given the definition of target markets in the overall strategy, is a conscious effort made to reward members of the organization for attracting and satisfying the "right" customers, i.e., those that reflect the strategy?

FIGURE 7–4
Questions Associated with the Cycle of Capability

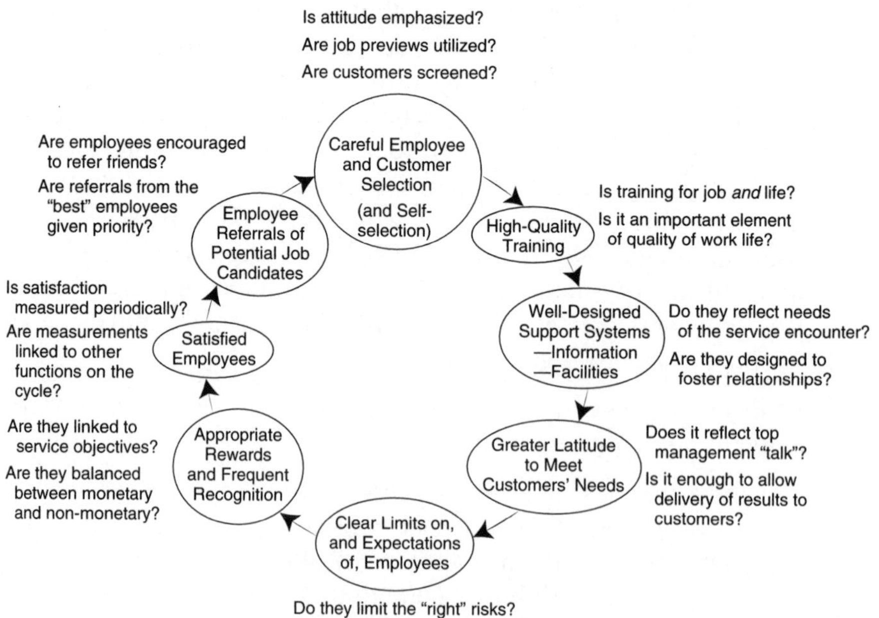

CONCLUDING COMMENTS

High-capability frontline organizations have a self-sustaining character. It is based on the principle we cited earlier that "winners" like to associate with "winners." Thus, in many of the organizations we have observed, referrals from existing employees are important sources of new employees. This is particularly true if such referrals are prioritized in terms of their source. (It is just as true that "losers" attract "losers.") It has important implications for any effort to achieve high frontline capability.

We would like to be able to report that Bugs Burger Bug Killers has sustained itself by carving a niche in the exterminating business that endures to this day. But Burger's business was brought to the attention of the S. C. Johnson & Son, Inc., producers of some of the world's best-known household cleaning and furniture-protection products, during the merger and acquisition mania of the late-1980s. Unable to resist a premium price of about $30 million for a business he had built from nothing, Burger sold.

But the forces of corporate bureaucracy at Johnson made short work of the Burger strategy and organization. The first thing to go was the name, hardly fitting for a large, respected company. The new name? PRISM, an acronym for Premises Integrated Sanitation Management. Next to go was the Burger guarantee, then the premium price strategy. Of course, without the premium price strategy or the guarantee, there was little need for, or money to support, the selection, training, and compensation practices of the former organization. Given these changes, PRISM began more and more to resemble its competition, although with a largely new management and frontline work force. The result was perhaps inevitable. The venture was written off several years ago by S. C. Johnson after several years of disappointing results.

In some ways, BBBK's "second chapter" provides just as important a lesson for us as the first. Well-thought-out strategies focused around high frontline capability do not respond well to tinkering.

"Winners" on the frontline both value and contribute to the most effective processes for carrying out their jobs. Process redesign has become a fetish in industry around the world. How it is approached may be just as important as what is achieved. These matters are the concern of Chapter 8.

8

Developing Processes That Deliver Value

Continuous quality improvement, reengineering, and process redesign are concepts that have dominated the thinking of managers in both large and small organizations for more than a decade. They have resulted in the development of as many techniques for such high-profile initiatives as there are consultants purveying them. The work has spawned arguments among the devotees of one process improvement philosophy or another—Deming, Juran, Crosby—about issues of whether the seven-step or the fourteen-step approach is best, or whether Hammer's approach to process improvement through reengineering is more effective than continuous quality improvement techniques.[1]

The concepts, techniques, and philosophies have all succeeded. And all have failed. Even more curious is the fact that some of the most successfully designed processes we know did not result from any of these concepts, techniques, or philosophies. From this it's easy to conclude that there are more important determinants of success at work in these efforts than the philosophy followed or the techniques chosen. And from this it is equally easy to conclude that quality and productivity improvement do not necessarily translate into processes that deliver value, our primary concern in this chapter.

The experiences of three very different organizations provide illustrations of what we mean. Two of these have become our constant companions since we first documented in case form the development of a little-known hospital specializing in fixing one kind of hernias in 1983[2] and a fledgling Japanese steak house concept in 1972.[3] The third became first a well-publicized model and then a lesson of what to avoid for other organizations contemplating the adoption of formal quality improvement initiatives.[4] In all, the experiences of Shouldice Hospital, Benihana of Tokyo, and Florida Power & Light help put in perspective the role of process improvement in the service profit chain in three very different settings. They provide convincing evidence that the role of process improvement is not just to deliver the highest quality or productivity, but to deliver the highest value and satisfaction to customers and employees alike, with resulting profits to investors.

BASIC TENETS OF PROCESS DESIGN THAT YIELD VALUE

Several universal lessons have resulted from all of the work to enhance value and improve quality and productivity through process redesign. They include:

1. The customer, not the service provider, determines and defines quality and value.
2. Because the customer determines and defines quality and value, these definitions are relative, not absolute.
3. Customer evaluations of quality and value are based on what was delivered as opposed to what was expected in terms of results, process quality, price, and the costs of acquiring the service.
4. Customer expectations are just as important an element of perceived value as what is actually delivered; it is important to manage such expectations.
5. Because customer perceptions of quality and value are relative, effective service delivery requires the adaptation of services to individual needs.
6. The most cost-effective way in which services are adapted to individual needs is through frontline employees or support systems, such as information technology, that recognize and respond to such needs.
7. Any decisions concerning quality and value that fail to take into account the customer are immediately suspect. This applies equally to techniques used in support of decision making.

For these reasons, efforts to enhance processes, quality, and value should have a profound impact on the very culture of an organization, forcing it to become more sensitive to the needs of customers, suppliers, and employees alike, resulting in the returns sought by investors.

Lest all of this sounds impossible to achieve, we have the example set by several organizations that have done the impossible, not always by consciously following highly accepted principles of continuous quality improvement or reengineering.

THE WORLD'S BEST HOSPITAL

We have yet to find a dissatisfied patient of the Shouldice Hospital in Toronto. Many have judged it the world's best hospital. Medical professionals may not agree, because they only do one thing at Shouldice, fix hernias—and only one type of external hernias (inguinal), at that. The service is based on an operating technique developed at Shouldice that involves arranging the muscles of the abdominal wall in three distinct layers that are overlapped at the margins in much the same manner as the edges of a coat might be overlapped when buttoned. The muscular wall of the abdomen is then reinforced with six rows of stitches under the skin cover. The result, in contrast to other techniques for fixing hernias, most often is a muscle structure that is stronger than for most people without hernias. As basic as this may be from a medical viewpoint, however, it is only one element in building patients' perspectives of Shouldice. The one thing they remember most is being invited to get up from the operating table after the operation and walk to the door of the operating room on the arms of their surgeons, the beginning of a remarkable recovery process that involves a stay of three to four days at the hospital and allows them to return to work twice as fast as for other methods. But even this doesn't explain what goes on at Shouldice.

New philosophies of medical practice have led to clinics where hernias are fixed on an outpatient basis, with same-day arrival and departure. Compared to a service that requires a three- or four-day hospital stay, one might assume that the same-day competitors are cutting into Shouldice's long waiting list. But they aren't even serious competition. Because at its core, Shouldice is not primarily a medical service.

In contrast to hospitals in which, according to one irreverent medical administrator who runs the patient-centered Riverside Methodist Hospital in Columbus, Ohio, Erie Chapman, "patients are subjected to excessive questioning, stripped of their usual clothing and possessions, placed in a subservient, dependent relationship to those attending to them, and allowed visitors only during certain hours,"[5]—in other words, treated worse than prison inmates—all processes at Shouldice are designed with patient and employee satisfaction clearly in mind.

Patients, many of whom are referred by doctors who have themselves visited Shouldice for hernia operations, supply all medical information about themselves once, at the time they make application for a scheduled time for the operation. Applicants are screened for obesity (a risk factor) and, if necessary, told to diet before applying again. So we see once again that Shouldice achieves both market focus ("low-risk" patients) and operating focus in its endeavors, two keys to outstanding service performance. It leverages this focus through the thoughtful attention its leadership gives to process design.

For those patients who are accepted at Shouldice, check-in time is minimized. They are examined briefly on arrival by the surgeon who will operate on them the next day. They are involved in, and held responsible for, their own recovery and the recovery of others throughout the process. No one carries their bags for them on arrival. They share rooms without the amenities that would reduce the amount of walking required to get to bathrooms, television sets, and even telephones. They even shave themselves in preparation for their own operations. Then they counsel other incoming patients several hours after their own operations. They exercise slowly but relentlessly, swapping stories with other patients, for two or three days following the operation. When this recovery (and patient bonding) process is finished, they are recovered sufficiently to return to their jobs—and prepare for the annual reunion of Shouldice patients that attracts about 1,500, many of them returnees for ten years or more. Several elements of the process are documented in the service maps shown in Figure 8–1, to which we will return.

The hospital facility itself reflects the philosophy of the organization. It is set on a country-club-like estate that encourages outdoor exercise. It doesn't look like a hospital, smell like a hospital (disinfectants are odorless), or feel like a hospital (carpeted floors being the rule to reduce falls). One of the few concessions to medical treatment are the low risers on stair steps to facilitate patients' movement from one floor to another (without routine access to elevators).

Surgeons at Shouldice are carefully selected for their ability to adhere strictly to an established technique and their tolerance for performing the same operation about 600 times a year. In return, they receive substantial compensation and work regular schedules, with operations in the morning and short patient examinations in the afternoon before heading for home around 4 P.M. They are rarely "on call" and are able, in the words of one, "to see their children grow up."

Nurses and housekeepers alike are selected not only for their skills but also for their ability to relate to patients, who require little logistical support typical of most hospitals. These are counseling, not "bedpan

FIGURE 8–1
Service Maps for Diagnosis and Booking, Arrival and Check-In, and Operation Processes at Shouldice Hospital

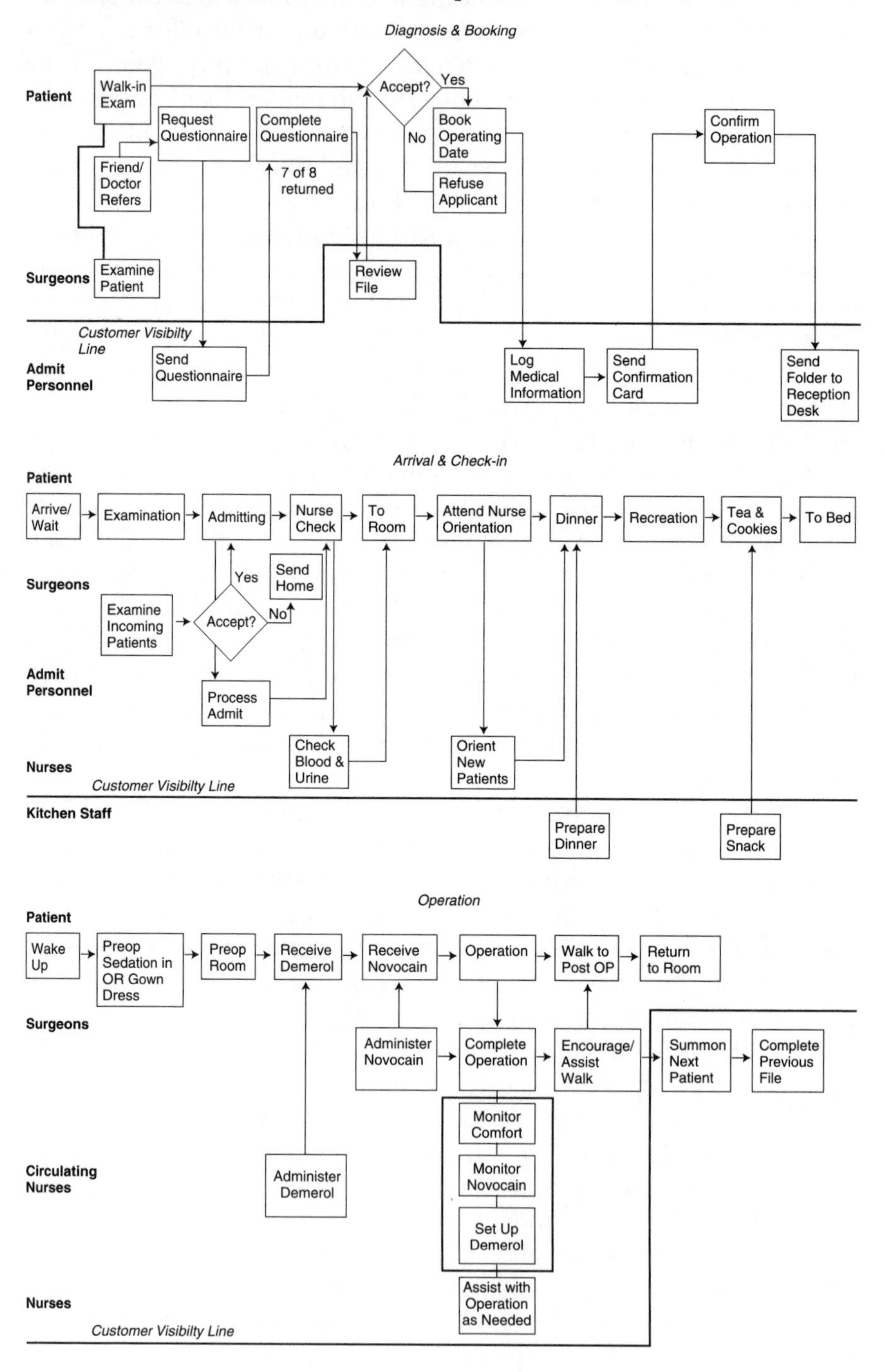

duty," jobs. As a result, they are some of most pleasant, satisfying jobs of their kind.

We would like to be able to tell you that this stunning combination of astute focusing of a service system, process design, and human resource philosophy resulted from the application of leading-edge techniques of the kind described later. Truthfully, the engineering of Shouldice's systems and processes resulted in part from the vision of the founder and in part from the trial-and-error application of common sense—but from the point of view of patients, not medical practitioners, a philosophy that is totally foreign to many medical service providers.

THE WORLD'S BEST DINNER SHOW VALUE

In 1964, a Japanese entrepreneur opened a steak house on the East Side of New York City that would influence a number of other restaurant concepts around the world. Today, Rocky Aoki's Benihana of Tokyo is taken for granted, confused with other "knock-off" restaurants as just another steak house. But the genius behind Benihana was an understanding of Americans' cautious attitudes toward, in Rocky's words, what they perceived as "icky, sticky, slimy" Japanese food, an ability to capitalize on those concerns, and an operating concept right out of the book of industrial firms like Toyota.

The first Benihana menus were huge in appearance but contained basically three items, shrimp, steak, and chicken, all cooked at a large hibachi by a chef personally preparing food, cooking it, and serving up to eight guests seated around the hibachi. Basically American food, cooked in full sight of patrons, relieved their uncertainties about what they were about to eat. But the carefully crafted Japanese decor and chefs brought directly to the United States from Japan provided just enough authenticity to make Benihana an exotic dining experience for those uninitiated in Japanese cuisine.

A potential investor might have given a restaurant concept featuring cooks who chopped and otherwise prepared food, served it, and even cleaned off the "stove" (hibachi) in front of the guests short shrift. But Aoki knew what he was doing, essentially creating a "dinner show" for less than $10 (at that time). His concept required significantly less kitchen space (22 percent vs. 30 percent of total space usually required for a more typical restaurant operation), allowing him to pay prime rents for great locations at a reasonable overall cost. The higher-priced meats could be supplemented with copious quantities of sprouts and other inexpensive vegetables, thus limiting his food costs while giving the appearance of large meals. But the concept had to facilitate the control of the other most important cost of food service, labor. This led directly to a need for process engineering.

The cooking and serving time for food items at Benihana was about twenty-five minutes. That meant that a chef working near capacity would have to serve more than one eight-person hibachi group. Presumably, this could have been achieved by having one chef serve two hibachis over a period of about an hour or three hibachis during a ninety-minute dining experience. The two-hibachi design had several advantages. First, a chef would be in front of his guests for about half of their one-hour dinner, enough to make them feel attentively served. Second, by "turning" hibachis every hour, greater numbers of guests could be served in a restaurant containing fourteen hibachis and 122 seats. Having made this basic decision, Aoki then began training chefs to "pace" their guests through a sixty-minute meal, entertaining them during much of this time by such things as flashing displays of circus-style knife work and an occasional shrimp flipped through the air right onto a lucky guest's plate. This ruled out "all you can eat" menu items, slow-to-consume items such as salads, and leisurely dessert consumption and after-dinner drinks at the hibachi. The trick was to make guests feel that they had been well fed and entertained without looking at their watches. In fact, in New York, some theatre-goers and others appreciated the dispatch with which they could complete dinner. And the concept was especially attractive to those wishing lunch in no more than forty-five minutes.

After having thought out the dining room so carefully, one would have thought that Aoki would have given similar attention to the bar. Instead, his first restaurant was opened with a bar that seated only eight people and had no lounge area. Concluding that this provided insufficient space in which to "inventory" customers and allow hosts to "construct" parties of eight persons for each hibachi, he doubled the size of the bar at his second restaurant. This was still too small.

At this point, Aoki's management began to observe guests' bar behavior and assess what would produce the greatest revenues per given time period. They concluded that an average patron consumed a first drink in about twenty minutes. It was to the establishment's advantage (computed in terms of bar revenue per minute of guest occupancy) to encourage a second drink but not allow the guest to consume it in the bar. Thus, the capacity of future bars would be designed to provide an average of twenty-three minutes of bar "capacity" for diners who would spend another sixty minutes at the hibachis. Given a 122-seat hibachi capacity, this would suggest the need for about forty-eight seats in the bar and lounge, roughly the number built into the design of Aoki's third restaurant. Results were immediate. While bar sales at his first Benihana had been 18 percent of total sales, they rose to 33 percent of sales at his third restaurant, which dictated the design for subsequent Benihanas opened around the world.

Note what Rocky Aoki did and did not do. He certainly understood his non-Japanese guests and what they needed, a safe but somewhat exotic dinner show. He did develop a process that was revenue- and cost-effective. In fact, his first restaurant paid for itself in six months. But he didn't get it right at first. Two trials-and-errors were required to balance the "production line" between the bar and restaurant "processes," probably not unlike what actually happened at Toyota and other auto manufacturers if the truth were known.

Could he have saved money on the authentic decor? Probably. But this is where Aoki's understanding of his employees' needs came to the fore. He claims that he spared no amount of money on the decor. This was not for the guests, who probably couldn't tell the difference, but for the chefs who had left their families behind in Japan and could appreciate subtle reminders of their culture in a foreign environment.

Rocky Aoki was an entrepreneur/engineer ahead of his time. His philosophy and approach ranks right up there with current process design gurus, if only he had chosen to document it. Instead, his experience suggests yet another approach to the design of service processes utilizing industrial concepts, totally appropriate in cases where the primary objective is to deliver a standardized service in predictable ways, regardless of how "impromptu" the service performance may appear to customers.

Both Shouldice Hospital and Benihana of Tokyo utilized unique process designs that were in large part the vision of their founders and a cornerstone for the early development of these businesses. This was not the case at Florida Power & Light, where process improvement was used as a vehicle for substantial change in a power utility operated by traditional industry methods for decades.

AMERICA'S FIRST DEMING PRIZE WINNER

John Hudiburg, CEO of Florida Power & Light (FPL), bought classic quality improvement procedures "hook, line, and sinker" and brought them to his company in 1981. He had been convinced of their usefulness when his organization used explicit quality standards proactively to construct a nuclear power plant in half the time, at less than half the cost, and with 50 percent more "energy availability" than the industry average. Reading Phil Crosby's *Quality Is Free;* organization of study missions to Japan, in particular to Kansai Electric, whose efforts had won it the coveted Japanese Deming Prize for quality improvement; attendance at seminars by such quality "philosophers" as W. Edwards Deming, Joseph Juran, and Al Gunnesou; and consultations with Japanese quality counselors led FPL's management to design its own "scientific" quality improvement program.

Formation of Quality Improvement Teams

FPL's effort began with the formation, on a voluntary basis, of ten pilot teams that rapidly grew to 1,400 functional, cross-functional, task (centered around specific problems identified by management), and lead (comprised of team leaders) teams five years later. Teams were instituted in layers, starting at the top of the organization. At first, many employees were skeptical of the process and were convinced only by early results. Some were convinced to participate by two initiatives, the introduction of what became referred to, almost religiously, as "The Process," and extensive training designed to communicate the purpose of the overall effort and an understanding of how to make The Process work.

Development of The Process

The Process adopted was right out of the books of the quality gurus. In FPL's case, it involved seven steps: (1) reason for improvement (to show the reason for working on a problem), (2) current situation (to describe the problem and set targets for improvement), (3) analysis (to identify and verify the root causes of the problem), (4) countermeasures (to select and implement measures to correct the root causes of the problem), (5) results (to confirm problem alleviation), (6) standardization (to identify steps to prevent the problem from recurring), and (7) future plans (to plan an attack on remaining components of the problem). But even with a clearly defined "process" in place, many teams got stalled, worked on poorly defined problems, or failed to analyze problem causes properly. This led to the adoption of a technique found at Komatsu, a Japanese manufacturer, of a storyboard format, shown in Figure 8–2, in which teams filled in the blanks as their work progressed. Storyboards became the centerpiece of the process and the pride of their creators. More important, they enabled executives touring FPL's facilities to note at a glance the status of the many team efforts underway. The storyboards presented the results of the application of several formal techniques that we have found useful and central to quality improvement. Foremost among them were root cause and Pareto analyses. These contributed to what became known as "management by fact" versus "management by gut" and a philosophy epitomized by a sign outside the door of the head of the Quality Improvement Department that read, "In God we trust; all others must bring data."[6] We'll return to these techniques shortly.

Employee "buy in" progressed well, especially since employees were assured that no jobs would be lost as a result of the process. But middle-management involvement continued to be a challenge, something that should have been no surprise. Middle managers had been told from the beginning to "stay away from the teams—you'll just stifle people." It was now necessary to involve them through training and deployment with the teams.

Policy Deployment

Until this point, teams identifying important problems had been encouraged to proceed with The (seven-step) Process with more emphasis on tools, techniques, process, and team dynamics than their contribution to specific business results. This led to the development of four major mid-term goals, to: (1) achieve customer satisfaction, (2) shape the environment, (3) strengthen organizational effectiveness, and (4) utilize resources effectively. Henceforth, priorities for proposed team efforts were set in terms of their contributions to these four objectives. It was expected that this would, for the first time, tie quality improvement efforts directly to corporate goals, as opposed to considering all quality improvement to be worthy of support.

Quality in Daily Work

The third important phase of FPL's company-wide initiative was to provide individual employees with a process for analyzing theirs and their departments' responsibilities and objectives, with a view to doing things better. For the first time, emphasis was placed on statistical quality control, mapping processes, and better understanding customers inside the organization and devising ways to improve service to them. In an effort to institutionalize practices and make them a part of the everyday effort of individuals, emphasis was placed at this point on the idea that quality improvement was not something employees were expected to do in addition to their regular work; it was the way they were to do their work.

Results followed. Between 1986 and 1989, customer complaints to the Florida Public Service Commission dropped 61 percent and reliability at the customer power meters improved by more than 30 percent. By 1989, the efforts of Hudiburg and his management team appeared to be paying off. The utility's operating income more than doubled in the ten years since Hudiburg had become President (and subsequently promoted). And later in the year, after prodigious efforts to meet stan-

FIGURE 8–2
Storyboard Format for Quality Teams, Florida Power & Light

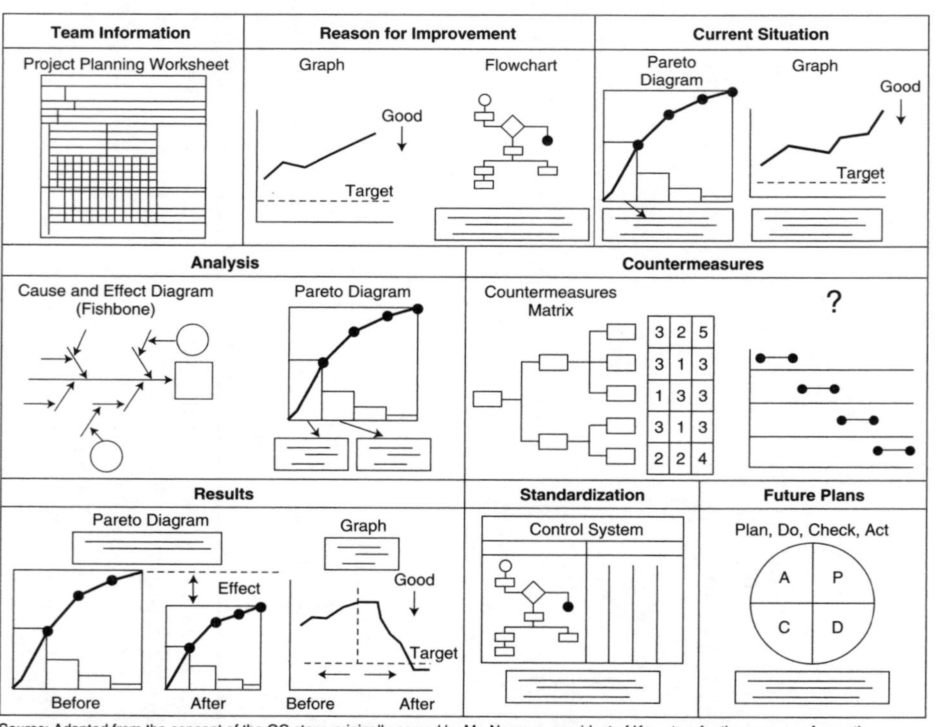

Source: Adapted from the concept of the QC story, originally named by Mr. Nogawa, president of Komatsu, for the purpose of reporting improvement activities. Professor Ikezawa and others expanded the procedure to include its use as a guide for solving a problem.

Christopher W. L. Hart and Joan S. Livingston, Florida Power & Light's Quality Improvement Program, Case No. 688-043. Boston: Harvard Business School, 1987, p. 11.

dards for the competition, FPL was awarded Japan's Deming Prize, the first ever given to a company outside Japan. It was not to be the last chapter in the FPL quality improvement journey.

IMPORTANT TECHNIQUES FOR PROCESS IMPROVEMENT

In part, we selected Shouldice Hospital, Benihana of Tokyo, and Florida Power & Light to illustrate important lessons in process design and improvement. In addition, we chose them because they provide excellent illustrations of several techniques for process improvement that have been particularly helpful to managers around the world.

Service Mapping

Service mapping is a first cousin to flow-charting techniques that have been employed for years in process analysis. These techniques were raised to a new level by concepts developed by Lynn Shostack that she called "blueprinting" of service processes[7] and Jane Kingman-Brundage's development of service mapping itself.[8]

The concept itself is very straightforward.[9] Unlike flow charting, the primary goals of service mapping are to chart activities from the point of view of the customer, insure that all aspects of the service add value to the customer's experience of the service, and identify points at which the service system might break down or otherwise fail to produce the intended value for customers.

Mapping can be as simple or complex as appropriate. A relatively simple map is shown in Figure 8–1 for several processes performed at Shouldice Hospital, including those for diagnosis and booking, arrival and check-in, and the operating procedure. The map itself is constructed by arraying the participants in the process down the left side of the chart and various steps in the process across the horizontal dimension. Several members of an organization can be involved in plotting a service map, often the more the better to elicit and debate the merits of different views.

Next a line of visibility is drawn through the chart, with all activities visible to the customer shown above the line. It may be especially critical to prepare employees to perform such high-visibility activities in ways that are acceptable to customers. The customer can be an extra force for quality improvement for processes that are visible. Further, processes with most steps visible to the customer are typical of those in which customer involvement is high, suggesting that customers are assuming responsibility for outcomes, a critical factor in the development of many outstanding services. All of this was likely the case at Shouldice

Hospital and contributed to the organization's outstanding performance in the eyes of its customers. The final step in service mapping involves the identification of the most likely fail points. These result, among other things, from: (1) steps in the service process that do not add value to the customer's experience of the service, often involving duplication of effort, (2) inadequate conditioning of customers' expectations in advance of the service, (3) steps that might confuse customers where their involvement and cooperation is important, (4) steps where employee judgment is very important, and (5) points at which the operations infrastructure (service delivery system) itself is poorly designed or has low reliability. For example, at Shouldice patients were asked to provide information only once, prior to their arrival in Toronto. They were provided with extensive information about what to expect before their arrival. Constant counseling while at the Hospital was intended to communicate to patients what would be expected of them in assisting in their own recovery and that of fellow patients. (What clearer signal of this could be given than to ask them to walk from the operating table?) Surgical decisions, typically involving the greatest amount of judgment, were reduced by rigid adherence to the Shouldice Method. And every aspect of the infrastructure was designed with the patients' needs in mind, from the extensive recreational facilities of just the right type (putting green vs. golf course) to the spartan rooms providing little encouragement to patients to stay in bed.

More complex service mapping may actually involve the measurement of time and costs associated with each step in the process. Whether simple or complex, efforts to get the service map right are basic to the success of succeeding steps.

Pareto Analyses

The importance of measurement and objective analysis as the basis for "management by fact" is illustrated by an experience of one of Florida Power & Light's quality improvement teams that was working on reducing power outages caused by lightning, a somewhat frustrating task considering the high frequency of electrical storms during certain times of the year in various parts of Florida. When questioned by their team leader about whether they had actually done a Pareto analysis, identifying the relative importance of various problem causes, they reported that there was little doubt that it was lightning striking power facilities. The Pareto analysis that was based on actual records disclosed otherwise. It is shown in Figure 8–3. To the surprise of the team, the most important cause in the region examined was found to be vehicles strik-

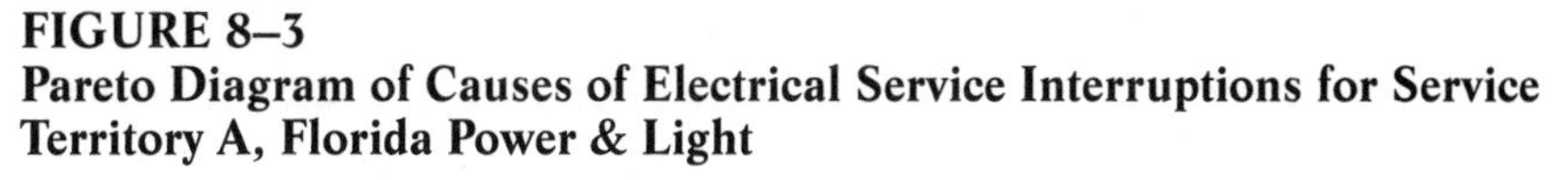

FIGURE 8–3
Pareto Diagram of Causes of Electrical Service Interruptions for Service Territory A, Florida Power & Light

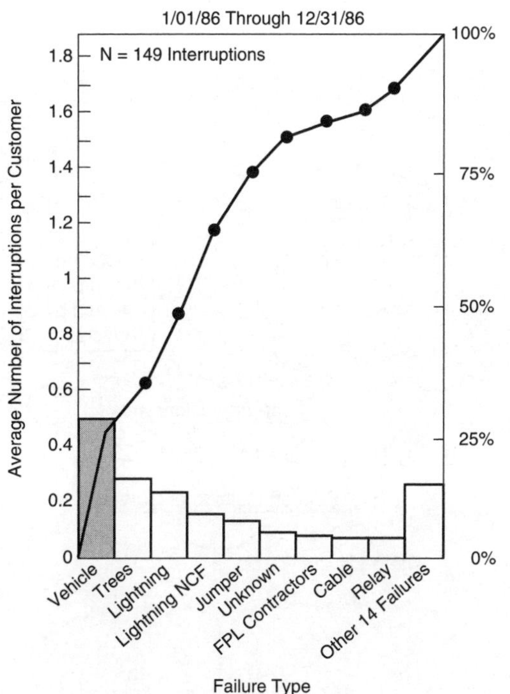

Source: Company data.

ing light poles. The team began to zero in on the problem by next turning to the construction of a cause-and-effect, or fishbone, diagram.

Cause-and-Effect (Fishbone) Diagramming

Fishbone diagrams similar to that shown in Figure 8–4 derive their name from the way in which they require information about root causes of problems to be organized. In the diagram in Figure 8–4, the "head" of the fish is the problem confronted by FPL's quality improvement team, "customer interruptions caused by vehicles," shown at the right of the diagram.

The primary "bones" of the fish describe various categories of possible causes, in this case "methods, man, or environmental" causes. Secondary "bones" describe all of the possible causes occurring to the team constructing the diagram.

This effort can be used to help in the organized investigation of pos-

FIGURE 8–4
Fishbone Analysis of Electrical Interruptions Caused by Vehicles, Florida Power & Light

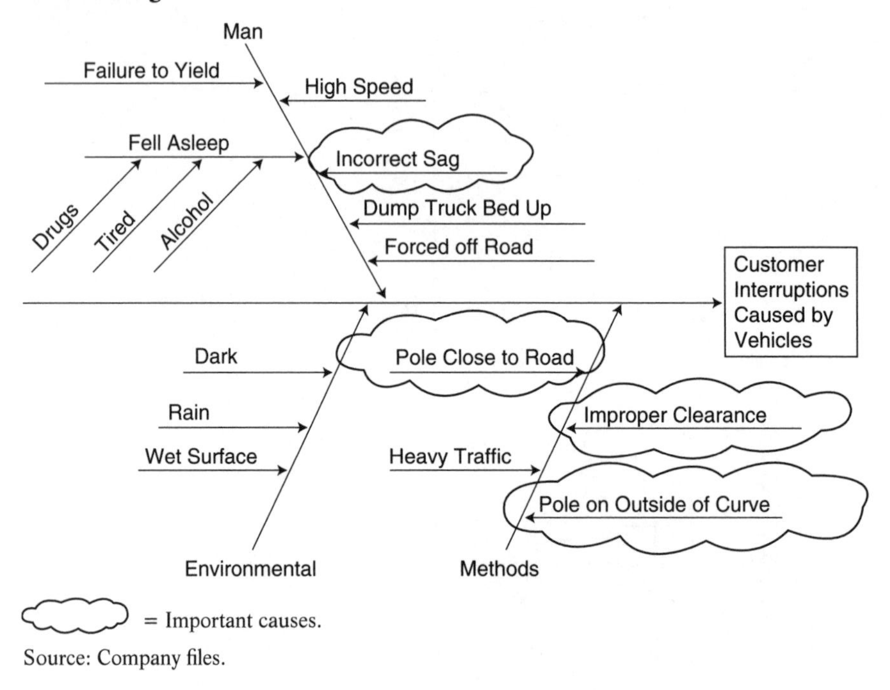

Source: Company files.

sible causes. In the case of FPL's power outage analysis, it led to an investigation producing a surprising disclosure, that the single most important cause of power outages due to vehicles was poles that were located on the outside edges of curves. This was followed by poles that were located too close to roads, and power lines with improper clearance or too much sag (resulting in their being broken by large vehicles).

Other Process Steps

The quantitative analyses described above provide the basis for management action. In the case of FPL's team, following the last four steps of the seven-step Process, it prepared a countermeasure matrix, measured results, took steps to "standardize" the corrective actions, and proceeded to the next set of problems.

Preparing the Countermeasure Matrix. The countermeasure matrix for "poles located on outside of curve" is shown in Figure 8–5. It provided the basis for analyzing each possible countermeasure in terms of: (1) its cost, (2) the degree to which it would solve the problem, (3) whether or not the team could implement the countermeasure, and (4)

FIGURE 8–5
Countermeasure Matrix, Electrical Power Outages Caused by Vehicles, Florida Power & Light

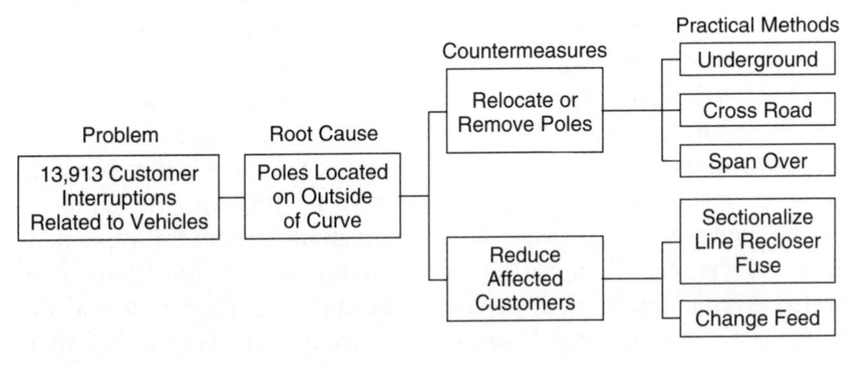

Source: Company files.

what other problems its adoption would cause. The countermeasure matrix in Figure 8–5 shows that the FPL team decided that relocating or removing the poles or taking steps to limit the geographic area over which power was lost might be the best alternative courses of action. Removal of the poles, however, would require that wires be placed underground, a very expensive alternative. Other alternatives proved to be more attractive from a comparison of results and costs. As a result, poles and lines were relocated and steps were taken to sectionalize the line to limit the impact of power outages when they did occur.

Measuring Results. Data from power "interruption reports" provided the basis for measuring the results of the team's actions. For the first nine months of 1987, as opposed to the same period in the previous year, it showed that power outages caused by vehicles had been reduced by 78 percent. In fact, vehicles had become the seventh most important cause of outages, ranking far below such causes as trees, faulty relay devices, animals finding their way into the equipment, and lightning.

Achieving Standardization. Once it was determined that the team's actions in relocating poles had indeed been effective and affordable, steps were taken to "achieve standardization," in effect to preserve the gains by changing the procedures for locating future pole placements, ensuring that the gains achieved could be sustained.

Making Future Plans. What started out as the team dealing with power outages due to lightning had become the team investigating power outages caused by vehicles, with emphasis on the location of power poles.

However, once that problem had been addressed, the team could turn its attention once again to power interruptions caused by lightning and falling trees, the next major causes. This required that it begin the seven-step improvement process again, but this time with the data and knowledge gained from its previous investigations. Multiplying this one team effort by 1,400 teams provides some idea of the impact that FPL's quality improvement initiative had on the company's management process and performance. At its peak, about a thousand quality improvement stories, represented by storyboards, were being presented to management by such teams. Most were accepted by management for implementation. Acceptance became the occasion for recognition, with most rewards given in the form of merchandise or pins, not money (which, according to many who have experience in these matters, is quickly forgotten). At the same time, employee suggestions of lesser magnitude increased twelvefold, to more than 12,000 per year, between 1981 and 1989. Employee pride, respect, and satisfaction increased as well.[10]

The seven steps in FPL's approach, summarized graphically in Figure 8–2, provided a way of implementing a basic philosophy right out of W. Edwards Deming's "book," PDCA, or Plan-Do-Check-Act (plan what to do; carry it out; check what you did; act to prevent error or improve the process, and repeat the PDCA routine).[11] This is characteristic of the simplicity (and memorability) required of all widely adopted concepts.

TRANSLATING TECHNIQUES INTO RESULTS

The experiences described in this chapter contain common themes that provide guides for the most effective application of process design thinking intended to increase value. They are of a higher order than such things as mere quality improvement techniques, and illustrate the importance of:

1. Encouraging leadership buy-in by calibrating the potential results from value improvements by benchmarking performance against the "best in the world" as opposed to merely the best in an industry. There are no hospitals against which Shouldice can benchmark its performance. It has to turn elsewhere. Similarly, Florida Power & Light turned to a Japanese utility and several Japanese manufacturers for its benchmarks. This is a pattern among other outstanding service organizations we have already mentioned. For example, auto dealer Sewell Cadillac, cited earlier for its outstanding service practices and accomplishments, turns to organizations outside auto retailing for service benchmarks and technology, organizations that face challenges most closely comparable to its own. In the case of Sewell, it's hospitals. In fact,

Sewell has adapted several medical technologies and devices for use by its mechanics in achieving better results in more complex car repairs.

2. Involving middle managers in the implementation of new value improvement approaches rather than "freezing them out" of such activities for fear that good ideas from frontline employees might be suppressed. Because it has to be done sooner or later, it's better done sooner through education and the shaping of expectations. Florida Power & Light learned this lesson the hard way. Why is this principle so often forgotten? Probably because senior managers forget how threatening value improvement is to those in middle layers of management. Too often value improvement has cost them their jobs.

3. Maintaining both a customer's and an employee's point of view in the design process, particularly for services for which there is a high level of perceived risk on the part of customers or in which employee satisfaction is critical to success. This is why service mapping is so important, whether done intuitively, as at Shouldice Hospital and Benihana of Tokyo, or more systematically.

4. Involving customers, where possible, in the design of the process. Patients at Shouldice assume an attitude of "ownership" during their stay at the hospital. They regularly mention things that could be improved from their viewpoint. And a number of their ideas have led to improvements in the value of the service to them.

5. Measuring and establishing facts at every step of the value improvement process. Without facts, assumptions and misperceptions will defeat whatever reason and good judgment can be brought to the effort. Resulting disputes will slow any such effort to a crawl. The leadership of Florida Power & Light learned this from their Japanese counterparts and applied the lesson well.

6. Shielding employees from the effects of value improvements that could cost them their current jobs. It's unrealistic to expect a wealth of new ideas from frontline workers whose jobs could be eliminated by successful value enhancement, especially if the emphasis is on reducing costs. To the degree that enhanced value is reflected in increased revenues, however, it should not be too risky to guarantee that value enhancement will not result in the loss of anyone's employment (as opposed to job). Again, this helped insure full cooperation of employees at Florida Power & Light.

7. Creating a "habit" of continuing value improvement that becomes second nature to people at all levels of the organization. Value improvement as a "way of life" in an organization can be achieved im-

plicitly, as at Shouldice or Benihana, or explicitly, as at FPL. The former approach runs the risk of loss of momentum with the loss of the visionaries, such as Earl Shouldice or Rocky Aoki, who devised the value-based strategy, structure, and techniques in the first place. That's why FPL's effort to make The Process a habit and the cornerstone of management thinking at the company is so noteworthy. The Process basically changed the way the company was managed, at least at lower ranks in the organization.

8. Actually expecting and seeking basic changes in the culture of an organization embracing such initiatives. As we will see later, managing a transition to profit chain thinking is no easy task. It requires vehicles for change. Value improvement initiatives can provide such vehicles, especially if they can become ingrained in management practice and thinking. It is doubtful that John Hudiburg could have achieved the changes he did without the thinking and practices encouraged by his company's Quality Improvement Program.

This all requires buy-in and enthusiastic support among an organization's leadership. In the words of Wayne Brunetti, FPL's Executive Vice President, who oversaw the effort, "From the board of directors to every supervisor, management must adopt the principles and language of quality, follow the processes, set examples and guide others."[12] Unfortunately, the FPL experience provides one additional lesson, perhaps the most important of all, the need to concentrate on goals and results, not process, to ensure that form doesn't triumph over substance.

VALUE ENHANCEMENT VERSUS QUALITY IMPROVEMENT PROCESS

By 1989, one business magazine called Florida Power & Light "America's best-run utility."[13] According to another account:

> Hudiburg saw himself as a pioneer in a movement that could restore U.S. industry. In fact, a Xerox vice president described FP&L as "the benchmark of U.S. quality." In 1987 Hudiburg helped persuade [the U.S.] Congress to establish the Malcolm Baldrige National Quality Award as a U.S. equivalent of Japan's Deming Prize, with Hudiburg as the Baldrige Foundation's second president. "I feel," says Hudiburg of the award's growing influence, "like the kid at the top of the mountain who kicked a little rock off, and it turned into an avalanche."[14]

But trouble was brewing at FPL. John Hudiburg's passion for Japanese approaches to quality improvement had led him and his associates to enlist the help of several consultants from Japan to assist the company in establishing team processes and prepare for competition for Japan's Deming Prize, requiring that everyone at FPL be able to answer questions about how he or she fitted into the system of serving customers, that storyboards and other indicators of process be of excellent quality, and that any manager be able to produce information requested by the visiting Japanese examining team in three minutes or less. In short, some of FPL's efforts became a triumph of form over substance.

The costs of FPL's effort to instill quality improvement processes became known to the public through the records of Florida's Public Service Commission. Because these costs became part of the basis on which electric rates were determined, they were of great interest to consumers, who were less aware of the savings achieved by FPL's efforts.

In addition, even though FPL's overall quality was improving, one troublesome nuclear power plant continued to produce complaints to the Nuclear Regulatory Commission, which had put the older plant on its "watch list." There were mounting concerns about whether, in its concentration on quality improvement processes, FPL's management had neglected to provide for enough capacity to serve its customers. And the company had begun to miss its monthly profit targets. By November 1989, when the Deming Prize was awarded to FPL, John Hudiburg had been replaced, in part because of the disastrous results from a diversification program instituted by his predecessor. The "wake up" chapter in the quality journey occurred. FPL's new Chairman, James Broadhead, issued an internal memo several months later acknowledging that "our quality improvement program is one of our most important tools," but asserting that:

> With the Deming examination behind us, it is time to go beyond our developmental emphasis on procedures and to accentuate those activities that have a more direct impact on the achievement of excellence. . . . The QI Story Seven-Step Process will no longer be a mandatory process to be followed for all problem solving. . . . Our Training Program, which is now overwhelmingly QIP [quality improvement process] related, will be redesigned.[15]

The "wake up" chapter in the journey continued in July 1990 when two FPL plants failed and the utility had to ask customers to forsake air-conditioning to avoid brownouts, an attention-getting request in the heat and humidity of a Florida summer.[16]

The FPL experience suggests that an organization culture can be changed with value improvement initiatives. But the procedure-oriented training and implementation necessary to create new habits can, if not controlled, take precedence over results-oriented efforts of greatest importance to customers and, in this case, regulators. This lesson may be John Hudiburg's most important contribution to the practice of value improvement. Once FPL reoriented its processes to be more flexible and cost-focused, it was able to improve quality while decreasing costs. The FPL customers' 1996 electric bill was less than in 1985, fossil plant availability had increased by 13 percent, and customer and shareholder satisfaction had been increased. It took a significant turn in the journey to reach this performance level.

QUESTIONS FOR MANAGEMENT

The most important of the many questions raised for management by the experiences of Shouldice Hospital, Benihana of Tokyo, and especially Florida Power & Light include the following:

1. In introducing quality or process improvement techniques to your organization, have the objectives of such initiatives been clearly identified and communicated at the outset?
2. To what extent have they emphasized value enhancement as opposed to merely quality or productivity improvement?
3. Have the initiatives adopted been customized to fit with the organization's culture or have they been designed with an eye to changing the culture?
4. Has the implementation of such efforts begun with the "buy-in" and participation of the organization's leadership?
5. Has adequate thought been given to such things as training and recognition for all participants, with emphasis on nonmonetary awards?
6. Has sufficient emphasis been placed on the achievement of results through measurement and "management-by-fact"?
7. What steps have been taken to reduce anxieties of various participants by: (a) involving middle managers in the "roll out" of such efforts and (b) considering assurances against job loss as a result of the implementation of recommendations made by employees?
8. What has been done to insure that emphasis on process and procedures remains secondary to substance and results in implementing value improvement initiatives?

Value enhancement results from various kinds of redesign efforts, including process, quality, and productivity improvement. In a service organization, these efforts are extended to the design of service delivery systems that enhance employee satisfaction, facilitate service, and ultimately influence customer attitudes toward a service. They are found, as we'll see in the next chapter, in the most unlikely places, even the offices in which the notorious MTV (Music Television) is produced.

9

Designing Service Delivery Systems That Drive Quality, Productivity, and Value

The offices of MTV, the producer and broadcaster of music video material aimed at 18- to 24-year olds in most parts of the world, contain a sea of television sets mostly tuned to MTV and blasting at high decibel levels.[1] Organization mores frown on one employee asking another to turn down the volume on her television set. What kind of working environment is this, you ask? Perfect, if all entry-level employees are recruited from the target "demo" (target customer demographic category) of 18- to 24-year-olds, especially if middle and senior managers carefully monitor the reactions of young employees to what is playing on the TV monitors and loudspeakers as everybody carries out their tasks. New employees are important "listening posts." It is important that a working environment is established that not only is comfortable for them, but contributes to effective product development and testing.

DEVELOPING SINGLE-FACILITY SERVICE DELIVERY SYSTEMS

You may find it odd that MTV provides an excellent illustration of service delivery system design. But a service delivery system is the sum of information- and noninformation support systems, location, layout, customer management devices, decor and ambience, and employee amenities, as shown in Figure 9–1. These components, in total, provide support for a strategic service vision aimed at attaining certain goals, expressed in terms of the service profit chain. Notice how this is achieved at MTV.

Music television has one of the shortest product life cycles of any business. Video popularity rises and falls with daunting speed. This is especially true of a music television business based on rock and roll, in which what is "cool" by definition has to change rapidly. As a former employee put it, "The thing I really miss is coming up with an idea on Monday, pitching it on Tuesday, writing the script on Wednesday, shooting on Thursday, cutting it Friday, and seeing it on the air on Saturday—that was the greatest high."[2]

That's why the leader in rock and roll video broadcasting, MTV, has such a difficult challenge maintaining its position. Many claim that the

FIGURE 9–1
Elements of a Service Delivery System

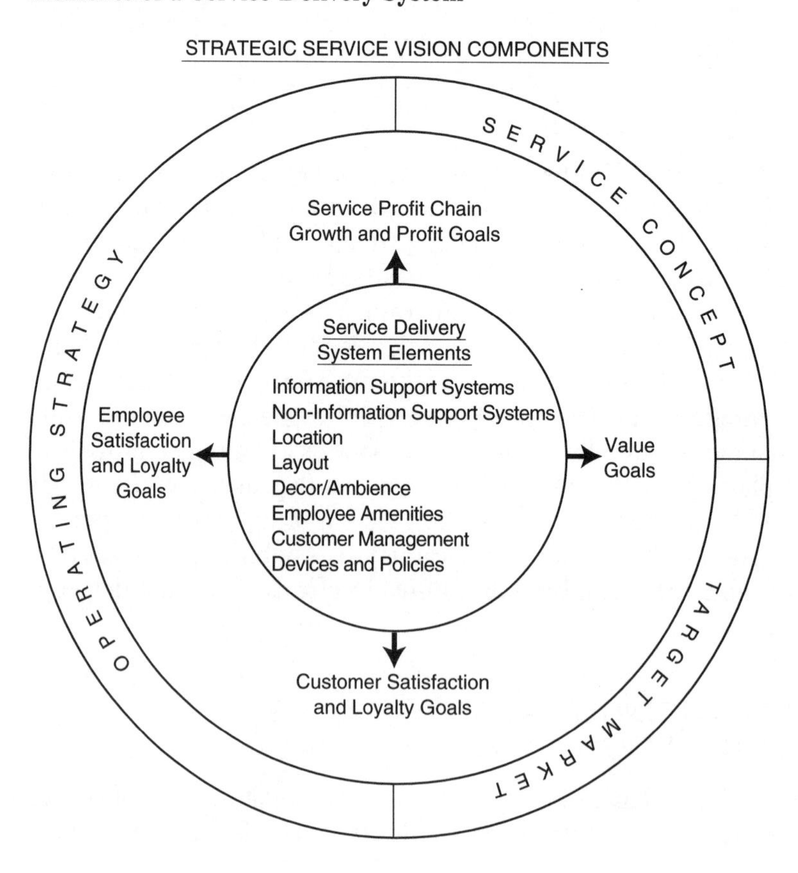

very nature of the business will claim MTV as one of its victims eventually. However, the organization has made sure that it has a good chance of surviving in its industry's revolving-door product development game by creating a strong organization culture, in part supported by its "hot house" for creating and testing new ideas on the twenty-fourth floor of the Viacom Building in Times Square in New York City.

The twenty-fourth floor is home to young production assistants and interns who are hired for little or no money, respectively, and given small cubicles in which to carry out their work, often involving nothing more than running errands. Instead, the company pays them in prestige among their contemporaries, a great source of dates, and the respect they are accorded on the job. New product is not approved if it doesn't pass muster with those "in the demo" (the 18- to 24-year-olds to which MTV is aimed), even if it is approved by more senior managers and the entertainers who are actually seen on-screen for MTV. To observe them, MTV's management has created an office environment in which broadcast material is continually observed and judged by the people to whom it is targeted. It's the service delivery system that supports MTV's operating strategy and strategic service vision.

In dryer, more academic terms, the location of MTV (in the middle of an exciting city in which to work), the layout of its production offices (on one floor to facilitate a sense of community and observations of "demo" members' reactions to the "product"), and the ambience of the office (personalized cubicles, blaring music, and a dress code permitting anything but nudity) all enhance the kind of quality, productivity, and value sought by MTV and provide a support system to achieve these results. In addition, because MTV hires its targeted customers and houses them the way it does, this combination provides one large information support system for middle- and higher-level managers in constant contact with the "demo." Nearly all the elements of a single-facility service delivery system shown in Figure 9–1 are addressed.

Planning System Designs for the Right Amount of Employee Latitude

Disney theme parks have been lauded for years for their effective human resource practices, particularly the selection and training of employees, many of them young and inexperienced, who provide the smiling faces that have impressed so many people. Human resource management effectiveness in the context of the Disney strategic service vision translates into extensive controls over the behavior of those of its employees who are "onstage" (carrying out their jobs in view of customers), called "cast members." This is done through numerous and explicit guidelines for such things as dress, hair styling, jewelry, and makeup, with the intent to create a model Disney onstage cast member in the image of Middle America's sons and daughters. It is communicated through the extensive training for which the organization is well known.

But so much attention has been devoted to Disney's human resource initiatives that we have largely forgotten another part of Disney's genius of which Walt Disney himself was so proud, the company's engineering prowess. Disney theme parks are designed to make Disney employees winners with customers. A "guided tour" through a simulated African jungle on a river boat supposedly steered by an appropriately costumed "guide" comes periously close to several dangerous situations. However, because the boat is on a track that takes it near packs of threatening but mechanical animals, the guide has to only pretend to steer while concentrating on relating to the guests in the boat, at least within the confines of the extensive script written for his or her "role." The experience is replicated time after time perfectly and with the appropriate amount of attention to human interaction.[3]

Perhaps our favorite illustration of the way in which Disney's service delivery system helps its employees fulfill the organization's mission is that of the role of the Custodial Host, Disney's euphemism for theme park janitor. Custodial hosts are selected from the same pool of shining faces that populate other "onstage" jobs. They are trained to be able to answer any number of questions that guests might ask about the park; in particular, they are trained to answer the same question a hundred times a day with the same smile. In order to do this, they must be able to establish eye contact with guests to encourage questions. They are aided in this effort by trash pans and brooms at the ends of long handles that enable them, with training, to sweep trash without looking down or bending over.

Contrast Disney, an organization in which cast members work "by the numbers," with Club Med, a company operating a chain of destination resorts in more than a hundred often-exotic places in the world, mostly on beautiful beaches or near ski slopes. As Jacques Giraud, former President of Club Med North America, points out, the Club Med "magic" is achieved by "allowing GOs (gentil organizateurs, or resort staff members) to do things 3-5-2-1-4 instead of 1-2-3-4-5, if that's the way they feel it."[4] In short, Club Med is an MTV with sand.

Club Med has planned its facilities to achieve its objectives of providing its guests with an escape from civilization and reality at modest costs (and higher value) compared with other vacation alternatives. In addition to a number of policies (such as carrying out all transactions at the resort in beads rather than money) instituted to reflect the objectives, the facility itself has to support GO efforts to achieve the objectives as well. The emphasis at a Club Med resort is on physical activities from dawn to dusk (and much later). Ideal GOs are those who are much like their guests; in fact, the best are often those who have visited and enjoyed one or more Club Med resorts as guests. They are expected to teach and participate in various sports during the day and entertain guests with songs, skits, and dancing at night. Training for these jobs is limited. There are no scripts. No two days or even two encounters with guests are alike. There is little time to devote to anything but guests. As a result, the physical facility has to be located in an inherently attractive place, designed and constructed for worry-free operation, and stocked with a wealth of sporting equipment to make the GOs' jobs doable.

Controlling Customer Behavior

Disney's high-control strategy extends to customers as well, although more subtly. Again, the service delivery system design plays the primary role. The theme parks are laid out for an easy, natural flow of traffic. Attractions are designed in such a way that, even though many of them are intended to thrill guests, they are engineered for maximum safety. No guest has been injured by a mechanical elephant on the Jungle Boat Ride or even seriously dampened with water.

Of perhaps greatest importance is that Disney recognizes that visitors will spend most of their time at the park waiting. It has become the world's champion at designing waiting lines so that queues that might discourage visitors are obscured from their view. In addition, visitors are provided with accurate information about the length of wait, entertained or otherwise diverted while in line, and often surprised when the wait is not as long as expected. In fact, Disney practices a number of "principles of waiting," explained several years ago by a former colleague of ours, David Maister. Based on experience and some research, they are:

1. Unoccupied time feels longer than occupied time. (This explains Disney's efforts to entertain guests in line with visits by Disney cast members in characters' costumes.)
2. Preprocess waits feel longer than in-process waits (explaining why some airlines find it effective to employ agents to work the "back end of the line" both to solve simple requests and make customers feel that their in-process waits have begun).
3. Anxiety makes waits seem longer. (Waiting for the dentist is more anxiety-ridden than waiting for a Disney attraction.)
4. Uncertain waits are longer than known, finite waits (explaining Disney's practice of informing guests about the likely length of their waits).

5. Unexplained waits are longer than explained waits.
6. Unfair waits are longer than equitable waits (providing a rationale for the growing practice of having customers form a single queue at airline counters, for example—even though the line may seem longer, it moves rapidly and is perceived as being more fair than multiple lines that move at different rates, often because unpredictably complicated transactions are mixed with more simple ones.)
7. The more valuable the service, the longer the customer will wait.
8. Solo waits feel longer than group waits.[5]

Club Med manages its guests, but in much less rigid ways. There is a regular routine for the day, especially for evening activities such as dinner, the singing and entertainment, and at least the beginning of disco dancing. Within this routine, however, guests are free to choose their activities and structure their day. Waiting, an activity of the "real world," is not tolerated to any degree by Club Med's guests. For this reason, there has to be an adequate "inventory" of activities and equipment to accommodate all guests at all times. This simplifies GOs' tasks of organizing and scheduling individuals' activities, freeing them up for what they do best, interacting with and teaching guests.

One important feature of a traditional Club Med facility is designed to deliver value through guest control. That is the tradition at many of its resorts catering to younger guests often traveling alone that guests rent beds, not rooms. As a result, two guests unfamiliar with one another at the start of their trip may be paired up to share a double-bedded room. Because little time is spent in the room, few object. Shared rooms contribute significantly to the vacation value that Club Med is able to deliver to its guests.

The Ultimate Customer Control Strategy: Self-Service

Facilities designed and built to encourage self-service are perhaps the most common form of customer control. Nowhere is this more prevalent than in retailing. Two examples of this are provided by Benetton, the global manufacturer whose retail store licensees operate fashion clothing stores in 120 countries, and Staples, the office supply warehouse chain in the United States that serves business offices and consumers through large retail stores.

Benetton's recent litany of problems in its U.S. market, to which we will return, has made us forget that the company literally revolutionized fashion retailing in Europe in the 1970s by encouraging licensees to open small stores selling Benetton fashions that invited customer browsing and self-service among stacks of colorful sweaters and other garments easily seen from the street.[6] Until that time, sales clerks had kept the merchandise behind counters for display only upon request by customers. Benetton's original stores were limited to a size that could easily be overseen by two employees, who spent as much of their time straightening merchandise as helping customers. On a much larger scale, much the same thing was accomplished at Staples.

Productivity in retailing is measured, among other things, in terms of sales per square foot. High sales per square foot can offset many other operating shortcomings. At Staples, an office supply store chain that serves both businesses and consumers, management has found a way to enhance sales productivity by redesigning its stores to facilitate self-service. Going beyond efforts to make sure that customers have a pleasant shopping experience, Staples has remodeled its stores with improved signage, wider aisles, and more lighting to make it easier for them to find the items they want faster and with less assistance from salespeople. Suppliers are asked to package merchandise so that shoppers can see what is inside. All of this allows Staples to transfer salespeople from other parts of the store to those departments selling electronics that require much more sales assistance and represent 40 percent of store sales. The result? An immediate 7 percent sales increase in the remodeled stores.[7]

As we saw at Shouldice Hospital, for certain services in which customers experience high degrees of perceived risk or traditionally poor service, encouraging customers to share responsibility for service delivery by helping themselves not only reduces cost, it may also produce higher perceptions of service quality.

Managing Information Support Systems to Enhance Customer Loyalty and Sales

Information support systems are central to the strategies of an increasing number of service providers. American Airlines originally developed its SABRE system to accept and process reservations while planning the yields (revenue dollars per seat mile flown) for each flight. This led directly to its use in pricing tickets to achieve the highest yield. When combined with its frequent-flyer program, SABRE provided not only a way of tracking customer loyalty but also ways of building it.

One of us experienced this directly on a flight through Chicago O'Hare's airport recently. Due to a torrential downpour one August afternoon, the main airport terminal experienced bad leaks that knocked out the system for displaying flight arrivals and departures.

Unable to obtain flight information, employees and travelers alike were helpless to do anything about the chaos that ensued. Even though it was beyond the control of the airline, members of the airline's AAdvantage frequent-flyer program received letters several weeks later from American Airlines apologizing for the inconvenience, acknowledging the fact that each had been at O'Hare airport on the day in question, and advising that, as a result of the inconvenience, several hundred miles would be credited to the AAdvantage account for each person.

A competitor, United Airlines, provides to the crew of each flight a list of passengers who have flown 100,000 miles or more with United during the last year. This allows the captain or a member of the crew to visit each valued traveler at his or her seat. In addition, pilots of this employee-owned airline are being encouraged to give out business cards to such passengers to thank them for their patronage. These relatively simple uses of management information systems have a positive impact on most passengers that is far greater than their costs.

Retailing now has its own version of such systems. For example, central to Staples' strategy from its very beginnings was the issuance of membership cards that offered discounts on all purchases to ensure their use. Why? Because this has allowed the company to build a data base of customer purchasing patterns that allows it to stock and even locate its stores according to customer needs. The data base not only provides Staples with information about the amounts and types of products purchased, it enables the company to offer discounts to customers surpassing a threshold amount of purchases and track those who have stopped buying from its stores.[8]

Providing Process "Visibility"

Service delivery systems and facilities that are designed to enhance the visibility of the process to customers provide one more incentive for high quality and productivity. Thus, auto repair service waiting rooms that enable customers to see their automobiles being repaired probably exert a bit of extra pressure on mechanics to at least create the appearance that they are doing their best for the customer. In any event, it is a feature of several high-service (and high-profit) auto dealerships with which we are familiar.

As we saw at Benihana, described in Chapter 8, in bringing the kitchen to the diners and creating a "show" out of the preparation of the food, management also made the delivery of the service totally visible. This not only provided an added control on quality, it also fostered an interaction between the food preparer and diners that enhanced the quality of the experience for customers.

Preventing Service Errors

Taco Bell, the Mexican fast food chain, has experimented with technology to improve the miserably low order accuracy often associated with drive-through services. You're probably familiar with the experience that goes something like this: You pull up to a squawk box; an unintelligible voice makes a sound; you assume that it is asking you for your order; you shout the names of several items into the box, changing several of them in the process; and the voice from the box says something that sounds like the charge for the food. Either you or the person at the other end may not speak English as a first language. The result? Two out of three drive-through orders are incorrectly delivered in some way. Errors, of course, often are not discovered until the customer is several blocks down the street, already late for an appointment and too busy to complain.

In an effort to combat this problem, Taco Bell has experimented with order takers with electronic order boards who approach each drive-through customer on foot to take orders. In other units, it has installed electronic menu picture boards which drive-through customers can touch to place their orders. Regardless of language or communication challenges, both of these methods have improved the accuracy of orders and order fulfillment dramatically.

These and other efforts to "fail-safe" services have been studied extensively by Richard Chase and Douglas Stewart.[9] Their work was inspired by the late Shigeo Shingo, known as "Mr. Improvement" in Japan, who devoted his attention to manufacturing processes and the efforts of production workers, devising what he called "poka-yokes" (from the Japanese *yokeru,* "to avoid," and *poka,* "inadvertent errors").[10] In adapting Shingo's work, Chase and Stewart point out that in many services, both customers and those serving them must be "fail-safed" because both contribute to service errors. (In a real sense, the developers of Taco Bell's electronic picture-board menu recognize this.)

Chase and Stewart describe a variety of devices for ensuring the accuracy and quality of service work, including: (1) trays with indented spaces that hold the array of instruments needed for performing a medical operation so surgeons can ensure themselves at all times that nothing has been left in the patient, (2) the practice of a Korean theme park that sews shut the pockets of new employees' trousers so that they do not offend customers by putting their hands in their pockets, and (3) strips of paper wrapped around towels so that hotel employees can tell if they are clean or not.

Customers make mistakes in preparing for a service encounter (not bringing the necessary information, for example), in the encounter itself (not following instructions or asking the right questions), and in the resolution of the encounter (failing to signal service failures, complain, or comment about the service). This has prompted companies like Digital Equipment to provide customers with instructions for making service calls, including the kinds of information to have ready. Other examples of customer "poka-yokes" are gauges at airline boarding ramps allowing passengers to test the size of their bags to make sure that they conform to carry-on limits and strategically placed trash bins encouraging customers to dispose of their own trash in fast food restaurants.

Any of these examples and devices can be applied in a single service establishment or setting. However, many services are network-based, creating a number of additional challenges in service delivery system design.

DEVELOPING AND MANAGING MULTISITE NETWORKS

Multisite service networks generally support knowledge (information) sharing, communication and logistics, or transactions, often more than one of these, as shown in Figure 9–2.

FIGURE 9–2
Basic Types of Multisite Service Networks

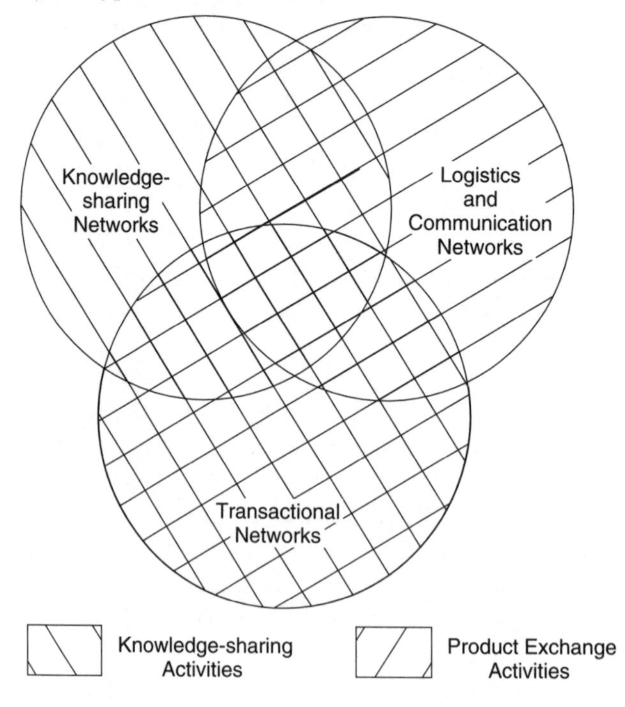

The Benetton story illustrates several of these points.[11] Benetton's networks facilitate knowledge sharing, communication and logistics, and transactions. While Benetton is a manufacturing company at its core, a former managing director of the company correctly identified it as a "service system." Why? Because while it maintains close control over manufacturing at plants located in eight countries, with 70 percent of its production in Italy, it subcontracts certain manufacturing processes to smaller firms located near its manufacturing facilities and ships product to nearly 7,000 stores located in 120 countries that are nearly all owned by licensees operating under the Benetton name. Thus the firm controls a huge transactional network, much of which it does not own, for the design, production, distribution, and retail sale of its products. While Benetton employs about 6,000 people, it is estimated that its transactional network provides employment for 40,000 more.

Knowledge sharing is critical to the success of Benetton's worldwide logistics strategy, supported by yet another network. Benetton shares its knowledge of fashion trends with its retail storeowners to help them place orders months in advance of a new fashion season. This enables Benetton to schedule much of its production in large, efficient quantities that can be shipped by slower, less costly means. Store owners are willing to do this because a system of dying assembled garments according to last-minute market preferences for color allows Benetton to replenish "hot"-selling items rapidly, providing a means by which retailers can adjust their inventories before the end of the season. Benetton provides them with a vehicle for selling a high proportion of their merchandise at full price while achieving low end-of-season inventories. This in turn enables Benetton to exact commitments from its retailers that they will buy only from Benetton and will not return merchandise once they have received it.

NETWORK CHARACTERISTICS

Networks have unusual characteristics. Often they are enhanced by size. For example, electronic mail becomes more valuable to a subscriber with each additional subscriber added to the network. Networks may require huge investments to build, often representing barriers to entry for those with insufficient money to invest. It's one reason why distribution networks typically serve the needs of many manufacturers, wholesalers, and retailers. Barriers have begun to come down in knowledge-sharing networks, where the cost of access to a common infrastructure provided by the Internet and World Wide Web has fallen rapidly. Similarly, network sharing has become more commonplace in transportation. Primary examples are the air traffic control systems in air transport and rail-sharing agreements among railroads.

In the past, exchange activities far outweighed sharing in such networks. But with the ascendancy of the importance of information, and the manner in which information is displacing tangible goods in the "mix" of the output and product of commerce, sharing activities are growing in relative importance, as shown by the shaded area of Figure 9–2. Suffice it to say that sharing is very different from exchange, essentially increasing the "capital" of both parties to a transaction and making both more productive.

FACTORS IN NETWORK DESIGN

In network design, questions arise as to the degree to which network design reflects and supports an operating strategy, the need for interconnectedness of the various "sites" or "nodes" on the network, the need for the standardization of the facilities at each site, and the degree to which managers of the sites are allowed latitude, particularly in issues regarding the preservation of brand value.

Degree of Support for Operating Strategy

At times, the service delivery system becomes an important element of the strategy itself. We saw this at Shouldice Hospital, where the hospital facility itself was designed to encourage patients to take part in the "do-it-yourself" recovery phase of their treatment, so essential to their fast recovery. In support of every great service is a not-so-obvious service delivery system that makes service delivery look easier than it is, insures consistency of service, and enhances the job satisfaction of employees as well as the satisfaction of customers.

Southwest Airlines carefully selects new cities to be served in terms of how well the terminal traffic and facilities will support the fast turnaround of aircraft, vital to the company's operating strategy. When possible, congested and delay-prone terminals are avoided. In addition, routes are constructed so that there are few flights of more than ninety minutes, critical to the operating strategy of an airline that limits in-flight catering to nothing more than beverages and peanuts and designs other of its services for frequent travelers desiring budget fares for trips that are relatively short in duration. In addition to these criteria, new cities are selected on the basis of the extent to which they will enable Southwest to hire the kind of people it requires to maintain a company centered around family, fun, and caring for customers and employees (in Southwest's terms, "luv").

Need for Interconnectedness

Network services relying on reservation systems, for example, require that as many sites as possible have access to the network. In fact, such networks often don't require that all sites be connected to all other sites. Instead, a "hub and spoke" system in which each site communicates only with the hub is adequate to support most reservation functions. It is when information and product is exchanged between sites that the need for interconnectedness increases.

Benetton for years operated a "hub and spoke" communications network, with company headquarters in Ponzano, Italy at the hub, and provided little encouragement for its storeowners to communicate with each other. The philosophy of the founder, Luciano Benetton, was that each owner should be free to operate as an entrepreneur, displaying merchandise in the most appropriate manner to each store and operating as a self-contained entity. Customers, used to exchange and other privileges provided by competing fashion retailers in the United States, quickly found that one Benetton store would not accept merchandise sold by another. Further, there was no easy way that one store could query another for a desired item that was not in its stock. Only in recent years has Benetton taken steps in the United States to help store owners organize themselves to provide competitive services that require greater interconnectedness in its knowledge-sharing, logistics, and transactional networks.

Need for Standardization

Automated teller machines and their operation are becoming more and more standardized as users access them over increasingly wider geographic areas. Standardization breeds familiarity among customers. And familiarity fosters usage, particularly for services involving high perceived risk.

Multisite services likely to be accessed at more than one location present a strong case for standardization, especially in the quality of products and services delivered. This is especially true for personal services. For example, the Holiday Inn chain of lodging facilities has used standardization as a major theme in its marketing programs to frequent travelers not wishing to familiarize themselves with new room layouts and gadgetry night after night.

Standardization is often driven by the need to establish policies resulting in consistent service quality and practices that lead to a set of expectations for service that doesn't vary greatly from one customer to another. Inconsistent policies from one site to another create havoc for employees. Inconsistent results create havoc for customers, and inevitably the service providers.

On the other hand, the standardization of all aspects of a service delivery system or the operating strategy it supports may be neither necessary nor desirable. For example, retail store designs for cold-weather climates may not be suitable for the Sun Belt, just as a common problem of large-scale retailers has been to provide overrides to computer inventory allocation programs to prevent snow shovels from being sent to all stores, regardless of climate.

Latitude Allowed Site Managers: Preserving the Core

Issues of standardization and the latitude afforded individual site managers in a multisite network in the final analysis depend on customer behavior and the need to build "brand equity." Where customers value diversity of image, layout, and amenities, as in some upscale hotels, managers may be given latitude to preserve an image by doing things in ways expected by loyal guests. But where the objective is to provide a consistent experience, latitude must of necessity be limited.

As we saw in Chapter 7, the Au Bon Pain chain of French bakery cafés confronted these issues by devising a Partner/Manager program designed to "enfranchise" managers by giving them strong incentives to improve profit and unusually wide latitude to manage their individual cafes in ways that would meet the profit improvement objective. This included moving walls, putting in new seats, refurbishing decorations, establishing employee selection, staffing, and compensation policies. Where did Au Bon Pain's management draw the line on such entrepreneurial behavior? On those items that were considered to be core to the concept, as shown in Figure 9–3. These included maintaining common signage identifying their units as members of a chain; insuring that certain items were common to all menus; having croissants, a staple of the concept, available at all times; and meeting standards for cleanliness and appearance at periodic inspections conducted by management.

Among determinants of core elements to be preserved across a network are those things that customers expect and value (at Au Bon Pain, croissants and cleanliness), that contribute to brand identity (signage and logo), and that facilitate and reduce the complexity of multisite operations (such as common menu items).

What is core to a company's operating strategy becomes especially important to the design of service delivery systems, the operating strategies they reinforce, and the results sought for customers when the objective is to serve customers in several countries and cultures.

FIGURE 9–3
Core and Peripheral Elements of Au Bon Pain's Operating Strategy

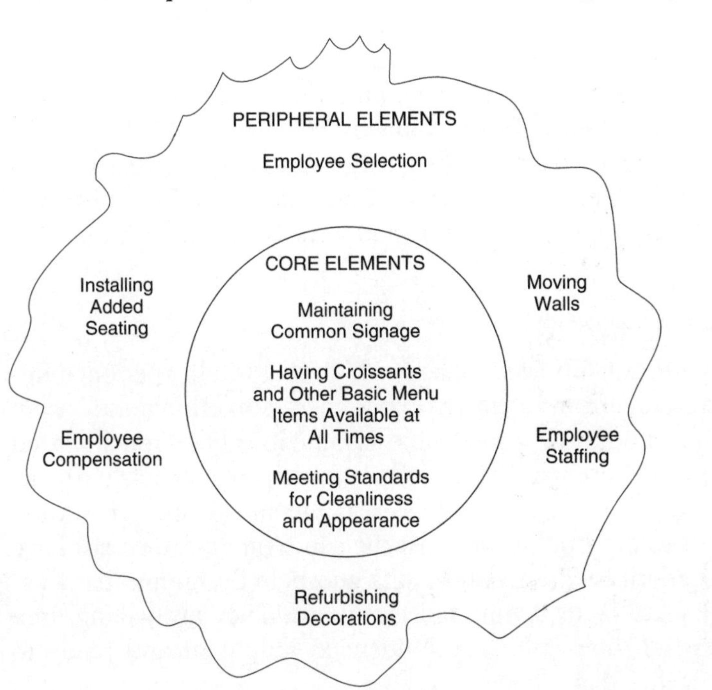

DELIVERING SERVICES GLOBALLY

Multinational, multisite services may or may not require customization to reflect local customs, cultures, and capabilities. To a large degree the decision is dependent on the target market in a particular country, the degree to which a service might be regarded as a "total experience" by its users, and whether or not the service/product package being provided is culturally sensitive. Benetton, Club Med, and Disney provide interesting examples.

The Target Market and the Need for Customization

Benetton stores worldwide have a similar appearance. The signage is the same. All advertising carries the same logo, "United Colors of Benetton," a reflection of efforts to convey through the faces of young people of many races and nationalities the upbeat, progressive, "one world" philosophy of the company in designing and distributing its fashions. The logo is even printed in English where it appears in 120 countries. How can Benetton possibly get away with this? Because it targets its fashions to men and women 18 to 35 years old who are most likely to break the bounds of tradition in their countries, are most likely to speak English, and most likely to regard fashion merchandise of Italian design as something above judgment according to the customs of their country. In short, Benetton has been able to create a global service system and brand because of the age, attitudes, and education of the customers it targets. This helps explain why MTV's viewership now extends throughout many parts of the world; it is just as popular with its "demo" outside the United States as it is domestically. MTV is designed for viewers who are quite likely to buy and wear Benetton fashions.

"Total Experience" Services

Vacationers go to a Club Med village, which is a total experience designed for an escape from reality, to experience "something else," even though they may not know what. Some assume it will be French, based on the origins of the company. Others may anticipate a beach-party atmosphere. Regardless of what guests assume in advance, it's Club Med's task not to disappoint them. At the same time, it does not have to take into account the nationality of its guests in designing many aspects of the facility or designing daily routines. They are willing, in a sense, to suspend their culturally influenced judgment and ready to enjoy whatever they experience.

A Disney theme park is a world of different worlds, inviting visitors to suspend their cultural judgments. Because most foreign visitors to EuroDisney in France or to Tokyo Disneyland in Japan expect to visit a slice of America, however, Disney does best when that is what it serves up. Efforts to Europeanize several Disney staples such as Snow White did not meet with great enthusiasm by visitors to Euro Disney who probably grew up with their own versions. Many of the problems with Euro Disney's service concept, which have since been worked out, involved mistaking core elements of the service with noncore elements and vice versa. For example, the conscious decision not to serve wine in France probably was regarded as a noncore matter by American executives. But to Europeans, the thought of not having wine available at the park was thought by many guests to be an annoyance and a design mistake. Nevertheless, wine or no wine, visitors came to the park and were impressed by the characters and the facility, not the presence or absence of wine, even though Disney did relent and begin serving it.

National airlines providing international transport are good examples of "total experience" services. This gives them the option of tailoring airplane and terminal decor, uniforms, food, and even certain services to reflect: (1) international, that is to say nondescript, tastes or (2) the cultures of the countries they represent. Those with distinct and interesting cultures, such as Air France, Alitalia, or China Air, may not always capitalize on them sufficiently in catering to business travelers with a preference for their particular cultures or pleasure travelers wishing to begin their vacation experiences when they set foot on board the plane.

In contrast, two "national" airlines that repeatedly receive accolades for service from travelers, Swissair and Singapore Airlines, have created services that reflect the cultures of the airlines' origins. In Swissair's case, it capitalizes on the reputation of the Swiss as excellent hoteliers and restauranteurs from a country where everything functions in an orderly fashion. In fact, the Swiss people have voted Swissair the most Swiss of all Swiss companies. Singapore Airlines, identified with a small city state known most for its strict legally imposed order, has created instead a renowned service that reflects most travelers' images of an exotic region, Southeast Asia. Whether Singapore Airlines, with its subtle and not-so-subtle "sexist" appeal to male travelers, is truly representative of Singapore is questionable. But it represents for many what Singapore must be or ought to be.

Culturally Sensitive Services

"Total experience" services are not as culturally sensitive as others, such as food service, medical practice, and professional services, that have to recognize different legal and accounting methods and customs in use around the world. For example, even a brand as venerable as McDonald's encounters local eating preferences that must be reflected in local menus. As a result, McDonald's facilities in some parts of Asia have to be designed and equipped to produce and sell seafood items that are not available elsewhere. While the hamburger must appear on the menu because it is core to McDonald's operating strategy and image, its sales are overshadowed by items reflecting local tastes in some parts of the world.

In extending its public accounting practice to Hungary several years ago, Coopers & Lybrand's management had to recognize that Hungarian accounting practices, much different than those in the United States, would have to be provided for some of its local clients while U.S.-based multinational clients operating in Hungary would require audit and other services performed according to both U.S. and local regulations. It required that the organization maintain two separate accounting teams who understood and were certified to provide auditing services for clients desiring each method.

Control over issues of standardization and customization are influenced as well by the degree to which a multisite organization engages in franchising.

INCORPORATING FRANCHISING INTO THE STRATEGY

Franchising is, of course, a vehicle for inviting many owners to contribute their money, real estate, and entrepreneurial enthusiasm to the development of a multisite service organization. In return for their investment, a franchise fee usually tied to revenues, and commitments to adhere to certain standards of construction and franchise operation, franchisees receive training, facility designs, the right to do business under the organization's brand, convenient sources for supplies they may need, and general support from the franchisor. The concept sounds wonderful in theory, and works best when franchisee and franchisor alike prosper. However, even the most sound of these arrangements requires careful administration, reflecting the different expectations held by the two parties to the agreement.

A franchisor seeks maximum control with minimum investment of financial and human resources in a multisite service organization. To the franchisee, on the other hand, the franchise represents an opportunity to be in business for one's self, the entrepreneur's dream, with no one telling him what to do. As long as performance and returns meet expectations, both parties typically are willing to live with this inconsistency. When expectations are not met, the degree of tolerance that either party will display often depends on the way in which the relationship has been structured and developed over time.

Business success helps explain why McDonald's has been so successful placing heavy reliance on franchising to fuel and maintain its growth in many countries over the years. But part of the success is explained as well by the way its relationships are structured and developed. First, in the United States, McDonald's has limited its franchisees to one or a small number of locations to encourage them to remain active in their businesses. In addition, it has encouraged them to gain work experience in another McDonald's unit and attend courses at McDonald's Hamburger University prior to assuming control of their first franchise. The network is supported with massive advertising, merchandising ideas, brand development effort, and a supply network that is capable of meeting most of the logistical needs of franchisees. This has resulted in a franchise network that is successful, reasonably loyal and cohesive, and with relatively little individual power when compared with the parent company.

Because of the need to place greater reliance on local knowledge and relationships in some non-U.S. markets, McDonald's has had to alter its policies to allow greater numbers of units to be operated by franchisees in some countries outside the United States. Where this has occurred, for example in Southeast Asia, franchisees have exercised more power in relation to their parent. This has led to local menu and other innovations supported by customized advertising that would be discouraged in the United States.

In keeping with its emphasis on entrepreneurship and local innovation, the Benetton organization has limited its support of "licensees" (as differentiated from franchisees) to the use of its name and graphics, store design and layout, and logistical support, primarily a complete line of fashions from which individual licensees can order. A limited amount of training has been provided by eighty-three agents working on behalf of Benetton worldwide, but it is meager when one considers that most Benetton licensees were selected because they reflected the spirit of Benetton and its targeted customers and had little or no previous retail experience.

The Benetton agreement, in contrast to most other franchise agreements, calls for no upfront fee or commission on store sales. Instead, it requires licensees to sell only Benetton products and refrain from returning any goods that are ordered and received. As a result, Benetton promises no territorial exclusivity that would shield licensees from potential direct competition, although it is often assumed by licensees. The fact that Benetton's retail network is administered largely by agents who are paid a 4 percent commission on product sold to stores, of which they are also part owners, means that Benetton's control over specific store location and licensing decisions is left largely in the hands of agents. Again, this reflects the entrepreneurial philosophy of Benetton's founder and head.

Perhaps inevitably, Benetton agents have made licensing and location decisions that have been perceived as damaging to the business of existing licensees, several of whom have brought suit against the company in the United States for failure to adhere to franchise law. Regardless of the nature of the complaint, poor business performance and failure to maintain constructive relationships by a franchisor are most often at the root of franchisee complaints and legal actions. In the case of Benetton, because its agreements do not conform to U.S. franchise laws that require fees to be paid in return for services, it has been difficult for franchisees to press their cases. Nevertheless, both franchisor and franchisees have suffered a decline of business.

"Employing" Franchisees

The lessons in heavily franchised networks that are provided by organizations like McDonald's and Benetton are quite clear. The most successful franchising relationships are those that involve agreements that insure that both parties benefit from the same actions to the degree possible, are based on a highly successful brand name that provides both parties with a high "stake" in its continued preservation, make clear the bounds within which franchisees can act on their own without diminishing the brand value for other members of the network, and provide continuing visible support that franchisees value and are willing to pay for. To some degree, the objective is to make franchisees feel a part of an organization comprised of managers with a common mission, to make franchisees feel like employees as well as owners. Having said this, above all, however, in maintaining successful franchising relationships, nothing succeeds like success.

"Enfranchising" Employees

Experiences of leading franchisers are informative for managers of all multisite service organizations. Comparisons of sales of company-owned and franchised units often are misleading, because they presume that the market opportunity afforded to each are comparable. More often, ownership of the highest-potential units is not passed on to franchisees. But it is probably safe to say that few organizations have been able to achieve in company-owned units the individual unit performance (in relation to market potential) and innovation attributable to franchise operations. For example, many of McDonald's new product ideas come from franchisees.

Efforts to encourage similar behavior from employees in company-owned stores, such as Au Bon Pain's Partner/Manager Program, in which unit managers retain a portion of profits achieved over a target amount, represent what we call "enfranchisement." It's the attempt to make employees feel like owners without requiring any investment in the business by giving them latitude to make decisions and paying them for results.

The employees at MTV, Staples, Disney, Club Med, stores carrying Benetton's name, and McDonald's all have something in common. They work in environments and with tools that have been carefully designed to insure that they achieve high levels of quality and productivity in delivering results and high value to customers. In short, they are supported by service delivery systems selected to help ensure total customer satisfaction.

QUESTIONS FOR MANAGEMENT

Service delivery systems are multi-faceted and broad-ranging in their nature, even when confined to a single facility. This is especially true in network-based service organizations. The questions and the appraisals they foster become even more complex when such network-based systems span international boundaries or support franchising strategies. The most basic questions arising from their design and maintenance are:

1. When is the last time the elements of your organization's service delivery system were appraised in terms of, among other things, the extent to which they:
   - Enhance or impede the quality and productivity of work carried out by employees?
   - Control customer behavior in ways that add to the effectiveness of service providers?
   - Involve customers in the successful delivery of the service?
   - Provide the right amount of latitude to service providers to adapt a service to local or even individual customer needs?
   - Provide fail-safe protection at critical points in the service delivery process?
   - Communicate a consistent message to customers about the nature of the service to be expected as well as the customer's role in delivering it?
   - Not only contribute to service workers' success in the eyes of the customer but also build loyalty among desired customers?
   - Generally support an operating strategy intended to deliver results to customers that are promised in the strategic service vision?
2. In multisite, network-based services:
   - Has the "core" of the offering, from which no deviation will be permitted, been identified and communicated to managers, employees, and franchisees?
   - Does the latitude offered unit managers in delivering the service reflect customer desires for consistency and the network's need for brand preservation and enhancement?
3. Is the cultural sensitivity of elements of your organization's international service offering reflected in the operating strategy and service delivery system?
4. Where franchising is employed, to what degree:
   - Does the agreement set expectations clearly and otherwise create compatible incentives, to the degree that is possible, for franchisee and franchisor alike?
   - Are franchisor services designed to provide continuing perceived value to franchisees in return for their fees and adherence to the agreement beyond the typical start-up "honeymoon" period of such contracts?

- Does it encourage the right amount of entrepreneurial and innovative behavior on the part of franchisees?
- Does it discourage "free rider" behavior on the part of individual franchisees that is detrimental to the "brand"?
- Does it insure that franchisees' expectations of success will be met, in terms of the nature of the service itself and the administration of the franchise agreement.

Our attention in the last two chapters has been focused on the design and delivery of services in what customers perceive as the "right" way the first time. But what about the inevitable situations in which this doesn't happen?

10

Attaining Total Customer Satisfaction

Doing Things Right the Second Time

The nearly universal quest for quality in the manufacturing sector has spawned a number of homilies, such as "do it right the first time." Motorola, for example, has compiled an enviable record in global competition in recent years by building at least a part of its competitive strategy around the principles of zero defects and six sigma (standard deviations above random quality levels) management goals. Motorola, in much of its manufacturing effort, is doing it right the first time.

In services, whether provided after the sale of manufactured products or not, there is ample evidence to believe that doing it right the second time in ways that exceed customers' expectations may produce higher satisfaction levels than services provided right the first time. The problem is that when given the opportunity to do things right the second time, too many service organizations drop the ball. They perform miserably. As one executive of the giant U.S. retailer Sears Roebuck put it recently in analyzing the impact of poor service on how customers felt after having their complaints at Sears resolved: "The implication is, even if we resolve a complaint, many customers won't come back."[1]

We have quantitative evidence to suggest just how costly this is. Each year in our service management courses, taught to graduate students studying for an MBA, we assign hundreds of students the task of writing and sending two letters resulting from their actual personal service experiences, one a letter of commendation and one a letter of complaint. The letters must include a description of the customers' expectations, how and whether they were fulfilled, and constructive suggestions for improvement that convey a sense of knowledge about how the service was performed. In short, the letters convey the impression that the writer is knowledgeable about service and contain useful suggestions to be taken seriously by the recipient.

The letters, hundreds of them, are composed and sent. And then we wait, sometimes in vain, for replies. Some replies contain apologies for poor service. Others contain defenses for practices observed. In total, the letters contain thousands of dollars of complimentary airline travel, free nights at hotels, and merchandise exchanges (including, in one case, a computer) and premiums, among other things. Many respondents are appreciative. Some actually indicate that they have implemented changes based on comments in the letters. Some are defensive, condescending, and even argumentative.

As the responses pour in, we ask our letter writers several questions about their experiences and the satisfaction they derived from the organizations to whom they wrote. The results are little short of astounding.

More than half of the students whose letters elicit responses to complaints tell us that they feel worse after attempts by service providers to recover than they did before they wrote their letters, that is, just after experiencing poor service the first time. This is *after* those receiving complaint letters, including well-known service organizations and manufacturers, have gone to some lengths to escalate complaints to higher levels in the organization, write expensive letters, and provide copious complementary services and products as compensation for the initial poor service they provided.

According to customers, service recovery in many of these cases apparently is without value. In fact, those attempting it might have saved money and achieved lower levels of customer dissatisfaction by not replying to complaints at all.

There is no need for this sorry performance, given the tools available to combat the "two strikes and you're out" malady. Several of these tools, including service contracting, effective recovery policies and procedures, and service guarantees, are the center of our attention in this chapter.

DOING IT RIGHT THE FIRST AND SECOND TIME

Service organizations that have patterned their quality improvement efforts solely on the basis of manufacturing concepts such as doing things right the first time often have come up short against competitors capable of effective service recovery. The experiences of UPS and Federal Express, two competitors in the overnight package and letter delivery industry, are instructive.

For years UPS has been the most profitable transportation firm in the world. Its performance record sets a high standard for any industry. As we noted earlier, it has fashioned its business around a highly focused operating strategy that, until recently, restricted UPS's service to the handling of packages of seventy pounds in weight and 130 inches of combined length and girth, in other words packages that could be handled easily by one person either in a package-sorting hub or at the point of pickup or delivery. This enabled UPS to engineer a series of processes to insure maximum productivity per unit of work from its people.

As a result, the company developed one of the largest and most capable industrial engineering departments among all service providers. This group redesigned, for example, delivery vehicles to conform to more effective work practices. UPS's delivery cars, built to the company's specifications, have carefully engineered seats, steps, and heights to facilitate driver movement and package handling. They have translucent roofs to provide interior light for reading package labels. And their construction facilitates easy and less expensive repair. Drivers are coached in practices that are intended to make their days more productive, right down to the gate at which they are encouraged to walk, procedures for honking as they approach a customer's place of business to enable the customer to prepare to receive a package, and the amount of small talk in which to engage with customers. The objective of these and other policies and practices is to produce a service that is done right the first time in a highly efficient way or, as UPS ads have claimed, in the manner of the "tightest ship in the shipping business."

In a sense, UPS borrowed from the practices of many leading industrial organizations in the early decades of the twentieth century and then exceeded the industrial engineering accomplishments of those organizations. Policies concerning extensive employee ownership, decentralization, communication, and managerial development; the unpretentiousness of its facilities; and its emphasis on customer service are contained in a document called *The Policy Book,* first published in 1929. It is testimony to the company's efforts to prescribe as many aspects of its employees' behaviors as possible.[2]

UPS's operating focus and engineering efforts have resulted in the development of one of the world's great service values, dependable, on-time deliveries at costs that were a fraction of UPS's major competitor in the early years of the company's development, the U.S. Postal Services's parcel post service. In deciding to enter into competition with a young and growing overnight package deliverer, Federal Express, UPS encountered a different kind of competitor.

The emphasis at Federal Express nearly from the start was on the use of technology as a primary driver of performance. Among other things, Federal Express was one of the first organizations to assemble technologies that enabled its drivers and package handlers to scan packages with bar code labels in order to track a package's progress at a number of critical points in its journey, feeding the information into a system that updates progress every thirty minutes. As a result, customers could be informed periodically where their packages were. Packages not delivered on time could be traced, triggering a service recovery process based on reliable information.

For years after entering competition with Federal Express, UPS did not have comparable package tracing capability. After all, its system was engineered to do it right the first time at very low costs, something that it accomplished in all but a small number of cases. But when service recovery was called for, UPS's information technology was inferior; the company had less information on which to act. Consequently, the company was not able to measure up to the recovery standards of its new competitor. In fact, only in recent years, with the expenditure of several hundred million dollars for new technology, has UPS begun to offer a capability to do it right the second time, something to which its industrial engineering department gave very little emphasis over the first eighty years of the company's existence. Now that it has the capability of doing things right both the first and second times, UPS has become an even more formidable competitor in its industry.

UPS and Federal Express are both fortunate in one respect. Customers quite naturally complain when they don't receive an expected package delivery. Most other service organizations are not quite so fortunate in their efforts to effect service recovery.

GETTING CUSTOMERS TO COMPLAIN: THE BRITISH AIRWAYS EXPERIENCE

The management of British Airways has engineered a remarkable turnaround of the airline since the appointment of Colin Marshall as chief executive in 1983, as we saw in Chapter 3. Under Marshall, a quality standard with a focus on "getting things right the first time" was developed that was communicated throughout the organization at the same time that the company was privatized. Quality initiatives included the upgrading of operational systems for ticketing and check-in; the renovation of physical space; the development of top quality brands (beginning with the Concorde class); changes in uniforms, aircraft, and marketing programs; and a series of "Putting People First" training programs that influenced how frontline service providers viewed the customer.[3]

It wasn't until several years later that management concluded that this was not enough. For one thing, the initiatives of the 1980s had lost their punch with employees. As one executive put it, "You can't go on selling the same old socks."[4] At this time, some internal research pointed in the direction of service recovery. BA discovered that as many as a third of its passengers were in some way dissatisfied with their service encounters with the company. Of these, 69 percent never registered a complaint. Another 23 percent complained at the time of their dissatisfaction to the nearest BA employee. And only 8 percent, representing the tip of the "complainant iceberg" shown in Figure 10–1, contacted customer relations where their complaints could be

FIGURE 10–1
The "Complainant Iceberg" at British Airways

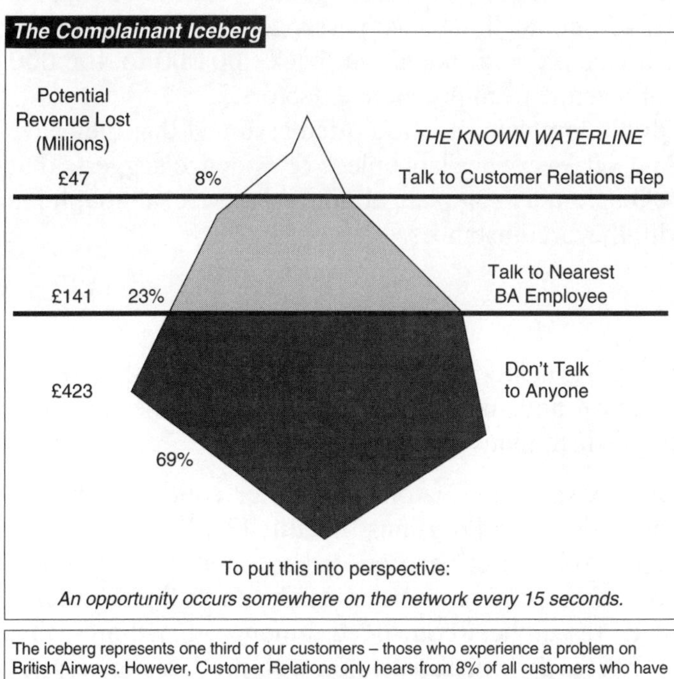

The iceberg represents one third of our customers – those who experience a problem on British Airways. However, Customer Relations only hears from 8% of all customers who have reason to complain (those at the "tip of the iceberg"). A further 23% claim to discuss the problem with the airline, but Customer Relations does not receive this data. Another 69% don't bother to complain; it's either too much hassle or they feel nothing will ever come of it. Delving further into complaint data shows that 90% of Executive Club members experience a problem – large or small – sometime during "the flying year."

Norman Klein and W. Earl Sasser, Jr., British Airways: Using Information Systems to Better Service the Customer, Case No. 395-065. Boston: Harvard Business School, 1994, p. 13.

dealt with in a systematic way and captured in the company's information system. Those who did encountered a customer relations organization, according to one BA executive, whose "aim was to either deny wrongdoing or find an excuse to explain away an incident."[5] If it was to win customer loyalty through service recovery, it also had to be able to act in ways designed to retain customers when problems occurred.

In order to do this, the airline trained frontline employees in ways of handling problems on the spot, created a Careline phone link to its representatives in its customer relations office who heard and dealt with complaints, developed CARESS (Customer Analysis and Retention System) to hold and organize customer-centered data files for use by customer service personnel, and extended the latitude of customer service employees to deal with customers' problems.

But after doing all of this, British Airways was still confronted with one of the most basic problems facing service providers today, getting people to complain or, as one BA executive put it, "melting the complainant iceberg." The payoff from this was big. Based on its experience with new service initiatives, BA's management concluded that for every 1 percent of additional dissatisfied passengers that it could get to complain to its service office, it could win back 200,000 to 400,000 pounds sterling in revenue from potential defectors.

If customers don't complain, it is too often assumed that they have been satisfied. And yet, every available piece of evidence suggests that only a minority of customers complain about bad service, although the numbers vary with the circumstances.

The Problem

The problem of eliciting customer complaints has to do with both the way customers behave and increasingly outmoded policies of complaint escalation on which many organizations rely.

Customer Behavior. A study of customer behavior conducted by the Technical Assistance Research Programs Institute (TARP) for the U.S. Office of Consumer Affairs has been quoted so often that its impact has been blown out of proportion to the research and its findings. Nevertheless, the TARP researchers concluded, among other things, that customers don't register their dissatisfaction with products or services because it requires too much effort for too little potential payoff. For face-to-face service encounters, it often involves unpleasantness that most people would rather avoid. And in some cases, there is a very real fear that a complaint will get a service provider, perhaps an acquaintance or at least someone a customer has gotten to know, into trouble.

Other dissatisfied customers don't know how or where to complain. And many others don't believe the organization will do anything if they do complain.[6]

Escalation and Invisibility to Top Management. Many organizations for years have followed the practice of "escalating" complaints to a higher level when they are not solved. This can represent a heavy burden to everyone if frontline employees are capable of resolving only a small proportion of complaints. A simple example based on the TARP study illustrates the point.[7] Assume that 40 percent of dissatisfied customers complain to frontline service providers such as sales or service representatives. The concerns of 25 percent of these customers are not satisfied and are "kicked upstairs" to middle management, to whom only one in five actually bother to escalate their complaints. Of those who choose to complain to middle management, one in five still remain unsatisfied. If half of those who are still dissatisfied escalate their complaints (or have them escalated) to a vice president, it produces the pyramid shown in Figure 10–2. Here we see that every complaint received by the vice president represents 500 dissatisfied customers.

FIGURE 10–2
The Complaint Escalation Pyramid

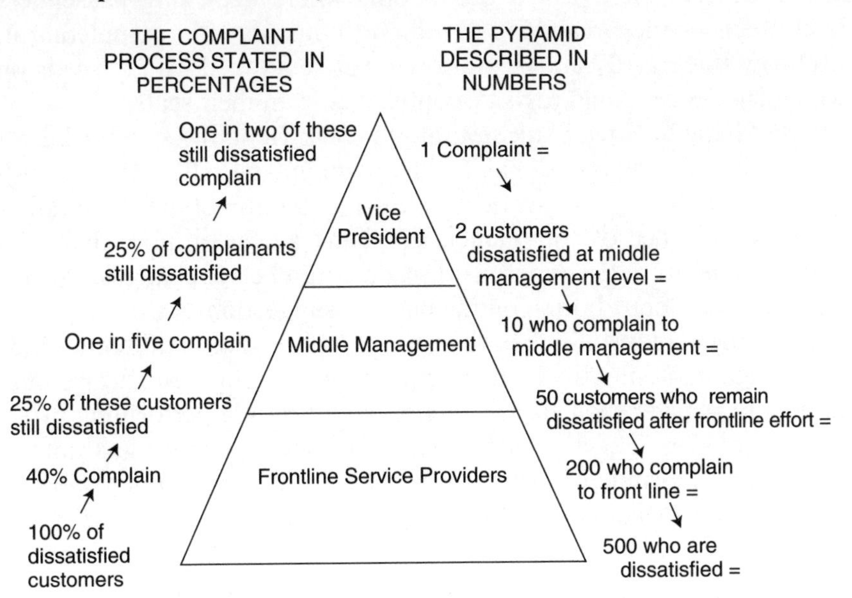

Source: Based on data presented in U.S. Office of Consumer Affairs, *Consumer Complaint Handling in America: An Update Study, Part II* (Washington, D.C.: Technical Assistance Research Programs Institute, April 1, 1986).

In the process of "protecting" senior management from dissatisfied customers through an escalation policy, organizations actually deny themselves important information that could trigger corrective action.

Failure of service organizations to elicit complaints or make them visible within the organization represents a waste of the "golden nuggets" that Japanese manufacturers so assiduously sought out from their customers more than a decade before the dramatic increases in the quality of Japanese products witnessed by the world in recent years. Such golden nuggets are the drivers of customer satisfaction in the short term and overall service improvement for many other customers in the long term.

Some Responses

British Airways, in order to encourage a higher proportion of dissatisfied travelers to provide such golden nuggets, has established several different kinds of listening posts. The CareLine phone connection to the service center was publicized. Global Free-Post Comment Cards that passengers could fill out and mail were introduced. "Informal chat groups" were organized by BA executives throughout the world. Highly valued customers were even invited to fly with BA's customer relations managers to experience the company's service together. The airline experimented with video booths where deplaning passengers could register their reactions to a flight moments after completing it. And new Boeing 767 and 777 aircraft were equipped with keypads on which customers could register complaints from their seats.

The Maine Savings Bank several years ago went one step further. It offered its patrons one dollar for every complaint letter written suggesting ways to improve service, a clear recognition of the value rather than the nuisance of complaints. The bank averaged more than 500 letters a year from customers and made a number of changes, including extending lobby hours, on the basis of suggestions.[8]

Still other organizations have begun to utilize several different kinds of management initiatives which, among other things, encourage customers to register their dissatisfaction about poorly performing products or services. They include service contracting, service guarantees, and carefully planned interactions between frontline service workers and customers leading directly to service recovery.

EXTERNAL AND INTERNAL SERVICE CONTRACTING

Service contracts can serve as a device for improving customer satisfaction, internal operations, and even supplier performance.

Customer Service Contracting

Many manufacturers now offer service contracts or extended service agreements on the products they sell. Too many have regarded this as a high-margin opportunity to capitalize on the fact that the products to which they relate, often offered under conditions of price competition, themselves do not yield sufficient profits. As a result, many service contracts have developed a poor reputation among consumer advisory groups.

There is another way of viewing the service contract, as not only a way of extending a relationship with a customer but also a device for eliciting complaints, information, and even new product ideas. Viewed in this way, even moderately priced low-profit service contracts can be justified.

Internal Service Contracting

In recent years, enlightened managements have begun to apply the service contracting concept to their internal processes, particularly those spanning two or more functional departments of the organization. This process encourages each department to ask itself: (1) Which other department(s) in the organization are our most important customers? (2) What are their needs, according to them? (3) What is the gap between their needs and our current performance? (4) What are the costs and payoffs of closing this gap?

Internal service contracting can be the answer to important cross-departmental challenges. For example, recently in one well-known casualty insurance firm, a question arose between the field sales force and the headquarters underwriting (pricing) department about the excessive length of time needed to process a new application for insurance. Customers, prone to having second thoughts about their application if required to wait too long, were canceling their "apps" with increasing frequency, producing wasted sales and underwriting effort. For its part, the underwriting department was swamped with so many applications that it could not process them with acceptable speed.

An internal contracting process was initiated in the underwriting department. Upon learning of the difference between the processing speed desired by the field sales force and what it was capable of achieving, it undertook to negotiate a solution. First, guidelines were developed for small contracts that enabled field salespeople to approve applications on the spot after eliciting the necessary information from a prospective applicant, thereby relieving the underwriting department of the burden of reviewing all applications. At the same time, information and communication technology was introduced that enabled field sales representatives to submit all information on applications electronically, eliminating the first step in the underwriting process that produced several days of delay. In return for much faster processing times, field sales representatives were willing to make the effort to provide information electronically. In fact, as a result of the contracting process, the application form was revised to facilitate the inputting of information, resulting in very little extra information input time required of field sales representatives.

Often, internal departments of an organization claim that they receive poorer service from their own colleagues than they do from outside suppliers. Internal service contracting is one way of correcting the problem. In fact, in one organization with which we are familiar, the effort has become known as the "Customer First" initiative. The concept has become so endemic to the way that departments of the organization deal with one another that the term has become a verb. When a problem arises within the organization, managers immediately conclude that they have to "Customer First" it.

Supplier Service Contracting

Internal contracting often identifies service and other quality levels needed from suppliers. Gaps between needs and actual supplier performance become apparent. The impact on supplier relationships can be profound. For example, many of the companies that have won the Malcolm Baldrige National Quality Award in the United States have required suppliers to at least compete for the award as the first criterion for maintaining a customer relationship. The same is true for companies achieving ISO 9000 quality ratings in Europe and elsewhere.

Supply chain contracting taking into account efforts to improve quality is a natural result of this process. In many cases, it has led to the demand for service guarantees to be incorporated into such contracts. Astute suppliers have anticipated such demands and have instituted their own quality improvement initiatives, including service guarantees.

SERVICE GUARANTEES

Service guarantees contain a promise to perform; conditions, if any; and a payoff to the recipient for failure to perform. They have become so prevalent and, in some cases, so superficial and poorly designed that they have gotten a bad name among some executives. But the fact remains that they are important to organizations like Lands' End, whose very simple guarantee, shown in Figure 10–3, supplies the level of trust necessary to encourage customers to buy merchandise sight unseen by catalog. If designed properly, they encourage complaints.

FIGURE 10–3
An Advertisement Featuring the Lands' End Guarantee

The world is full of guarantees, no two alike. As a rule, the more words they contain, the more their protection is limited. The Lands' End guarantee has always been an unconditional one.
It reads:

> *"If you are not completely satisfied with any item you buy from us, at any time during your use of it, return it and we will refund your full purchase price."*

We mean every word of it. Whatever. Whenever. Always. But to make sure this is perfectly clear, we've decided to simplify it further.

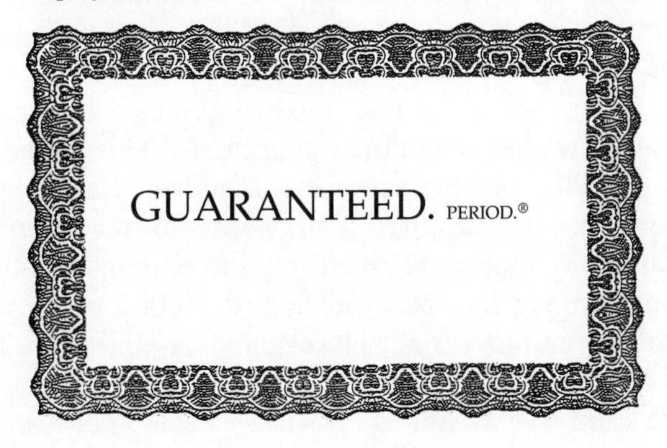

And they can provide significant encouragement to customers to demand great service and to service providers to supply it.[9]

Questions in Guarantee Design

Managers who become enamored of the idea of offering a guarantee often fail to ask themselves several simple questions: (1) Is the primary purpose for the guarantee marketing or operational improvement? (2) Should we have one? (3) Should it be unconditional or conditional? (4) Should it be total or specific? and (5) Should it be explicit or implicit?

What's the Primary Purpose?

"Satisfaction guaranteed or your money back" has been a byword in many marketing campaigns for years. Often it has been applied to products of little value sold to customers who perceive little risk in their use and who are not likely to put forth effort to invoke the guarantee even if they are not satisfied. It is, pure and simple, a guarantee designed to sell product. Such initiatives have, by and large, diminished the concept in the minds of many consumers.

However, for an organization offering a professional service whose quality can't be judged in advance, a service guarantee may be an important marketing tool, significant to the potential client who may be incurring a substantial risk. For an organization such as Lands' End, it is critical to establishing customer trust and loyalty.

At the same time, organizations may use a service guarantee as a way of improving operating procedures and outcomes. A guarantee involves the customer in the task of process improvement, but it also highlights the importance of good service in the minds of service providers. It can have an important positive impact on organization pride and morale if a guarantee carries with it the implication that an organization is the "best in the industry."

Most organizations, of course, hope to obtain both marketing and operational improvement from their guarantees. This has been the case at Delta Dental Plan of Massachusetts, a managed-care dental insurance company that has captured a large share of the group dental insurance market in that state, insuring more than 2,000 corporate organizations ranging in size from five to 10,000 employees.[10] In a process involving employees at all levels of its organization, Delta Dental decided to offer seven guarantees, all involving the administration of insurance contracts, including "no hassle" customer relations, accurate and quick turnaround of ID cards, and a minimum of 10 percent savings on claims paid to its participating dentists. The Delta Dental promise on each of these guarantees ranges from specified results to total satisfaction, as defined by the customer. For example, if a corporate customer is dissatisfied for any reason with the conversion from its current insurer to Delta Dental, the payoff is the cancellation of a month's administrative charges. Monetary payments result from other kinds of failures to meet guaranteed levels of performance.

Shortly after the introduction of these guarantees, Delta Dental attracted new accounts that enabled it to increase revenues by 15 percent over plan, the number of sales leads by 50 percent, the number of quotes to potential clients by 400 percent, and its "close" ratio on bids to 66 percent over target. Shortly after the introduction of the guarantee, its account retention rate rose from 95 percent to 97.1 percent. Just as important, however, was the fact that Delta Dental was able to implement a number of new process improvements suggested by clients who invoked the guarantee, process improvements that have produced significant reductions in administrative costs. Employees have also developed and implemented internal and external customer satisfaction surveys to provide more data about the insurer's performance. And they have formed a quality group to provide feedback to claims-processing operators and analysts with the goal of eliminating rework. These are the kinds of marketing and operating improvements that a guarantee can stimulate.

Should We Have One? Most organizations asking themselves the following questions would discard the idea of having a guarantee in the first place:

1. Are we good enough? The cost of a guarantee to a poorly-performing organization can be prohibitive. Organizations hoping to find a way of improving on low levels of service quality would do well to consider other alternatives.
2. Do we have enough "surface" credibility with customers? Whether or not a guarantee is believable may depend on whether people generally regard an organization as capable of delivering high quality.
3. Does it matter enough to customers? Unless the cost of the service or the perceived risk of using it is sufficiently high, customers may perceive little need for a guarantee.
4. Will it raise few suspicions about service quality? Airlines don't guarantee safety. There is no point in raising apprehension levels about something assumed by passengers as being part of the basic requirements of flying.
5. Can we manage the internal aspects positively? If employees are penalized when customers invoke guarantees, they will either improve their service levels, find a way to discourage customers from invoking the guarantee, or become more dissatisfied with the job and less loyal to their employer. Two out of three of these outcomes are undesirable. As we saw at Bugs Burger Bug Killers, whose guarantee was described on pages 124 and 125, employees whose customers invoked guarantees and canceled service were reimbursed for their lost commissions until such time as the lost business could be replaced. When it happened more than once, supplemental training was provided to the employee. This positive reinforcement contributed to the success of the guarantee.
6. Will it give us a service edge through better incentives and controls? The service edge resulting from Bugs Burger's guarantee was sufficient to allow it to charge four to six times the fees of its competitors, the very best measure of a service edge.

Once these questions are answered adequately, others relating to the nature of the guarantee to be instituted have to be addressed.

Should It Be Unconditional? An unconditional guarantee can expose its sponsor to claims resulting from service failures over which it has no control.

Lands' End has realized many benefits from its unconditional guarantee, shown in Figure 10–3, not only because the guarantee is critical to mail order sales but also because the company's management controls most factors associated with product quality and service. And by and large, its customers have little tendency to take advantage of the spirit of the guarantee by returning merchandise they have worn for some time. Those who do are generally such a small percent of all customers that the organization can support the design and delivery of its service guarantee. As a result, the design of the guarantee is influenced by those who honor it rather than the small number who take advantage of its spirit. These are the factors influencing an organization's decision to remove all conditions from a guarantee and give the customer latitude in invoking it.

The reasons that conditions, often in the form of "fine print," creep into guarantees is that they are often passed through many organizational "screens," including those set up by operating people who are concerned about whether they can deliver on the guarantee and a legal department that desires to limit all possible liability. However, conditions often diminish the impact of a guarantee on a potential client, make the guarantee more difficult for frontline service providers to administer, and engage the firm in potential litigation over the terms of the guarantee itself.

Should It Be Total or Specific? When a guarantee covers all aspects of a service or product, little time is lost arguing with customers, either on the frontline or higher in the organization, about whether the guarantee applies. Because of the inability to control all aspects of a service, it may be necessary to make a guarantee more specific. For example, at Delta Dental, only the quality of the insurance services, not the dental service itself, is guaranteed.

Under conditions such as this, a specific guarantee may be more appropriate. Where limits are clearly specified, service workers know more exactly what is expected of them, "cheating" by customers is discouraged, and customer expectations of service standards are more clearly formed.

Should It Be Explicit or Implicit? This question brings us back to the issue of the original objective of a guarantee. Those using it to attract customers, help shape their expectations of the service, and create incentives to improve internal operations will want to make it explicit or highly visible to customers. On the other hand, implicit guarantees communicated only to employees enable service workers to effect service recovery on an individual, customized basis and impress customers with service that exceeds expectations. They may create more service worker job satisfaction while producing positive longer-term marketing results through favorable word-of-mouth advertising. For every Lands' End guarantee there is one like Nordstrom's, which is widely understood by customers to allow employees to accept merchandise returns without question and provide other forms of service and relief even though the "guarantee" is never mentioned in Nordstrom's advertising.

Internal Guarantees

Internal service guarantees can provide effective means for encouraging service improvements between departments of the same firm. Often they may be associated with an internal service contract.

For example, the management of the GTE Corporation's Management Education and Training Group, responsible for managing the giant communication company's Management Development Center at Norwalk, Connecticut, concluded that one way to insure the maintenance of its outstanding facilities and high service levels would be to indemnify itself against customer dissatisfaction by initiating the following guarantee for other of the company's divisions: "GTE Management Education and Training guarantees that you will be satisfied with any GTE Management Education and Training sponsored course delivered at the GTE Management Development Center, or we will refund the tuition, room and board." In announcing the guarantee to the rest of GTE's organization, Jerry Tucker, Corporate Director of Education and Training at the time, commented: "Establishing a moneyback guarantee sets clear standards. . . . The service guarantee will help in generating additional feedback and define what we must do to satisfy our customers. The guarantee challenges us to do better."[11]

At one of the Marriott Corporation's resort hotels, the human resource department decided to combat its most important continuing problem of unfilled frontline positions, encompassing 70 percent of all the employees at the facility, by guaranteeing that all positions not filled in fourteen days would be staffed on day 15 with temporary helpers paid by the department. Within several weeks, the average number of open frontline positions (including those staffed by temporaries) at the hotel dropped from forty to five.

Impact on Suppliers

Guarantees leading to the improvement of service levels often place increasing pressure on suppliers to improve their service levels as well. We were confronted with this phenomenon several years ago when, after returning from a visiting year on our campus, Prof. Richard Chase returned to the University of Southern California to initiate a new course in service management. Enamored of the idea of a service guarantee to stimulate interest in his new course and force him to practice what he would be teaching, Chase offered to buy back his students' books and pay them $250 for tuition costs if they decided that they were not satisfied with their learning experience in the course. To Chase's surprise, more than three times as many students as he expected signed up for the course. Having assigned one of our books as the text for the course, he naturally contacted us to ask if we would stand behind his guarantee for those students who invoked the guarantee. But it probably had a positive influence on the quality of Chase's teaching (and, we hope, the quality of our subsequent writing).

The Economics of Service Guarantees

Few descriptions extolling guarantees contain hard numbers that allow practical managers to appraise their usefulness. However, those with which we are familiar are very encouraging.

For example, the benefits of increases in sales leads, quotes, and the rate of sales "closes," along with increased customer retention and the development of several improved processes for administering insurance contracts at Delta Dental, described earlier, all were obtained at a cost of only $36,007 in payments for service failures to 238 accounts in the first year after Delta's guarantee was introduced.

Bugs Burger Bug Killers claimed that it had paid for its full guarantee only once, but incurred payouts of about $2,000 per month to restaurant diners and hotel guests for pest sightings. However, this represented less than one-tenth of one percent of revenues received from customers in any given year. In return, the organization enjoyed a sterling marketing device that distinguished it from less reputable competitors in an industry incurring a great deal of customer distrust. It was able to use the guarantee as an incentive to managers and employees to improve the quality of their methods, materials, work, and relationships with customers.

But perhaps the most detailed accounting of the costs and benefits from its service guarantee is provided by Hampton Inn, a subsidiary of the Promus Corporation offering economy lodging to business and pleasure travelers throughout the United States. The unconditional guarantee was developed several years ago and is shown in Figure 10–4.[12]

One year after the introduction of the guarantee, Hampton Inn's management undertook a detailed analysis of its economic results. Based on the results of a survey of "frequent stayers" (eleven times or more during the year) in which 2 percent of them indicated that they stayed at a Hampton Inn because of the guarantee, management was able to calculate the number of room nights at an average of $46 per night that this represented throughout the chain, which at the time was renting 7.85 million room nights per year. This represented an increase of $7.2 million in annual revenue. In addition, 45 percent of the 7,465 dissatisfied guests who invoked the guarantee during the year came back, with 61 percent of them indicating that they returned to Hampton Inn because of the guarantee. They represented another $1 million in annual revenue. On the other hand, Hampton Inns' costs of refunds to dissatisfied customers during the year approximated $500,000. And roughly $300,000 above the normal budget was spent to advertise the guarantee. Nevertheless, the ratio of increased revenue to increased cost for the hotel chain was about 10 to 1, a huge payout in a business in which the contribution from incremental sales of hotel room rentals can be as much as 80 percent.

FIGURE 10–4
The Hampton Inn Unconditional Service Guarantee

The "soft" payout from the guarantee was measured in terms of employee reactions. Fully 66 percent of those surveyed said that employee pride had improved, 75 percent said that Hampton Inn was a better place to work, and 85 percent said that they were motivated to do a better job as a result of the guarantee.

As a result of this experience, Michael Rose, the Promus Company's CEO at the time, stated: "Unconditional service guarantees are the wave of the future. Those companies choosing to ignore them or refusing to implement them are doomed to surrender their competitive edge to those who stand full behind the services they offer."[13]

The story doesn't end here. Because roughly 90 percent of the more than 200 inns being operated under the Hampton Inn name at the time the guarantee was initiated were franchised, questions were raised about whether the guarantee could be implemented and, if it could, whether it would have much impact on quality in franchised inns. In order to deal with these questions, Hampton Inn agreed to share all penalty payments 50-50 with franchisees for the first six months of the program. In addition, advertising costs were paid out of the pool to which both the corporation and franchises contributed.

To track the effectiveness of the guarantee, the company stepped up its customer satisfaction surveys in order to obtain measures for each of its inns, franchised or company-operated. This provided it with data similar to that shown in Figure 10–5, data that was used in managing relations with franchisees to raise the quality of Hampton Inn's customer satisfaction. For example, franchises achieving high measures of customer satisfaction and low numbers of invoked guarantees were celebrated. Those experiencing low measures of customer satisfaction and high numbers of invoked guarantees were provided with management help to solve their problems. But those producing both low customer satisfaction levels and small numbers of invoked guarantees became targets for possible "buy-outs" or franchise revocation, given the strong indications that they were neither delivering good quality nor cooperating with the program.

One indication of the success of this guarantee is the fact that the guarantee is still the centerpiece of Hampton Inn's advertising several years after its introduction.

Putting Guarantees in Context

Service guarantees have an immediate and strong appeal to many executives we encounter. For many, they represent the ultimate "quick fix" for marketing or operating problems. Nothing could be further from the truth, for a guarantee developed and introduced without at-

FIGURE 10–5
Possible Management Actions Resulting from Service Guarantee and Customer Satisfaction Performance

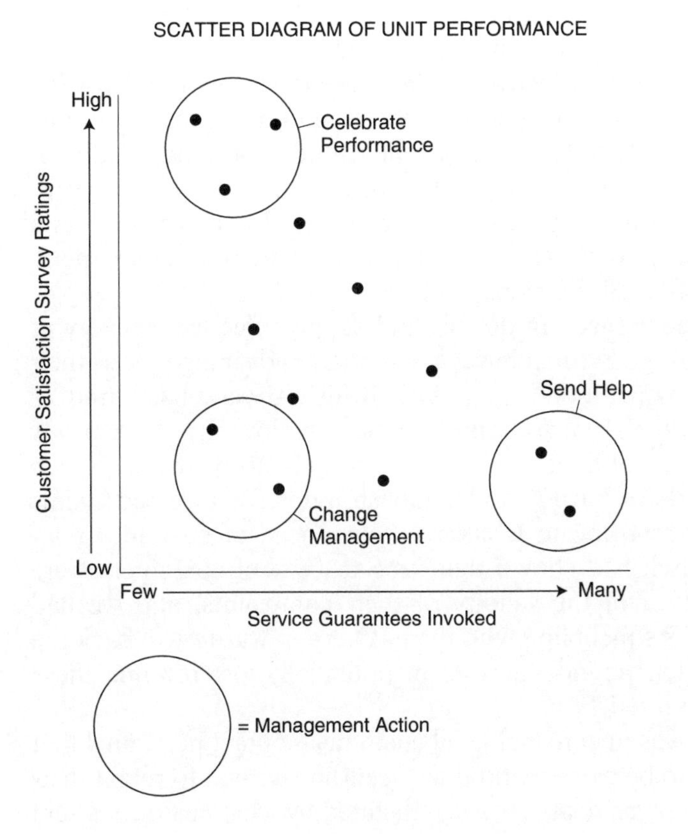

tention to all other elements of a service strategy can lead to disappointment or, worse, bankruptcy.

The Hampton Inn experience is a good example of the need to adapt guarantees to the business and the management context in which they are to be used. Because they require effective communication, frontline job descriptions and authority that make appropriate response possible, high existing levels of service quality, and customer credibility, guarantees are components of very complex strategies. They should be used with caution.

SERVICE RECOVERY: A CASE FOR CAPABILITY

Total customer satisfaction can be achieved without the perfect design and delivery of services. But it requires a kind of capability that has been overlooked in the manufacturing sector, the capability to recover from poor service incidents. As we have seen, the most effective recovery is fast, customized, and personalized. The fastest, most customized, and most personalized service recovery takes place at the point of contact between customer and service provider, the service encounter.

Organizations aspiring to achieve total customer satisfaction cannot rely too heavily on service recovery. They have to be very good at what they do, delivering results for customers day after day, time after time. This requires a very high level of capability centered around good people selected carefully for the frontline jobs they occupy who are supported and motivated by outstanding methods, incentives, and technologies, and who are able to exercise judgment and remain flexible when unanticipated things happen.

But organizations that can do this and supply effective recovery as well when things go wrong have a particular advantage over their "merely good" competitors. That is what British Airways has found.

Under the airline's previous management philosophy, BA's newly developed methods for handling customer complaints would have been used for investigative purposes to establish a defense to avoid claims payments. But according to Charles Weiser, head of customer relations, "BA research had shown that 98% to 99% of customers were sincerely convinced of the validity of their complaints, and we had nothing to gain by squabbling with them. Our aim was to win back the almost 400 million pounds sterling in potentially lost revenue these customers represented."[14]

The first step was in convincing all customer-contact personnel that customers were to be trusted and that the airline wished to retain their business. The rest was relatively easy, dictated by what customers said they most wanted: (1) an apology, (2) to be asked what they wanted as a solution, (3) a quick resolution of the complaint or (4) assurance that the problem was being fixed, and (5) solutions by CareLine phone calls if possible.

This reflects what our students told us as the result of their experiences with the letter-writing campaign described at the outset of this chapter. They wanted quick, personal, and customized responses to their complaint letters as opposed to lavish recompense often viewed as "buyoffs." Their reactions told us that hastily scrawled messages faxed to complaining customers are much more effective and less costly than carefully composed and beautifully typed letters sent days later. And form-like letters completely missed the mark, were a waste of everyone's time, and more often generated more badwill than good.

Reasoning that the most effective way of dealing with customer complaints, if possible, was on the initial phone call (as opposed to a thirteen-step investigative process before the development of the

CARESS data base and information system), British Airways first trained a cadre of CareLine customer service representatives to do what customers said they wanted done. Next it gave them the latitude to rectify problems in ways that customers desired, including spending significant sums of money if necessary.

THE SERVICE RECOVERY PAYOFF

It's natural to ask whether an organization can afford initiatives such as those described here. The evidence strongly suggests that managers can't afford *not* to invest in service recovery.

For example, when TARP explored the question "How many of your unhappy customers will buy from you again?" under several circumstances, it obtained results that suggest the potential cost of poor service or service recovery.[15] They are shown in Figure 10–6. For major purchases, TARP found that the proportion of dissatisfied customers making major purchases who would buy again rose from 9 percent for people who didn't even bother to complain to 19 percent for those whose complaints were not resolved to 54 percent whose complaints were resolved to 82 percent whose complaints were resolved quickly.

The stream of income over the lifetime of a customer relationship, when augmented by the favorable word-of-mouth resulting from effective recovery (and in some cases the avoidance of regulatory interven-

FIGURE 10–6
Dissatisfied Customers' Repurchase Intentions under Various Conditions

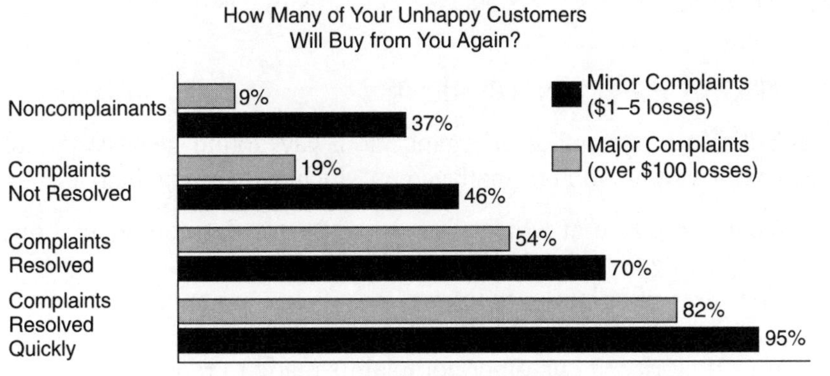

Source: U.S. Office of Consumer Affairs, *Consumer Complaint Handling in America: An Update Study, Part II* (Washington, D.C.: Technical Assistance Research Programs Institute, April 1, 1986), p. 50.

tion as a result of dissatisfaction), often can be several times the cost of handling complaints and providing effective service recovery.

The management of British Airways found out several very important things as a result of its service recovery initiatives: (1) The faster the response time, the lower the monetary rewards that were required to satisfy customers, (2) as CareLine customer satisfaction indicators rose into the mid-90 percent range, the staff were actually awarding 8 percent less in customer compensation, and (3) for every pound spent on customer retention efforts, the airline was retaining two pounds in revenue that it would have lost. Perhaps just as important, as we saw in Chapter 3, job satisfaction measures for customer relations staff members at BA rose from the low teens to 69 percent, with part of the satisfaction resulting from the extra training they received in "life skills" such as negotiation, influence, decision making, and anger diffusion.

The CARESS supporting technology (costing nearly $7 million) paid for itself in one year in the "hard" measures of increased repeat business for British Airways. But the payoff was probably much greater in "soft" measures. First, CARESS allowed the airline to collect many more complaints and catalog them in ways that could be used with "root cause analysis" associated with continuous quality improvement efforts. Further, it could be programmed to assist letter writing, if needed, by maintaining an up-to-date set of the most effective phrases used in communicating with customers.

But perhaps of greatest interest, CARESS made it possible for British Airways to trace complaints to shortcomings of its suppliers, thereby facilitating the kind of "supply-chain" problem-solving contracting that we discussed earlier. This extended the urgency of "doing things right the first and second times" to the airline's suppliers as well, further enhancing BA's service levels to its customers.

QUESTIONS FOR MANAGEMENT

What British Airways and other organizations have found suggests several questions for examination by management. Included among them are:

1. What is the rate at which dissatisfied customers complain about your products or services? How do you know?
2. How are complaints encouraged by your organization? What kinds of incentives are provided to customers to complain?
3. Are a majority of customer complaints made to representatives of the organization who can do something about them? If not, what has to be done to insure that this is the case?
4. Are the reactions of dissatisfied customers assembled in one data

base (a consolidated "listening post") for management information, planning, and longer-term action?

5. Based on information from dissatisfied customers, what is the potential for renegotiating agreements both across relevant departments of your organization and with "supply chain" partners?
6. What does fast, personalized, customized recovery mean in your business? What has to be done to achieve it in your organization?
7. To what extent has service contracting been employed within the organization and with other organizations in the supply chain?
8. How could a service guarantee help your organization elicit complaints, provide an incentive for effective service recovery, and serve as a vehicle for improving service operations?

Efforts to attain total customer satisfaction have little prospect of success without proper measurement—measurement that not only tells an organization where it's been but also where it's going. We turn to it next.

11

Measuring for Effective Management

Service profit chain management is affecting the way managers measure, track, and, most important, predict the performance of their organizations. It influences what managers measure: profit and growth, of course—but increasingly, customer and employee satisfaction and loyalty and the drivers of these phenomena. It influences how managers measure, with increasing sensitivity paid to issues of worker morale and objectivity in measuring results. It influences how frequently managers measure: from annually to increasingly greater frequencies, even daily. And it influences how the results of such measurements are used and fed back to all levels of the organization.

We see it happening all around us. Some of the most interesting examples are provided by the managements of First Data Corporation, USAA, AT&T Universal Card Services, Fairfield Inn, Federal Express, and Xerox in the United States and Swedbank in Europe. All have developed highly customized efforts, underscoring the importance of fitting measurement to strategy. The managements of several of these organizations have been inspired to act by yet one more measure, the lifetime value of a customer.

ESTIMATING THE LIFETIME VALUE OF A CUSTOMER

As we have seen, customer loyalty is one of the most important drivers of service profit chain performance. One of the most graphic reminders of this is the lifetime value of a customer to any supplier of goods and services. That's why, as we saw earlier, Carl Sewell took the trouble to estimate that it was $332,000 for a customer of his Village Cadillac dealership in Dallas, or why Phil Bressler calculated it at $4,000 for one of his Domino's Pizza customers. These were not sophisticated calculations. They were estimates based on experience intended to motivate managers to become interested in the retention of customers. Estimates of this kind have been a useful tool for us as well in getting top management interest in initiating efforts to increase customer retention.

In Chapter 4, we said the simplest "back of the envelope" estimates of lifetime value can be made on the basis of assumptions about the average "life" (loyalty) of various customers and their average annual consumption rates for services and products. Further efforts can be made to estimate price sensitivity and the profit streams resulting from a customer relationship over time. Yet other analyses may include estimates of the number of new customers that may result from the referrals by a loyal user of an organization's output, as shown graphically in Figure 11–1. Obviously, the more complete the estimate, the more dramatic the result. At Intuit, the creator and marketer of personal finance software selling for $40, we saw that the total revenue stream for prod-

FIGURE 11–1
Factors Determining the Lifetime Value of a Customer

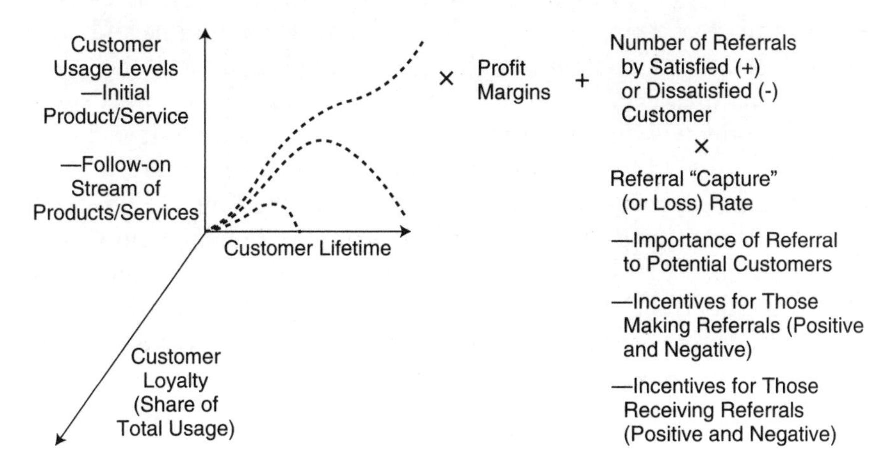

uct, related suppliers, and electronic transaction services could grow to thousands of dollars over a customer's lifetime with the company. In the computer service industry, for example, the number may be well up into the millions of dollars. If the purpose is shock value and drama for jaded senior executives, this kind of measurement will do. For decision-making purposes, more careful, detailed analysis will be necessary.

Two subsidiaries of First Data Corporation, for example, take somewhat different approaches to the measurement of customer lifetime value, illustrating both methods of calculation and uses of the results. First Data's TeleCheck International, which is the world's largest check acceptance company, provides a range of check guarantee, check verification, and collection services to retail and financial clients. Its management's approach to calculating lifetime value is shown in Figure 11–2. By factoring in such things as increased revenues from its base product (FastData) as well as declining per-unit service costs (from both customer and supplier learning effects), the increased sales from purchases of a new product (FirstPursuit), and estimated profits from referrals by a satisfied customer, TeleCheck International's management estimated that a 20 percent annual increase in revenue from its base product could produce a 33 percent annual increase in operating profit from the customer relationship. The total five-year stream of operating profit, nearly $86,000 in the hypothetical example, would more than justify the $6,600 expense incurred to acquire the customer prior to the first year of the relationship.

If instead the purpose of lifetime value measurement is to determine the amount of time and money that can be spent on maintaining or improving customer retention rates, the effort may be focused on the analysis of various levels of loyalty for a group of customers. For example, First Data's Integrated Payment Systems, Inc. (IPS), a check and money order processing service for large financial institutions and utilities, has developed a detailed method for estimating not only the value of a new national account, but also the value of a "book" of existing business under varying assumptions regarding customer loyalty, as shown in Figure 11–3. The organization realizes fee income for each check processed, revenue from the float during the time the check is held for payment, and positive cash flow from tax-reducing amortization. The value of a customer depends on its transaction volume, the "life" of the float, the average transaction size, and of course the life of the account. From these estimates, others related to fixed and variable costs must be subtracted to produce estimates of profit after tax, discounted for the time value of money (in this case, 8.25 percent per year).

FIGURE 11–2
The Calculation of the Lifetime Value of an Average Customer at TeleCheck International, Inc.*

	Year 0	*Year 1*	*Year 2*	*Year 3*	*Year 4*	*Year 5*
Revenue:†						
QuickResponse	—	$33,000	$39,600	$47,520	$57,024	$68,429
FastTrack	—	—	5,500	6,600	7,920	9,504
Costs:						
QuickResponse	$6,600	$24,090	$28,908	$34,690	$41,627	$49,953
FastTrack	—	—	4,152	4,983	5,980	7,175
Lifetime Customer Value:						
QuickResponse Profit	($6,600)	$8,910	$8,910	$8,910	$8,910	$8,910
Increased Purchases of QuickResponse	—	—	1,782	3,920	6,487	9,566
Profit from Added Products (FastTrack)	—	—	1,348	1,617	1,940	2,329
Reduced Overhead Allocation‡	—	—	1,155	1,486	1,663	1,995
Profit from Referrals§	—	—	1,100	1,650	3,300	6,600
Total Profit	($6,600)	$8,910	$14,295	$17,583	$22,300	$29,400

*Product names and data have been disguised. As a result, profit on these products is overstated.
†Assuming revenue increases on both products of 20% per year.
‡Declining at the rate of 15% per year in relation to revenue, to reflect lower costs of customer relationship associated with both customer and supplier learning curve effects.
§Estimated, based on assumptions concerning: (1) the importance of referrals to new customers from old customers, (2) the frequency with which satisfied customers refer new customers, (3) the size of customers referred, and (4) the lifetime value calculations for new customers.

Estimates of the lifetime value of existing customers under various assumptions regarding their loyalty helps the organization calibrate expenses to retain customers. For example, the recent analysis of a base of 819 customers at IPS, shown in Exhibit 11–3, indicated that an 8 percent customer defection rate cost the company $18 million after tax more than a 0 percent defection rate over a five-year period. This suggests that the company can invest a considerable sum of money to reduce customer defection rates below their current levels.

Once lifetime value has been estimated and management convinced that service profit chain management does indeed have some merit, the next step is the design of the measurement system to encourage the right actions to manage relationships important to the chain.

FIGURE 11–3
Lifetime Value of 819 Customers at Varying Rates of Defection, Integrated Payment Systems, Inc.* (Dollar Figures in Thousands)

	Year 1	*Year 2*	*Year 3*	*Year 4*	*Year 5*
At 0% Rate of Defection					
Number of Customers	819	819	819	819	819
Transactions (000)	62,295	62,295	62,295	62,295	62,295
Total Revenue†	$55,362	$57,106	$58,910	$60,779	$62,713
Total Expenses	23,755	24,580	25,435	26,319	27,235
Pre-Tax Profit	31,607	32,526	33,475	34,460	35,478
Net Income After Tax	18,333	18,865	19,416	19,988	20,578
Add Back Amortization	1,350	1,350	1,350	1,350	1,350
Nominal Cash Flow	19,683	20,215	20,766	21,338	21,928
Discounted Cash Flow‡	19,683	18,675	17,722	16,821	15,969
Lifetime Value (Net Present Value of Discounted Cash Flow)	24,030	46,800	68,490	89,010	108,540
At 8% Rate of Defection					
Number of Customers	819	753	693	638	587
Nominal Cash Flow	19,683	18,337	17,055	15,831	14,662
Discounted Cash Flow‡	19,683	16,939	14,553	12,479	10,678
Lifetime Value (Net Present Value of Discounted Cash Flow)	24,030	44,730	62,460	77,760	90,720
Differences Between 0% and 8% Rates of Defection					
Number of Customers	—	66	126	181	232
Nominal Cash Flow	—	$1,878	$3,611	$5,507	$7,266
Lifetime Value	—	2,070	6,030	11,250	17,820

*Data has been disguised.
†Assuming growth in the value per transaction.
‡Cash flow is discounted at the rate of 8.25% (present value factor).

FITTING MEASUREMENT TO THE BUSINESS

The service profit chain provides the broad guidelines for a management information system centered upon financial measures of profit and revenue growth; customer satisfaction and loyalty; the value-cost relationships of services and goods delivered to customers; and employee satisfaction, productivity, and loyalty. We are often asked whether it is necessary to maintain ongoing measures of every element of the service profit chain, particularly in view of the costs associated with getting some of these measures. The simple answer is yes. Would anyone ask such a question about measuring profit? And yet the basic elements of the chain are determinants of profit. They should be measured in some form regularly. Having said this, it is important to recognize that measures have to be adapted to the peculiarities of particular businesses and business strategies.

For example, customer loyalty in AT&T's Universal credit card business can be measured either by the stream of purchases charged to the card or the proportion of the estimated total card usage that AT&T's card enjoys. The first is easy to track but doesn't tell the entire story; the latter is less precise. These measures, however, don't work well for the Swedbank organization, offering commercial and retail banking services in Sweden. In banking, for example, most consumer transactions are not profitable. A loyal customer who only uses the bank for checking services may be of limited value. Instead, what is important for long-term profitability is what is called the "depth" of the relationship, the number of banking services utilized by the customer. Thus, depth of relationship is measured as a surrogate for customer loyalty at Swedbank.

In many organizations, employee loyalty is a simple measure of how long an individual has been associated with the organization. This suffices, for example, at organizations like USAA, the supplier of financial services to military personnel and their families. At economy lodging chain Fairfield Inn, as we saw earlier, this isn't sufficient. In a business where employee absenteeism is one of the greatest problems, it's important to track employee loyalty in terms of attendance on the job. As a result, Fairfield Inn not only tracks it carefully, but provides incentives, in the form of fully paid "earned leave" away from the job, for those employees who either show up for work or make sure that a suitable substitute does.

In some businesses, there is such an immediate linkage between employee and customer satisfaction, for example, that it may be sufficient to measure one or the other, especially where neither is a leading indicator for the other. This, however, is rarely the case. So to be able to predict customer satisfaction in the future, it is important to measure employee satisfaction today.

The most difficult of the profit chain measures to track is value. Customers may be asked to comment regularly on value as part of their expression of satisfaction. This is especially important where value is a critical element of strategy. For example, at Fairfield Inn, guests checking out were asked to respond electronically by means of a touchscreen computer program called Scorecard to four questions, one of which was, "How do you rate the overall value of your Fairfield Inn stay?" That is one measure of output, or results achieved for the customer, as viewed by the customer. In order to appraise efforts needed to achieve such value, regular measures of the quality of goods and services and the productivity with which they are created provide additional information about current and future value.

FITTING MEASUREMENT TO PURPOSE: RELEVANCE

Measuring elements of the service profit chain provides an overall indication of how an organization is doing, particularly on dimensions deemed important to a business. If used solely for this purpose, it is probably sufficient to make sure only that such measures are approximately accurate and obtained in a consistent manner for comparison with earlier periods of time. If such measures are intended to be used as the basis for evaluation and compensation, however, the care with which the task must be planned and carried out must be increased considerably. Consider the following examples.

The Xerox Experience

Xerox, as part of a more extensive organization-wide initiative titled Leadership Through Quality, described earlier, developed a monthly customer survey (shown in Figure 5–1) designed to measure the level of customer satisfaction with the Company's products and services.[1] A monthly frequency was appropriate for tracking general trends in performance. The stakes associated with this measure were raised significantly, however, when Xerox began incorporating results of the survey into individual evaluations and compensation. For one thing, it became necessary to increase the number of customer questionnaires mailed monthly to 40,000 in order to get the 10,000 returns thought necessary to provide valid measures of the satisfaction levels achieved by individual Xerox field sales and service districts.

The AT&T Universal Card Experience

AT&T's Universal Card division was faced with the need to put in place a customer service organization in a short period of time.[2] The company, founded only in 1990, offered the first advertisement for its credit card, offering low annual fees and low interest rates on outstanding month-end balances, during the television broadcast of that year's U.S. motion picture industry Academy Awards. In the following twenty-four hours, the organization responded to more than 270,000 requests for applications and information. In just three years, the division became the second largest issuer of credit cards in the U.S., with nearly 12 million accounts. Given its objective of "delighting customers," management instituted a measurement system designed to fit with the pace and quality required of its customer service department.

First, a Customer Satisfier Survey was administered to determine what cardholders cared about most. Once this was determined, management put in place measures to highlight each satisfier. Most were associated with the service provided by the company's 300 telephone service representatives. This led to the development of a measurement system designed to: (1) locate problem processes, (2) promptly address any problems discovered, (3) constantly assess how well customers were being served, and (4) reward exceptional performance. Measures were constructed from inputs from a daily performance survey constructed around a "bucket of measures" related directly to the customer satisfiers in ways illustrated in Figure 11–4. In addition, monthly surveys of about 3,000 customers who had recently contacted AT&T Universal Card were performed to measure trends in overall customer satisfaction with the service they had received.

By the middle of 1991, a Relationship Excellence team was tracking a "bucket" of 120 measures. To increase the impact of the measurement and provide incentives for corrective action, the team set specific standards for each measure and began rewarding every employee in the company when a certain proportion of the standards were met on a daily basis. For example, if 95 percent of the standards were met in a given day, employees were said to "earn quality" for the day. For every day that quality was met, a quarterly bonus was paid to everyone. According to Deb Holton, the Manager of Quality, "It is virtually impossible to be in this building for 10 minutes without knowing how you did the day before."[3]

The use of performance measures to determine bonuses created special needs for the measurement system. Many measures, such as length of call, numbers of calls accepted per day per employee, customer call wait times, and the proportion of customers hanging up before having their calls taken, could be compiled electronically. Others were constructed from extensive call monitoring carried out by managers. Rather than using broad service profit measures, the organization concentrated on many very specific measures relevant to its strategy. Its success earned it the 1992 Malcolm Baldrige (U.S.) National Quality Award just two years after the company's founding.

TAKING PROCESS INTO ACCOUNT

The question of who should determine measures or set standards is an ongoing one. At both Xerox and AT&T Universal Card senior management teams assumed the responsibility. In an effort to encourage bot-

FIGURE 11–4
Relationship between Customer Satisfiers and Selected Elements of the "Bucket of Measures" at AT&T Universal Card Services

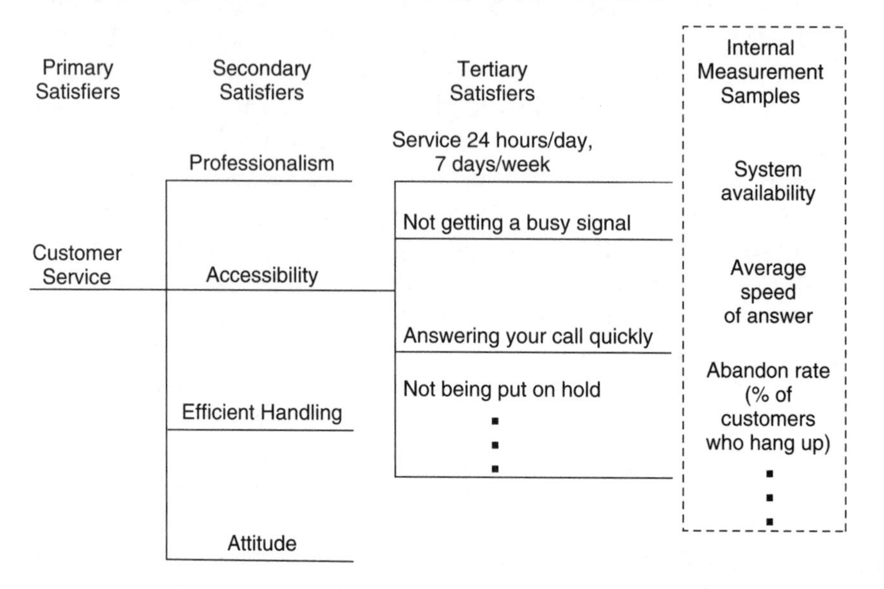

Susan Rosegrant, A Measure of Delight: The Pursuit of Quality at AT&T Universal Card Services (A), Case No. 694-047. Boston: Harvard Business School, 1993, p. 16. Copyright © 1993 by the President and Fellows of Harvard College. Reprinted by permission. Note that tertiary customer satisfiers and internal measurements are shown for only one secondary satisfier, "accessibility."

tom-up initiative, USAA took a different approach. It supplemented its annual evaluations of individual employees with what it called a "Family of Measures" initiative, based on the belief that people wanted to be measured according to standards they themselves had set.[4] The primary purpose of this effort was learning and improvement, not compensation.

At the time we observed it in action, The Family of Measures initiative at USAA had five dimensions, each of which was tracked monthly. They were: (1) quality of work, (2) quantity of work completed, (3) service timeliness, (4) resource utilization (the percentage of available hours that a group actually spent working), and (5) customer satisfaction. Where appropriate, individual employees received monthly reports of results. For other measures, groups received the reports.

Members of each working unit decided the aspects of their jobs that should be tracked, based on four criteria: (1) whether the activity was under the group's control, (2) the significance of the actitivity, (3) whether the activity was measurable with data the group could collect, and (4) whether the results could easily be analyzed. In the policy service group, comprising policy service representatives who provided phone service to USAA's insurance policy holders, the Family of Measures offered group feedback on service timeliness (for example, the percentage of calls answered in 20 seconds), resource utilization (the ratio of hours worked to hours paid), and customer satisfaction (based on responses of a sample of customers, called "members" at USAA, who had recently been served by a policy service representative).

Measures for quality and quantity of service were individual. Quality was measured by the monitoring of phone calls, correspondence, and resulting transactions to identify both problems and examples of outstanding performance. Quantity was simply the number of transactions handled. For purposes of individual evaluation and feedback, the policy service group members decided that quality should receive a 60 percent weight and quantity a weighting of 40 percent. Individual standards varied by grade level and experience, with more experienced employees expected to achieve higher levels. The ratings provided the basis for recognition or decisions to provide training for those not improving fast enough.

The process itself insured a great deal of involvement on the part of all of USAA's employees, something that the company felt translated into higher employee satisfaction that was transmitted to some degree to customers with whom employees largely interacted by phone.

DETERMINING THE FORM IN WHICH RESULTS WILL BE TRANSMITTED

The form in which the results of performance measurement efforts are communicated to the organization may affect the urgency with which people act. A classic example of this is provided by Federal Express, an organization handling millions of packages per day.

For a number of years, the company measured the percent of the time packages were delivered on time in good condition. These seemingly impressive percentages, often ranging between 99 percent and 100 percent, were stated in tenths of percentage points and were reported weekly. But it occurred to CEO Fred Smith that a 99.5 percent accuracy level for a volume of 2 million packages meant that 10,000 packages per day were being misdelivered or delivered late. To impress the importance of quality on his organization, Smith had the reporting of the measure changed to actual numbers of packages that Federal Express had failed to deliver as promised; saw that all percentages associated with these numbers were stated in hundredths of percentage points, not tenths; and insured that the number was widely distributed daily. In fact, package tracking systems were devised later that could actually predict the number of packages that would not meet standards for delivery during the day of their scheduled delivery, allowing Federal Express's customer service representatives to notify customers of potential problems on a proactive basis before customers called them. Smith's actions highlighted the importance of quality to employees who already thought that the quality of their performance was extremely high.

OTHER CRITERIA FOR EVALUATING MEASURES AND METHODS

In addition to their relevance for a particular business or strategy, those measures and methods we have found most useful have been designed to be simple, consistent, timely, and fair.

Organizations that have constructed elaborate measurements and methods often find that the cost of maintaining them and difficulty of understanding them defeat their usefulness and guarantee that they will fall into disuse. Such approaches often lead to the kind of tinkering that changes measures from one period to the next, making it impossible to track progress. Because of the difficulty of gathering information for some measures, they may not be prepared sufficiently frequently or with the timeliness needed for decision making.

The issue of fairness arises when measures are used for performance evaluation and compensation. For example, store managers at Au Bon Pain, the chain of French bakery cafes, complained that appraisals of various aspects of the quality of store management such as cleanliness were based too heavily on the reports of "mystery shoppers" who tended to visit stores during the busiest times when it was most difficult to keep the stores clean. Whether this is true or not, the perception created dissatisfaction among the managers.[5] These same store managers had been less interested in "mystery shoppers" when reports from these surprise visitors previously had little effect on incentive compensation.

In order to deal with the issue of fairness at Fairfield Inn, where employees (essentially receptionists and housekeepers) received bonuses of up to 10 percent of their wages based on customer feedback, it was necessary to devise a better feedback method than that used in other hotels operated by the Marriott Corporation, of which Fairfield Inn was a subsidiary. Comment cards placed in the rooms to be filled out voluntarily by guests, typically producing a 1 percent return rate, simply would not do.[6] This resulted in the development of Scorecard, the electronic touchscreen devise on which customers could respond to four questions about friendliness, cleanliness, and value in ten seconds or so during checkout. The response rate, 60 percent at some units, was sufficient to provide credibility with employees whose compensation depended on the results. The system proved so workable that Marriott installed a version of the system on the in-room television monitors of some of its other hotels. This has probably resulted in more objective customer evaluations, because it was not solicited on a face-to-face basis by employees whose work was being rated. But it also resulted in much lower response rates, of less importance in hotels in which bonuses were not tied to customer feedback.

DESIGNING THE BALANCED SCORECARD

Like other banks, Sweden's Swedbank, resulting from the consolidation of several other government-owned banks with 4.5 million individual and 100,000 business accounts, measured its performance largely in financial terms. But as the bank approached privatization, with the sale of its stock to the public, questions were raised by management about what umbrella measures would be needed to help reverse the bank's unprofitable performance going forward.[7] Its CEO, Göran Collert, had to find a way to bring organizations with very different cultures together around a common set of goals and measures. Management first identified three clusters around which performance weaknesses existed and new initiatives could be structured. They were "people value-added" (PVA), "customer value-added" (CVA), and "economic value-added" (EVA). When measured at the branch bank level, it was found that high-performance branches ranked highly on all three dimensions, leading management to conclude that the measures could be used not only to bring about a cultural change but also significant improvement in economic performance as well. The result was the development of three "families" of measures focusing on financial performance, customer satisfaction, and employee satisfaction. Management performance would, in the future, be measured on these three overall dimensions, with individual operations adopting some form of each for its own evaluation. When combined with increased latitude for frontline employees, new product development and introduction, increased training, and the introduction of a new management information system, these initiatives began to produce results that were monitored on what Swedbank calls a "branch report card," a copy of which is shown in Figure 11–5. The widely distributed report cards tracked actual-to-target performance on a number of measures related to PVA, CVA, and EVA. By 1995, the bank's performance had sufficiently improved to the extent that it was able to successfully list its stock on the Stockholm Stock Exchange.

FIGURE 11–5
An Example of a Branch Report Card Used to Report Performance at Swedbank, 1996

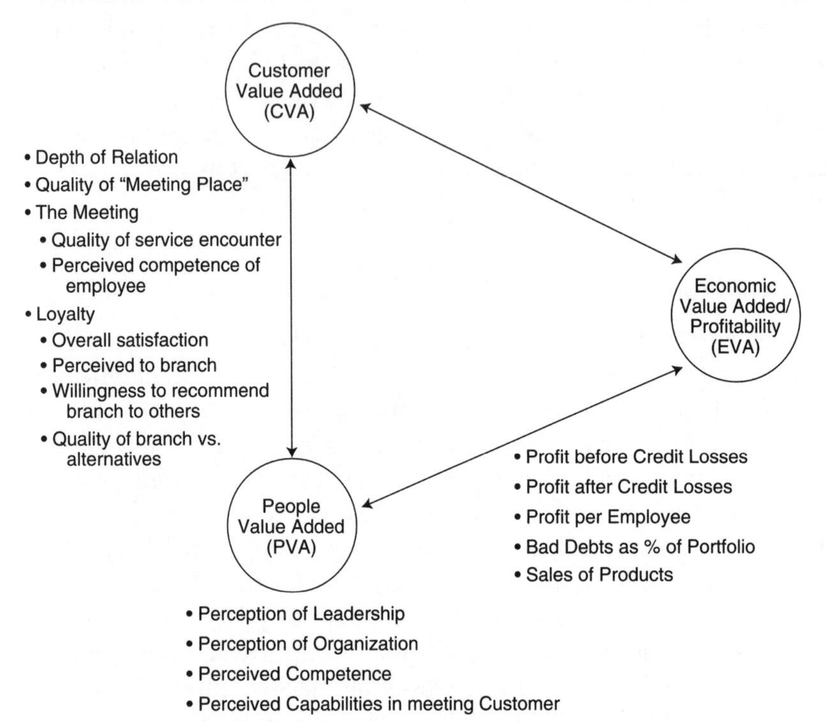

Adapted from Stefan H. Ennerfelt, Mikael A. Paltschik, and Erik G. Tillberg, *Verktyg for framtiden* [Tool for the Future] (Stockholm: Ekerlids Forlag, 1996).

This effort is an example of what Robert Kaplan and David Norton have come to call "the balanced scorecard."[8] It is of great interest to us, because the elements of the service profit chain constitute a form of the balanced scorecard. A balanced scorecard system of measurement provides management with some unique tools and capabilities when compared with traditional systems of financial measures, as suggested in Figure 11–6.

The most important contrast between conventional financial measures and the balanced scorecard is that the former look back, whereas the latter looks ahead. Conventional financial measures track history, something about which management can do nothing. Balanced scorecard (and service profit chain) measures, on the other hand, enable managers to predict future organization performance, as indicated by current measures of employee and customer satisfaction and loyalty. In addition, they challenge managers to make "balanced" assessments of problems and possible corrective actions, rather than acting only with a short-term interest in "meeting the financial numbers" for the current period.

FIGURE 11–6
Comparison Between Traditional and Balanced Scorecard Performance Measures

Traditional Performance Measures	*Balanced Scorecard Performance Measures*
Financial in Orientation —Profit on Investment —Growth —Cash Flow	*Also* Nonfinancial in Orientation —Customer Satisfaction and Loyalty —Employee Satisfaction and Loyalty —Rate of Innovation —Safety
Stated in Monetary Terms	*Also* Stated in Nonmonetary Terms
Reflective of Past Performance	*Also* Predictive of Future Performance
Show Profit and Growth Results	*Also* Show Profit and Growth Determinants
Provide Basis of Recognition for Past Accomplishments	*Also* Provide Basis of Recognition for Enhancing Potential Future Performance

A scorecard reflecting elements of the service profit chain encourages managers to think about the totality of a business. In addition, it can be implemented at successively lower levels in an organization as cross-functional teams apply it to encourage effective decision making in the face of conflicting outcomes and interests, particularly between short-term and long-term interests and outcomes. It has been used as well for the development of personal scorecards, particularly for managers with broad responsibilities.

Its use requires that an organization find and train managers capable of shaping and employing the scorecard, not only in everyday decision making, but in setting longer-term strategy for the company. In short, the effective implementation of a balanced scorecard may well provide an organization with nothing less than a new approach to and philosophy of management.

QUESTIONS FOR MANAGEMENT

Because it is so critical to performance, measurement raises a number of questions for a management team deciding to orient its efforts around the service profit chain. Among the most important of these are:

1. How could each element of the service profit chain be translated into one or more measures of performance that are relevant to your business?
2. To what degree are such measures used in your organization to either measure performance or provide the basis for rewarding incentive compensation now?

3. How do measures used for performance appraisal in your organization rate in terms of relevance to your business or strategy, simplicity, appropriate frequency, and fairness?
4. To what degree are such measures determined by the employees to which they are applied?
5. What impact would the adoption of service profit chain measures organized in the form of a balanced scorecard, either for employee appraisal or compensation, have on your organization?

Performance measurement and tracking is just one element, but a very important one, in comprehensive initiatives to reengineer entire organizations. We'll see next how it fits into such efforts.

Part III

Putting It All Together

12

Reengineering the Service Organization for Capability

Gains and Pains

At one extreme of efforts to change service organizations and the way they function are those that begin by shuffling boxes on an organization chart and people in jobs. This rarely works, so advocates of this approach do it again and again, following the "organization of the year" strategy, with growing frustration at all levels in the organization. At the other extreme are reluctant leaders who practice delegation to the extreme and entrust the management of change to those who are most likely to be affected by it, in a sense, turning the chicken house over to the foxes. They are then surprised by the slow rate or entire lack of change. Both of these approaches are based on simplistic views of change. Neither work.

Accounts of organization reengineering efforts often emphasize the gains while glossing over the pains. This is perhaps especially true for services in which many levels of management have been created between the top and bottom to accommodate rapid growth in the numbers of operating units in particularly successful multiunit service organizations.

Fortunately, leaders of a select group of service organizations understand the psychology and dynamics of change, appreciate its complexity, and have the ability to convince others of its importance and the patience to see it through. They teach the rest of us. Three of these are John Martin, William Bratton, and Arthur Martinez. They probably don't know each other. They don't compete with each other. And each knows little about the other's business, except how to transform its organization from a "merely good" to an outstanding performer. Martin, former CEO of Taco Bell, knows tacos. Bratton, former Police Commissioner of the City of New York, knows police work. And Martinez, the CEO of Sears, knows the retail merchandising of everything from power tools to socks. But they all know organizational reengineering, the core of the change management process, firsthand. Together, they provide an interesting study of "work in progress" with strikingly similar strategies.

THE THEORY OF MANAGING CHANGE

Those who have studied the management of change have produced a very simple model of the elements that must be assessed in determining whether change is possible to accomplish. It is that the feasibility of achieving change varies to the degree that:

$$(D \times M \times P) > C$$

where D = the level of dissatisfaction with the status quo, M = the existence of a model or vision for change, P = the availability of a process for change, and C = the costs of change to various participants in the process.[1]

Note that the determinants of the model are multiplicative, not additive. In other words, if one of these values is zero, so the model goes, the presumption is that change will be difficult, if not impossible, to achieve. Clearly, many leaders would have benefitted from an objective use of this model before beginning their unsuccessful efforts. Others have probably been dissuaded too easily by it from attempting a change process. Once again, the model represents a simplistic view of the change process intended to provide only the broadest of guidelines for undertaking it.

Fortunately, our subjects in this chapter must not have paid too much attention to it. For their organizations were not on the brink of disaster at the time they began a process of organization reengineering. For Martin at Taco Bell, the process began in 1988. For Bratton in the NYPD, it began on January 1, 1994. And for Martinez, it didn't begin until he was named CEO-to-be in November 1994. It is fair to say that Martin's vision for change was less clear than that of the other two. But even with a clear vision for change, the perceived costs of change by managers in all three organizations probably outweighed the cumulative weight of a perceived crisis, a clear vision, and a process for change. How, then, do we explain the success to date in these three situations?

ORGANIZATION REENGINEERING WITHOUT A CRISIS

The contrasting situations faced by Martin, Bratton, and Martinez and the similarities and differences in the way each dealt with them provide a study in reengineering a service organization in the absence of a crisis.

Taco Bell, in 1988, in John Martin's words today, "was a Mexican ethnic fast food chain."[2] He doesn't say it, but executives at fast-moving parent Pepsico's headquarters probably thought Taco Bell's logo, a sleeping Mexican under a sombrero, was probably appropriate. The chain was recording modest year-to-year sales and profit gains, but not up to the demanding standards of other Pepsico operations, such as the soft drink and snack food divisions. In his first five years at the head of Taco Bell, Martin had done the usual things to refurbish operations. He had changed the decor, the signage, and uniforms, and made other largely cosmetic changes. But he knew that corporate management was getting restless, even though there was no sense of urgency among managers at Taco Bell. Even Martin would probably admit that he did not have a clear vision for the organization at that time.

Bill Bratton knew that he would be Police Commissioner of New York if Rudolph Giuliani won his election race with incumbent David Dinkins in November 1993. He had several weeks to outline a strategy for reengineering the New York Police Department, having earlier served as the Commissioner of the Transit Police and learned the challenges of police work in the City before assuming office in January 1994. New York, along with other major cities, was seeing modest declines in major crimes at the time, having experienced a peak in 1991. Bratton inherited a department in which the work ethos was, according to one consultant to the Department, "keep your head down, hand out a reasonable number of summons, and collect your pay." There was no perceived need for change in anything but increased pay levels and better policing equipment by those in the ranks—all in all, not a very promising climate for change. But the new Mayor had waged his successful election campaign on the platform of balanced budgets, an improved educational system, and reduced crime. This perhaps explains Bratton's head start in putting together a strategy to deliver on at least one of these promises.[3]

Between the time that Arthur Martinez was hired to run Sears' merchandising group in August 1992 and the time that CEO Edward Brennan announced in November 1994 that Martinez would become CEO of the entire organization, Martinez had done what any good retailer would do. He began a $4 billion program to remodel run-down stores, upgraded the merchandise, and added private-brand apparel and cosmetics.[4] He changed marketing programs to reflect a newer, fresher, more-focused image for the store that once advertised that "Sears Has Everything." The price of Sears' stock responded with a more-than-50-percent increase over that time period. Investors apparently concluded that Sears had righted itself from the tailspin that had cost it its leadership position among American retailers. A sense of satisfaction pervaded the organization. But as Martinez assumed his new position, one indicator continued to bother him, the relatively low customer satisfaction numbers that Sears' surveys disclosed compared with rivals Wal-Mart, J. C. Penney, and Kmart.

Students of organization change would conclude that none of these represented situations ripe for change. And yet, the results to date for each are highly encouraging.

JOHN MARTIN AND TACO BELL

Between 1988 and 1992, John Martin and his organization literally changed the face of fast food service in the United States. The process began with two insights. The first was obtained at no cost when a Taco Bell franchisee provided management with the information that would reshape the industry. The franchisee lowered prices by 25 percent and found that sales jumped by at least 50 percent. The laws of economics really did apply. This signaled the beginning of a new era in value, with customers sending the message that price in relation to quality mattered. The second insight was gained from an extensive (and expensive) consulting study that produced startlingly predictable conclusions that the customers Taco Bell's management had decided to target as a result of the franchisee's findings (penny-pinching HFFUs, or heavy fast food users seeking value) wanted FACT: fast food *f*ast, *a*ccurate order fulfillment, *c*leanliness, and *t*emperature control—hot food hot and cold food cold. Not worth the effort you say? Taco Bell's management was more impressed with what customers did not emphasize: the need for a kitchen in the restaurant, for example. These two insights provided the basis for a multifaceted strategy that Martin's organization implemented in Taco Bell's 1,800 company-owned stores (out of a total of about 3,200, with the remainder operated by franchisees at the time).

Actions

In order to attract and retain penny-pinching HFFUs, Martin's team decided to lower prices by over 25 percent in all 1,800 company-owned stores in 1988. With no change in quality, this meant that food costs went from 25 percent to 33 percent of sales. As a result, Taco Bell would have to squeeze eight percentage points of overhead costs out of the 13.6

percent it was then experiencing. Putting it another way, it would require some combination of overhead cost reductions up to 60 percent or dramatic increases in sales with no attendant increase in overhead costs.

The next two years saw Taco Bell's management implement K-Minus, the "restaurants without kitchens" concept in which food preparation except for final assembly and heating was moved to centralized commissaries. This more than doubled table space for customers in a restaurant to 70 percent of the total from 30 percent. It also relieved restaurant employees of a job they didn't like and freed them up to spend more time with customers. During this same time the TACO (Total Automation of Company Operations) information system was introduced in stores to relieve managers of up to fifteen hours of administrative work per week while improving their controls over their businesses. By walking down the street and copying the concept from McDonald's, Taco Bell redesigned its food delivery process by assembling some popular items in advance of demand rather than making them to order. This speeded up service during the busy lunch hour by 71 percent (to thirty seconds) and increased restaurant sales capacity by 54 percent during this time period.

By 1991, experimentation with carts and kiosks in airports and offices convinced Taco Bell's management that it could operate "restaurants without walls," greatly expanding what it began to refer to as "points of access." In fact, once walls were no longer thought indispensable, it became clear that the company could eventually serve people at as many as 100,000 places in the United States alone. But this would not be possible without reengineering the organization. It would require a totally different view of frontline work organization, the role of supervision, and attendant spans of control and numbers of middle managers.

The first step was to change the job of the restaurant manager to that of a general manager with the capacity to manage units without the day-to-day supervision typical of the industry. Wage and bonus packages were increased to about 60 percent more than those of competitors to attract the kind of managers needed to accomplish the change. Only two-thirds of Taco Bell's existing managers were deemed to be qualified for the new jobs. Three levels of middle management were then replaced with a position called "market manager." Market managers would help restaurant general managers do such things as plan strategies for capturing larger shares of their markets. But they would no longer provide close supervision or approve even capital requests of several thousand dollars. Instead, they were to serve as consultants to as many as twenty restaurant general managers, roughly twice as many as their predecessors. In return, they could earn up to $110,000 per year, or at least twice that paid by competitors for traditional "command and control" middle-management positions. How much they earned depended on the degree to which they were able to grow the number of points of access in their territories.

But even this kind of change would not be enough to manage a "chain" of 100,000 points of access. It would require managers able and willing to help work teams hire, discipline, schedule their work, and handle money. The company set out to implement this with a program called Teaming at Taco Bell.

Managers and employees alike were trained to spend less time on operating matters and more time on the front line with customers. To drive home the new operating strategy in a memorable manner, thousands of Taco Bell's employees spent time on the job studying and understanding the strategy and its implementation by "playing" a board game, called Domination, designed for the purpose.

The goal was the creation of a completely restructured organization, as shown in the hypothetical example in Figure 12–1.

Gains

Between 1989 and 1993, Taco Bell's sales increased rapidly, producing profit gains roughly three times those of its major competitors. The company was on target to achieve its goals of 250,000 points of access (including 150,000 supermarkets selling branded Taco Bell products) and $25 billion in sales by the year 2000. Customer satisfaction increased each year. The turnover of managers declined rapidly as Taco Bell began hiring from among the best of its competitors for restaurant general managers and MBA graduates as market managers.

Pains

Spans of control were doubled and restaurant and middle-management jobs changed quickly. This was deliberately done to discourage traditional command and control managers from hanging onto their jobs by working harder. Taco Bell wanted them out. When confronted with the drastic change in job definition, at least one in three of Taco Bell's best command and control managers left the organization. There was a great amount of dislocation for those who remained. Training costs skyrocketed.

WILLIAM BRATTON AND THE NYPD

Commissioner Bratton assumed his new job with the benefit of already having initiated a significant change process in the New York Transit

FIGURE 12–1
The Economics of Restructuring a Multisite Service Organization

	Year "X"	*Year "X + 7"*
Sales	$1.5 billion	$20 billion
Retail Outlets (Points of Access)	1,800	100,000
Organization:		
Level 1	1,800 restaurant managers at $35,000 annual wage = $63 million	5,000 restaurant general managers at $70,000 annual wage = $350 million
Level 2	300 district managers at $50,000 annual wage = $15 million	250 market managers at $150,000 annual wage = $37.5 million
Level 3	50 area managers at $80,000 annual wage = $4 million	None
Level 4	10 division managers at $150,000 annual wage = $1.5 million	None
Level 5	2 division vice presidents at $250,000 annual wage = $500,000	12 business unit managers at $500,000 annual wage = $6 million
Level 6	1 vice president, operations at $500,000 annual wage = $500,000	1 vice president, operations at $1 million annual wage = $1 million
Total Compensation:	$84.5 million	$394.5 million
Compensation as a % of Total Sales	5.7%	2.0%
Average Compensation, First Two Management Levels	$37,000	$74,000

Police organization, which was due to be merged with other police units in the first year of his administration. The formula for change there had gone far beyond cosmetics, although it did include equipping officers with new, more powerful weapons and new uniforms. Bratton carefully selected the team of officers that would change Transit Policing in New York. Of greater significance was that officers were judged on the results they achieved in reducing crime on New York's subways, including "social" crimes such as spraying graffitti on the cars. He took his cues from a 1982 article[5] that presented evidence for the "broken windows" theory of policing based on the idea that if a broken window is not fixed, soon all windows in a building will be broken. As a result, Bratton's force began to detain "fare jumpers" who had failed to pay, searching them for weapons and paint cans, checking their police records (on the theory that people who commit one misdemeanor or crime are more likely to have committed others), and arresting many. In just two years, Bratton's team helped transform a somewhat demoralized force policing a transit system featuring dirty, graffitti-covered, unsafe trains into an effective deterrant to crime as well as defaced equipment and declining ridership. Bratton planned to do the same thing with the much larger organization he had just inherited.

Polls taken at the time of the election that led to his appointment told Bratton and his team what the citizens of New York wanted: reduced crime, defined in terms of both major crime and the kinds of misdemeanors, such as panhandling, painting graffitti, and urinating in public, that were perceived as adversely affecting the "quality of life." Surveys of police officers disclosed a low level of morale and a perception of police work defined in terms of effort, not results.

Actions

Bratton believed that crime could be "managed" to lower levels, a view not shared by all of his seventy-six precinct commanders. Those deemed unable to adapt to a strategy aimed at achieving results instead of goals based on effort were reassigned to other jobs. This was particularly significant, because a decision had been made to provide precinct commanders with a wider range of resources and hold them accountable for crime in their respective precincts.

At the same time, steps were taken to obtain larger fifteen-shot ammunition clips, improved protective vests, and more distinguished uniforms for police officers. Several occasions arose in which Bratton could come to the defense of officers charged with excessive force, communicating his image as a "cop's cop."

Two other important efforts were undertaken in the first months of his new administration. One involved an extensive survey of officers' attitudes toward their jobs, designed to get officers trained to defend the Department to admit that problems might exist, intended to help identify potential areas for improvement. Out of this evolved a massive reengineering effort involving 300 members of the Department organized into twelve teams to, in Bratton's words, "reengineer . . . an underperforming organization."[6] For example, one team found that there were 8,000 forms in active use within the Department. Another found that officers were on duty during desirable working hours, not when crimes were being committed. Yet a third resulted in the introduction of new video conferencing technology to save fourteen hours of overtime associated with the average arrest by making it possible for officers to testify in front of judges without waiting in courtrooms during off-duty hours. In all, 600 practical crime-fighting ideas were proposed by the teams. Many were incorporated into six "strategies" around which the Department would organize its effort: (1) Getting Guns off the Streets of New York, (2) Curbing Youth Violence in the Schools and on the Streets, (3) Driving Drug Dealers out of New York, (4) Breaking the Cycle of Domestic Violence, (5) Reclaiming the Public Spaces of New York, and (6) Reducing Auto-Related Crime in New York.

The other major effort concerned the computerization, organization, and rapid reporting of cumulative crime statistics. Computerized maps reported crime daily. The data were used as the basis for twice-weekly ComStat (computer statistics) meetings led by two deputy commissioners to plan strategies for reducing crime with precinct commanders. As the effort gained publicity, ComStat meetings were visited by police administrators from all over the United States and other countries. The era of management by, and accountability for, facts in the NYPD had begun.

Resulting strategies were based on the knowledge that high-crime areas occurred at the confluence of three conditions, the presence of guns, drugs, and people with criminal records. Since these locations could be identified, police resources were reassigned (to the degree the other communities would allow it) to high-crime areas. At the same time, a drive against petty crime, in which those committing misdemeanors were stopped, searched, and checked for police records, was initiated not only to improve the quality of life but also identify some of those who might be capable of committing more serious crimes.

Results-oriented performance measures replaced those measuring effort. They were reported every day. As Bratton put it, "Can you imagine running a bank if you couldn't look at your bottom line every day?"[7]

Gains

During the first two years of Commissioner Bratton's administration, murders in New York City declined by 39 percent, auto thefts by 36 percent, and robberies by 31 percent. These were much larger reductions than in other major U.S. cities. In fact, the reduction in the absolute number of crimes in the City accounted for more than half of the total for the entire United States during these two years. Misdemeanors declined just as sharply. Public perceptions of the quality of life in New York City were measurably improved. Officers exhibited more pride in being associated with the Department.

Pains

Eventually, three out of four precinct commanders were reassigned to other jobs, most because they were not able or willing to manage toward results- versus effort-oriented goals. Absolute pay levels were reduced as efforts to cut overtime through such things as improved technology resulted in a $34 million (roughly 30 percent) decline in this annual expense, equivalent to a pay cut of almost $2,000 for every officer on the force with arresting authority. Although morale on the force was up, complaints about no pay increases due to City budget cuts were mounting.

Complaints of excessive force by police officers increased about 40 percent. Some of the increase may have been due to more diligence on the part of police in stopping people who were observed committing petty crimes. But it led to the creation of an additional strategy titled "Rooting Out Corruption: Building Organizational Integrity in the New York Police Department."

ARTHUR MARTINEZ AND SEARS

After 25 years of experience at Sears, Arthur Martinez knew what needed to be changed when he assumed his CEO's position. He decided to do it under the theme of making Sears "a compelling place to shop/work/invest." Three months after assuming leadership, he issued a clear challenge to his senior colleagues, characterized by one colleague as "leave or change." A number of efforts were on his list for immediate implementation.

Actions

Near the top of the list was the organization's command and control philosophy, characterized by a 29,000-page manual of policies, rules, and procedures. Store managers were given little information with which to make decisions. Instead, they were required to spend up to 80 percent of their time preparing reports. Little wonder that Sears, in spite of merchandising and store improvements, still had a long way to go to become customer friendly.

One of Martinez's first actions was to get rid of the company manual, replacing it with, according to one account:

> . . . a folder called "Freedoms and Obligations." Measuring about an eighth of an inch thick, it contains a one-page letter from . . . [Martinez]; a one-page list of "shared beliefs" (like "we recognize our obligation to shareholders: profitable growth and superior total shareholder return"); a 16-page booklet outlining leadership principles for managers ("reward people who add value to Sears"), and a 17-page code of business conduct for every employee ("we must always describe products and services accurately").[8]

At the same time, reporting requirements were being changed to significantly alter the job of the store manager. According to Patricia Recktenwald, Vice President for Store Operations:

> Some of our managers didn't know how to work a register. . . . They had moved up because they filled in reports well. . . . Store managers were spending 20 percent of their time on the sales floor. . . . Now they are spending 80 to 90 percent of their time on the floor.[9]

Four large management task forces were formed to study the operations of three of Sear's major store types and the work of the headquarters support staff. This was indicative of a philosophy of involvement that had not characterized Sears' management for many years.

Simultaneous to these efforts, training was instituted for every one of the Company's 300,000 employees to begin communicating concepts and signals that a new operating culture was coming. Training for this many was accomplished through the use of the same kind of learning maps employed at Taco Bell. The first, completed by everyone in mid-1995, emphasized the new competitive, value-oriented environment for retailing as well as the need for Sears to deliver more service, convenience, and value. It was followed with a learning map-centered exercise dealing with building customer satisfaction. And in early 1996, yet a third learning map was used to explain sources and uses of funds at Sears, an exercise intended to make Sears employees more conscious of the economics of the business to be able to make better-informed decisions at the frontline level, where job latitude was being expanded.

Measurements and the basis for incentive pay was changed to reflect Martinez's view that "for a long time, we gave lip service to the customer. But at the end of the day it was 'Did you make your numbers?'"[10] As a result, Sears implemented what resembles a more balanced scorecard for measuring and paying bonuses to the top 200 executives in the company. Only half of their bonuses was based on financial measures. The other half was calibrated on the basis of customer satisfaction and employee evaluations. At the same time, a larger number of managers were introduced to 360-degree performance evaluations, with each receiving feedback from those reporting directly to them as well as their peers and superiors.

Gains

In 1995, Sears' sales increased 5.9 percent, a distinct turnaround. Profits increased more than 10 percent. And its stock price increased 71 percent. Customer satisfaction began to climb. And Sears had begun to take market share away from its closest competitors.

Pains

Early in 1996, middle-management jobs were reviewed, with the prospect that many would be changed and their occupants removed or reassigned. This followed changes that had already taken place in senior management ranks. Of the top 100 executives, apparently sixty had convinced Martinez that they could change. But forty of the architects of the new Sears were people hired from outside the organization. The same kinds of challenges confronted store managers, who were expected to begin spending nearly all of their time on the sales floor, a distinct contrast with the past. Just a year after Martinez assumed his new job, half of them already had been replaced.

Nor will change take place without stress at other levels in the organization. According to Anthony Rucci, head of human resources and administration, "a compelling place to work does not mean a nice place to work. We want people to feel some degree of anxiety, the stress of achievement-oriented people."[11]

PUTTING ORGANIZATION REENGINEERING IN CONTEXT

Reengineering is a term coined by Michael Hammer and others to describe an approach to the redesign of processes and the organizations that perform them through interfunctional and task-oriented team coordination.[12] The primary focus of such efforts is to change the way work is performed by ignoring current practice; organizing around outcomes, not tasks; and placing decision rights in the hands of those performing the work. It often results in the reshaping of the organization along with process design.

Organization reengineering concentrates on the latitude provided frontline employees, the forms of support provided to them, the way they are compensated, and the shape of the organization in which they work. It is especially important to multisite service organizations because of the large numbers of frontline employees and unit managers engaged by such organizations, numbers that have been assumed in the past to require an extensive hierarchy of management levels, both to provide guidance to the front line and to offer opportunities for promotion and development. Consider, for example, that at the time the efforts described here were initiated, the Taco Bell organization and its franchisees employed over 75,000 people operating 3,000 stores (separate, self-contained operating units), the NYPD encompassed 38,000 people staffing seventy-six precincts, and Sears had about 300,000 employees responsible, among other things, for 1,700 retail outlets. Organizations of this size and shape offer different opportunities for reengineering than exist in industrial organizations with many fewer operating units. In the latter, as reengineering accounts suggest, the focus is on enhancement of quality and productivity through the introduction of the right amount of technology, the elimination of duplication in jobs and tasks, and the general objective of doing more with fewer frontline people (machinists, office workers, etc.). In multiunit service organizations, the focus is instead on changing and rationalizing jobs at all levels in order to increase spans of control and reduce the need for middle management, in a sense reshaping (hence reengineering) the organization.

Experiences of these organizations as well as others we have observed allow us to identify stages that more or less describe the process by which such organizations remake themselves. The stages are presented in graphic form in Figure 12–2.

Applying Cosmetics

Change can be announced through cosmetic change. At Taco Bell it was new decor and new uniforms. At the NYPD it was new equipment as well as darker uniforms that appeared more authoritative. At Sears it was a refurbishing of stores. If this is all that happens, there may be some short-term change in customer reactions as well as employee morale followed by business as usual.

At the same time, a "theme" or "slogan" may be adopted for the change effort, although this rapidly becomes another "program of the month" if not followed quickly with something of substance. At Taco Bell, it was FACT. At the New York Police Department, Commissioner Bratton himself provided the slogan by repeatedly telling audiences that the Department was engaged in "taking the City back from criminals one block, one street, and one neighborhood at a time." Arthur

FIGURE 12–2
The Stages of Organization Reengineering

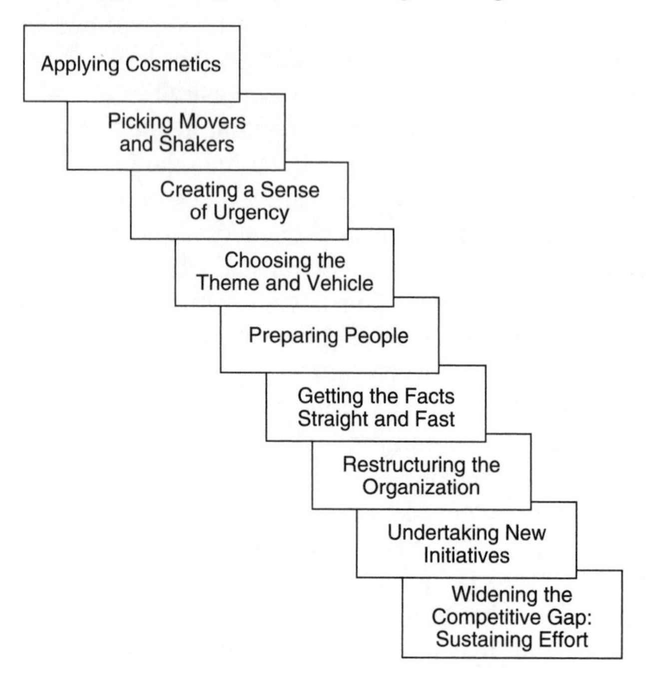

Martinez verbalized Sears' initiatives in terms of making Sears "a compelling place to shop/work/invest."

Don't get us wrong. Cosmetics are important. If not followed with something of substance, however, they have about as much impact as a cotton candy lunch.

Picking Movers and Shakers

The people who are going to drive change are identified at the outset. This does not necessarily mean the organization is changed. There may be few or no immediate changes in titles. But in addition to whatever else they do, they become part of a team that will determine the direction of change and get it done.

Unlike the first, this step is painful. It requires that old relationships be changed and new faces identified. At Taco Bell, it involved bringing some members of John Martin's new team from other parts of the Pepsico organization. At the NYPD, William Bratton hired several of his close associates who had been involved in the transformation of the New York Transit Police. At Sears, it meant the immediate creation of a new policy group.

At the same time, jobs were identified that would be important to the change process. At Taco Bell, the jobs were created. They were called market managers. At the NYPD, the decision was made at this point to focus the frontline change efforts at the precinct commander level. At Sears, the top 100 positions as well as store managers would be most critical.

From this point forward at each organization, personnel changes began. At Taco Bell, only two out of three middle managers were found qualified to assume the position of market manager. At the NYPD, only one out of four existing precinct commanders were able to convince Bratton and his team that they would be able to lead a change from an effort-driven organization to one centered around results. At Sears, only about 40 percent of existing top management and 50 percent of store managers eventually would qualify for jobs in the new environment.

Managers at all levels unwilling to stand this kind of pain never make it past the first stage.

Creating a Sense of Urgency

With the change makers in place, Martin, Bratton, and Martinez took several steps to create a sense of urgency in their organizations. Customers and constituents were polled to find out what they expected of each organization. At Taco Bell it was FACT. At the NYPD, it was safe streets and an improved quality of everyday life. At Sears, it was more attentive, knowledgeable salespeople.

It takes more than an expression of unfilled customer needs to create a sense of urgency in an organization. Only at Sears had the organization suffered anything resembling a competitive crisis, losing its position of largest U.S. retailer to Wal-Mart in the process. This provided a ready-made opportunity for Martinez to make his moves at Sears. Martin and Bratton, however, had to create their own crises.

A 25 percent price cut followed by a whirlwind round of employee meetings to communicate the need for new ideas for administrative cost reductions at Taco Bell were John Martin's ways of stirring a somewhat complacent organization. To cap it off, he made commitments to the parent Pepsico leadership that appeared to his colleagues to be nearly impossible to meet.

The attention given the NYPD by news and entertainment media had made it the best-known organization of its kind in the world, hardly conducive to creating a climate for change. As a result, William Bratton had to resort to calling in a consultant to conduct focus group sessions with police officers that represented the equivalent of what one journalist called a ". . . bureaucratic AA [Alcoholics Anonymous] meeting. You had to admit you had a problem, and you had to recount for everyone else in the group how long you'd had the problem and how serious it was."[13]

Choosing the Theme and Vehicle

With the gap between customer expectations and current accomplishments firmly implanted in everyone's mind, the lead teams then could set about to restate the mission and goals of the organization (at Taco Bell, to become a "feeder" rather than a "Mexican fast food chain"; at NYPD, to become "results-oriented" vs. "effort-oriented"; and at Sears, to become "a compelling place to shop/work/invest") as well as to begin to define the strategy by which the goals would be achieved. The most public of the strategy statements naturally occurred at the NYPD, where the strategic initiatives were not only defined but printed in booklets for distribution to police as well as other interested citizens. But they received a great deal of attention at Taco Bell and Sears as well.

Among the means by which changes would be conceived and implemented were the twelve reengineering teams at the NYPD and the four task forces at Sears.

Preparing People

Training had always been an important initiative at Taco Bell, the NYPD, and Sears. But it took on a new importance with the initiatives described here. In all cases, it encompassed every member of these organizations.

At Taco Bell, training for the new initiatives called for an innovative device, designed like a board game, in which all employees could participate. In addition, regular training in the skills demanded by various jobs continued.

The same approach was adopted by Sears, whose task was to communicate the nature of change and the company's new dedication to its mission to 300,000 people. This was accomplished by designing the same kind of game boards used at Taco Bell. By early 1996, three such "learning maps" dealing with the retailing environment, customer service, and sources and uses of funds at Sears had been played by every member of the Sears organization. This supplemented ongoing training.

The challenge at the NYPD was to raise the standards in order to recruit more highly educated officers, then incorporate training about the Department's new strategies into the Police Academy curriculum. In addition, training sessions on the strategies became a regular feature of training sessions both in the precincts and among those specializing in detective, narcotics, and other work.

Getting the Facts Straight and Fast

Just as we saw in the last chapter, measurement became one of the cornerstones of each of these efforts, as a prod for change, as a way of tracking past progress and predicting future performance, and as the basis for recognition. New information systems, in addition, served to free up managers and employees alike from previous time-consuming tasks of analysis and reporting of information.

Customer and employee satisfaction surveys were regarded as "safety nets" by the management of Taco Bell. Their results were factored into bonus payments for management personnel. TACO, the company's information system, relieved unit managers of many of their previous reporting tasks, making information available at all levels of the organization much faster than in the past and, in addition, providing information-system support for unit-level hiring, scheduling, and compensation.

Computer-generated crime and related information became the basis for the twice-weekly ComStat meetings of precinct commanders and senior staff at the NYPD at which short-term operating strategies for attacking crime were actually worked out. Its availability not only discouraged the opinion-based rationalizations that had pervaded such discussions in the past, it also greatly reduced the time required for the preparation of reports at the precinct level. In addition, it provided the basis for measuring performance and recognizing those achieving exceptional results.

At Sears, it wasn't until information was provided to task force members that enabled them to prepare profit-and-loss statements that included allocated corporate overhead and took into account the cost of capital that they began to realize the low profitability of what they had been managing and the importance of what they had been asked to undertake. It spurred their efforts to seek improvements.

Restructuring the Organization

Once initiatives have been launched to increase the capability of organization members through improved selection, training, and support systems, efforts can be made to change the shape of the organization and the nature of work in it. If the more extensive experiences of organizations like Taco Bell (and, for example, Xerox, described in Chapter 5) are any indication, this involves:

1. Providing frontline employees with much greater latitude.
2. Encouraging the reorganization of frontline work so that it can be performed by teams, preferably those that manage themselves.

3. Extending the span of control for frontline managers to several operating units, each of which is staffed by a work team.
4. Restructuring middle-management jobs into a smaller number that emphasize counseling and consulting rather than a large number that require commanding and controlling.
5. Eliminating one or more levels of the organization, particularly those in which managers manage managers with essentially the same job descriptions.
6. Dramatically increasing the compensation for larger middle-management jobs carried out by fewer, more highly qualified people.
7. Shifting a larger proportion of the total compensation bill for the organization to the front line.

In sum, these kinds of changes can alter the structure of an organization in ways illustrated in Figure 12–1.[14]

This stage has yet to be undertaken at the NYPD and Sears, although pressures confronting both organizations suggest that the issues will have to be addressed soon.

Undertaking New Initiatives

How often have you encountered opposition to a new business initiative from colleagues who claim that the organization is incapable of implementing them? Organizational reengineering frees up managers to undertake new initiatives. No longer do the hiring and development tasks required by such initiatives seem so daunting, particularly if the basic ratio of managers to the total organization has been changed dramatically. In a sense, the "confidence" of the organization in its ability to take on new challenges is renewed.

Well into the reengineering process at Taco Bell, the organization determined that it could develop its brand and concepts in many ways. In addition to dramatically expanding the number of "points of access" that the organization could support, Taco Bell's management undertook a project with its sister Pepsico company, Frito-Lay, to develop a line of Mexican food items to be sold from supermarket shelves. It also acquired and developed several new chains, such as California Pizza Kitchen and Chevy's, offering casual dining to those desiring white tablecloths and a pleasant social experience. At the same time, it was developing new technologies to analyze store layouts and work processes as well as a taco machine capable of assembling to order 900 tacos an hour with higher quality than those made by humans.

At the NYPD, once the organization began delivering results, it was next necessary to turn to efforts to improve productivity, given the

City's limited budget and the growing need for increased compensation for a force that had not had a pay increase for several years. At the same time, the Department was able to target specific problems, for example mounting a major effort to reduce narcotics-related crime.

As part of the organization reengineering effort at Sears, managers identified a new business opportunity, the provision of various services to the seventeen million homes that Sears' appliance installers and maintenance people entered in a given year. Thus, the Home Service Division was created to expand on the opportunity.

Widening the Competitive Gap: Sustaining Effort

The biggest challenge facing Martin, Bratton, Martinez, and leaders in similar situations is that of sustaining efforts within their organizations. As Jack Maple, Deputy Commissioner of the NYPD under Bratton put it, "Armies like to fight short wars."[15]

At the very least this requires adequate recognition and compensation for progress, something that Taco Bell and Sears have been able to achieve in their management ranks. At the NYPD, constrained by budget and union contracts, the effort has been limited to recognition.

To the extent that continuous improvement becomes a way of life in an organization, the momentum that it provides helps sustain effort. But additional incentives, such as service guarantees or other commitments to customers, may help in this regard. After following the steps described above, for example, Xerox introduced a total guarantee of satisfaction to dissatisfied customers and provided frontline service and sales representatives with the latitude to take action to respond to customers' needs under the guarantee.

At Taco Bell, John Martin continued to challenge his organization (and the competition) by vowing publicly at an industry meeting that the company would not raise prices for at least five years. After two years of dramatic crime reduction, Commissioner Bratton announced a goal of a further 10 percent reduction in major crimes for 1996. While Arthur Martinez was just reaching the point where some kind of sustaining commitment would be required, it was clear that he too would have to come up with one if Sears were to continue to change under his leadership.

OBSERVATIONS

Strictly speaking, organization restructuring is confined to only several of the stages described above. On the other hand, organization reengineering spans all of them. Whichever way these initiatives are viewed, it is important to keep in mind that reorganization, per se, is far from the first task undertaken. Further, it is done in a much wider context of efforts which must be coordinated into a kind of master plan, some of the components of which are carried out sequentially and some simultaneously. The master plan may evolve, based on successes and failures in its execution and the changing environment in which it is carried out. But its basic components do not.

We know that John Martin and the ideas of his management team have had an enormous impact, not only on Taco Bell but the industry in which it competes. We can conclude that William Bratton and his organization have probably changed the face of police work in the United States and even other parts of the world. If the eventual outcome of the work of Arthur Martinez and his associates is as dramatic as their initial efforts, it will transform one of the world's largest retailing organizations into the operating powerhouse that it was at one time.

In spite of these accomplishments, it is impossible to tell what the future holds for these three leaders. At Taco Bell, an effort to combat reports of high fat content in Mexican food with a new line of product, Border Lights, aimed at the health-conscious may well have driven away some members of its core customer group, penny-pinching HFFUs, with a dampening effect on performance. Someone else will have to deal with this challenge; John Martin has been reassigned within Pepsico. After its remarkable accomplishments, the New York Police Department confronted problems of the need to cut the budget, the inability to provide pay increases reflecting the performance of its officers, and a rapidly declining morale, presenting even greater challenges than those faced two years earlier when the Commissioner assumed his job. It would have to confront them without him, because he had assumed a job in private industry. And it is much too early to tell whether Arthur Martinez and his colleagues at Sears will face similar stumbling blocks largely unrelated to their organization reengineering efforts. But whatever the fortunes of these three management teams and their respective organizations, they have provided significant roadmaps for others.

These massive efforts to reengineer entire organizations pose questions best asked before undertaking such changes.

QUESTIONS FOR MANAGEMENT

1. How critical is the need for reengineering your organization?
2. How widely is the need for change perceived both within and outside the organization?
3. Can a crisis be "created" or other levers for change be devised?

4. Have the top management team leaders and middle-management focus points for change been identified?
5. To what degree will cosmetic changes be used to signal that the organizational reengineering process has begun?
6. Have the theme and objectives for the change effort been identified? To what extent are they based on marketing research of customer needs and the degree to which the organization is or is not satisfying them?
7. Has the "vehicle" for change, such as continuous quality improvement or reengineering, been established?
8. Have information systems and training been upgraded to support organization reengineering?
9. Are you prepared to alter the shape of the organization rapidly once you have begun, losing one-third to one-half of your best command and control managers, while simultaneously redefining jobs and altering compensation?
10. Do you really believe it is important to raise frontline pay levels significantly in order to reduce overall labor costs?
11. Once these efforts are achieved, what new strategic initiatives will the organization be in a position to undertake that are beyond its capabilities today?
12. What kind of public commitments to customers or internal commitments to employees will you make to sustain the change effort?

In this chapter we have observed three leaders in action, at least in terms of what they've done and what they've accomplished. It is just as important to understand the leadership qualities and behaviors that characterize some of the more successful proponents of service chain management. We give these attention in the next chapter.

13

Leading and Living Service Profit Chain Management

The service profit chain focuses management thinking on just two very important ideas: (1) do what is necessary to detect the needs and insure the satisfaction and loyalty of targeted customers and (2) achieve this, in most cases, by giving employees the latitude and support necessary to deliver high value to desired customers. If this is so obvious, why don't more organizations achieve service profit chain success? Often the explanation is a leadership gap, a failure to incorporate service profit chain thinking into the core beliefs and culture of the organization, a tendency to confuse the organization with too many messages and too little focus, and an inability to lead by word and example.

The accomplishments of the organizations cited in our examples didn't happen by chance. They didn't happen completely by excellent planning and design either. They resulted from extraordinary leadership by a small group of exceptional people who understood implicitly the relationships embodied in the service profit chain, who put them to work to create organizations capable of detecting and adapting to changing customer needs, and who have seen to it that cultures have been created in their organizations that will sustain them during future ups and downs.

Leaders of these organizations do and say things that others don't, things that demonstrate their concern for drivers of organizational performance. And they do and say them over and over in ways that management sophisticates often regard as corny or boring. Each time they do and say these things, service profit chain leaders act as if it is the most important thing they do. Take, for example, Wal-Mart, founded and led for many years by the legendary Sam Walton.[1]

SERVICE PROFIT CHAIN LEADERSHIP AT WAL-MART

Talk with Wal-Mart executives and attend one of their management meetings and the tenets of service profit chain leadership become very clear. From CEO David Glass on down, the main mission of Wal-Mart employees is serving as an "agent for the customer." Think for a moment about what that means. When Wal-Mart merchandisers negotiate for suppliers, they are known as being very tough (but fair). Why? Of course, because they have the clout of the world's largest retailer behind them. But more important, they are on a mission as an agent for the customer. They try to achieve things in the service of the customer that representatives of other retailing organizations would not attempt. It was reflected during a visit we paid to Wal-Mart in the responses of a class of new graduates from the management class at the company's Sam Walton Institute who, when asked by Don Soderquist, Company Chief Operating Officer, who comes first, shouted in unison, THE CUSTOMER. And it is reflected in the large electronic scoreboard on one wall of the auditorium where Wal-Mart's management meetings are held. Instead of clicking off a running estimate of Wal-Mart sales, the board calculates estimates of second-by-second savings generated for customers.

What Wal-Mart provides the customer is, of course, value. In this case, value is defined in terms of "Everyday Low Prices" combined with cheerfully delivered service in conveniently located stores. How does Wal-Mart's leadership know this is what customers want? By spending an inordinate amount of time with them and the people who serve them directly.

The customer may come first at Wal-Mart, but there is clear recognition that it all happens because of satisfied, loyal employees. Wal-Mart is run, according to the philosophy of its founder, like a family. First, all senior managers from the CEO down spend three or four days a week in the field with store personnel and customers, returning to headquarters in Bentonville, Arkansas for Friday's merchandising meeting and Saturday's management meeting. Communication is personal; where that is impossible, it takes place by means of the most extensive in-company television network anywhere. Signs in the Company's headquarters proclaim things like: "Communications Keep Us Together" and "Communicating Always Produces Results."

Today's leaders, CEO David Glass and COO Don Soderquist, have assumed the role of cheerleading that Sam Walton did so well. Each meeting of employees is a pep rally, punctuated by the Wal-Mart cheer ("Give me a W, give me an A, give me an L, give me a squiggly, and so on"), something that many executives could not repeat over and over with a straight face. Managers and employees alike are flown to the Saturday morning management meetings, to which all employees and their families are invited. The result is a weekly gathering of nearly a thousand people for a combination of an economic review, presentation of new merchandise, discussion of specific issues, and a general bonding. The concept of the organization as family is not new. The remarkable thing about the Wal-Mart "family" is that it encompasses 560,000 people. And yet, Wal-Mart's leadership has achieved the seemingly impossible. It has maintained a palpable feeling of family in this vast organization. The same is true at Southwest Airlines, although it plays out in somewhat different ways.

SERVICE PROFIT CHAIN LEADERSHIP AT SOUTHWEST AIRLINES

As we saw earlier, the focus at Southwest Airlines is on high value for customers who need frequent transportation over relatively short distances at fares comparable to the cost of driving their own auto. For these customers, the airline means high quality, reflected in frequent departures and on-time arrivals, as well. High quality also means first-name recognition by loyal employees (a form of the Company's emphasis on "luv") who have worked Southwest's ticket counters long enough to be able to recognize literally hundreds of frequent flyers by name. Thus, Southwest, like Wal-Mart, often substitutes close, continuing contact with customers for more formal marketing research.

As we saw earlier, Southwest doesn't get sentimental about customers, especially when they mistreat its employees. When Herb Kelleher, CEO of Southwest Airlines, says: "When we encounter a customer like that, we say to him, 'We want to see you again because of the way you treat our people,'" he is communicating core beliefs important to the preservation of employee satisfaction and loyalty at Southwest.[2] He personally calls passengers who have been abusive to Southwest employees. It sends the message that their organization stands behind them.

The Southwest Airlines family comprises more than 24,000 employees, nearly a thousand of whom are literally married to each other. (The only rule at the airline is that they can't report to one another.) The thousands of photos displayed at company headquarters suggest that they spend a great deal of time together off the job, partying and serving in charitable activities, led by Kelleher. There are so many photos that it was rumored that Southwest's picture framer was thinking recently of taking his company public. Hugging is a serious activity among employees at Southwest. A casual walk between offices at headquarters becomes an extended exercise in getting caught up on business and personal affairs. It slowly dawns on a visitor that these people aren't putting on an act; they really like each other. It may explain why they are able to work approximately 20 percent more productively than employees of other airlines for about the same amount of pay, which in turn explains why Southwest is able to deliver such high value to its customers. And it explains why Herb Kelleher's sidekick, Colleen Barrett, holds the title of Executive Vice President-Customers (who include employees at Southwest) and heads up the group responsible for maintaining the Company's culture.

Herb Kelleher will tell you that his most important task is insuring that the organization remembers these two important sources of focus: high value service to customers who appreciate what that means at Southwest Airlines and the preservation of a sense of family in the Company's organization.

There are many common elements in the way the leadership of these two organizations has interpreted, and managed by, principles of the service profit chain. Given this, it should probably not surprise you that one of the companies against which David Glass, Don Soderquist, and others at Wal-Mart benchmark their practices is an airline. You guessed it, Southwest. Nor should it be too surprising that Herb Kelleher, Colleen Barrett, and their colleagues at Southwest Airlines tailor many of their practices to those used by a major retailer. Right again, Wal-Mart. Has is worked? Absolutely. Even though both organizations have suffered their competitive ups and downs, during the decade of 1982 to 1992, they ranked one-two (with Southwest Airlines first) in terms of total return to investors among all Fortune 1,000 firms. What a coincidence.

LEADING SERVICE PROFIT CHAIN MANAGEMENT

Leaders who subscribe to service profit chain management stand out like orchids in a patch of thistles. First, they insure that desired customers are served well by their organizations. Second, to achieve this, they know that a primary concern must be for employees who influence customer satisfaction and loyalty. Third, they devote a great deal of effort to the creation and preservation of core values promoting adaptive behavior through the careful continuing attention paid to the needs of both customers and employees. They have little time left over to worry about next quarter's earnings or growth. But it isn't necessary. Taking care of employees who take care of customers who take care of earnings and growth seems to work.

Through interviews, their writings, and other reports, we can piece together a profile of these leaders that provides a template against which others can assess their leadership philosophies and qualities. What they believe and do and how they do it are important. Their beliefs and behaviors allow us to highlight what they do differently from other leaders, as opposed to presenting here a complete manual on organizational leadership.

WHAT SERVICE PROFIT CHAIN LEADERS DO: SUPPLYING THE "EXTRAS"

Standard leadership "manuals," of which there are many available today, emphasize the importance of establishing or preserving some kind of culture (customer-driven, time-based, continuous-improvement-oriented, you name it), putting in place an effective strategic planning process, preserving focus in marketing and operations, instilling in the organization a sense of cohesion, and providing continuing examples of desired behaviors, among others. Leaders of organizations from which we have drawn our examples have read these manuals. And, of course, they insure that these tasks are accomplished.

And yet, our leaders bring something extra to their organizations, something that is hard to describe. At the heart of this "something extra" is a strong belief in a results-oriented approach to management, measurement, and reward, one that focuses on doing a few important things well. But this is far too simple an explanation. In addition, our leaders are able to inspire large numbers of people to manage by the guidelines provided by the service profit chain. They do it by emphasizing a few themes, using a language system that is so repetitive that it is boring to those forced to listen to it more than once, and demonstrating by example that it works.

BELIEVING IN AND COMMUNICATING THE BASICS

Closely held beliefs are at the core of service profit chain leadership. But not just any beliefs. The pattern of beliefs held by leaders we have mentioned is as tight as the pattern of shots on the target of an expert marksman. They include the beliefs that: (1) customers buy results, (2) employees with the right attitude, the right incentives, the right training, and the right amount of latitude who will listen to customers are the key to designing and providing services that create such results, (3) because financial performance is the result of past performance, measurement and incentives must concentrate on determinants of future performance, customer and employee satisfaction and loyalty, and (4) the real payoff from listening to customers is not just results-driven service design and delivery that produces outstanding current performance, it is the maintenance of a strong, adaptive organization culture that insures continued excellence.

These beliefs lead naturally to some predictable and some counterintuitive leadership behaviors toward employees, customers, and investors in organizations like Wal-Mart, Southwest Airlines, ServiceMaster (a supplier of support services to hospitals, schools, and industrial plants), Rosenbluth International (one of the world's largest corporate travel agents), Taco Bell, and the Girl Scouts of the USA. The behaviors are reflected in the measures by which performances are tracked in these organizations.

Putting Employees First

As we've seen, employees warrant careful attention and recognition in service profit chain management. Nowhere is this articulated more explicitly than at Rosenbluth International. Hal Rosenbluth, CEO, is fond of saying, "The customer comes second."[3] This doesn't mean that Rosenbluth International ignores customers. To the contrary, the assumption here is that the employee is the pathway to the customer's heart, something that Rosenbluth's customers experience over and over. Putting employees first requires that managers spend unusually large amounts of time on the service front lines with employees, personally lead developmental efforts, spearhead efforts not only to redesign frontline jobs to provide greater latitude but also to introduce technologies and other supporting mechanisms to make frontliners more successful at what they do, and actually support higher wages as a means of lowering overall labor costs in relation to revenues.

Spending Time on the Front Line. It's not by chance that our service profit chain leaders spend unusually large amounts of time talking and working with employees. Chairman William Pollard and his colleagues at ServiceMaster clean customers' toilets and hospital operating rooms at least one day a year. As Pollard says, "It reminds all of us what our business is all about . . . no matter what job we're in, we're not too busy to serve."[4] The memories of these days are vivid; in Pollard's case, he has never forgotten having had a door opened in his face by an unapologetic surgeon who was not even able or willing to acknowledge Pollard's presence in the operating room that Pollard had just cleaned. All remember the times as unit operating managers when they regularly personally served refreshments at training meetings for hospital and school custodial people who had never been served by anyone, let alone their manager. The immediate result of these practices is an unusually high level of senior management support for the redesign of methods, equipment, and materials both to make frontline employees supervised by ServiceMaster's managers more productive and successful at what they do as well as help them preserve as much dignity as they can on their jobs.

How much time can an organization's leadership afford to spend in activities like these? As much time as it takes to send the message to the entire organization that because employees come first in efforts to serve customers, the primary job of managers and leaders is to serve those who serve customers.

Leading Personal Development. In addition to spending a great deal of time on the front line, our leaders invest personally in the development of a core of promising managers. Hal Rosenbluth and John Martin have regularly led seminars for new managers at Rosenbluth International and Taco Bell, respectively. But teaching requires an even higher level of commitment at ServiceMaster where the rule is "If a manager is too busy to teach or learn, then he or she is too busy to be a manager at ServiceMaster." Chairman Bill Pollard sets the example by teaching regularly in the Company's senior management program, the pinnacle of an extensive curriculum of training programs offered at ServiceMaster's state-of-the-art training facility. In addition, however, he leads a program that involves the Company's managers in reading and discussing a number of books on management and philosophy, sending the signal that teaching and learning warrants a high priority. At one recent retreat for board members and senior managers, Pollard could be found enthusiastically organizing small group discussions of a stack of assigned books around questions that he himself had crafted.

The Girl Scouts of the USA, with more than 330 councils comprising nearly 5,000 volunteer board members, is one of the world's largest leadership training ventures. Most of the GSUSA's volunteer leaders, including thousands of troop leaders, have never had leadership experience. This has required that the national headquarters staff develop extensive training materials and devices that allow board members not only to learn about leadership but to determine how well they are performing. It has resulted in the development of a 126-page director's manual from which many for-profit organizations could benefit. It helps explain why Peter Drucker once labeled the GSUSA one of the best-managed organizations anywhere.[5]

Supporting Greater Job Latitude. Service profit chain leadership supports the design of jobs with greater latitude for employees, leading to the investment in technologies and organization designs that broaden jobs and responsibilities.

Taco Bell, confronted with a shortage of capable restaurant managers to staff its remarkable growth, has instituted a program, Teaming at Taco Bell, in which teams of trained, qualified employees are encouraged to take on greater responsibility with the guidance of their coach manager. When supported with a store-level information system called TACO that facilitates decision making and reduces administrative reporting requirements, Taco Bell has found that self-managed teams help select, train, and discipline their teammates; schedule work; manage cash; and even find time to develop innovative new technologies more effectively than traditionally staffed restaurants. Typically, team members train each other in all the jobs, trading off responsibilities from time to time to reduce boredom. One such innovative team developed a technique called "Aces in Your Places," which has spread to other stores. During peak business hours, a team leader calls out the command, sending those who are most expert in each task in the restaurant to their "battle stations," thus increasing a typical store's capacity by about 40 percent. John Martin, former CEO, described self-managed teams as a "win-win proposition for both the employees and the company."[6]

The Girl Scouts of the USA substituted a circular organization "web" for the more traditional form, an example of which is shown in Figure 13–1, to accommodate frequent job rotation designed to enhance the development of the organization's permanent, paid employees. The organization also reflected then-Executive Director Frances Hesselbein's belief that the concepts of vertical "promotions" and reporting relationships had to be discarded to facilitate the headquarters organization's ability to reflect the changing needs in the field.

The eight-step process for cleaning a hospital room developed by ServiceMaster implicitly involves expansion of the job of the custodial worker. As Bill Pollard puts it, "A housekeeper in a hospital is just not there cleaning a floor but . . . should also be concerned about the welfare of the patient. . . ."[7] Instead of being the unseen, unheard menial laborer of hospital tradition, those working under ServiceMaster's supervision are encouraged to take the time to greet patients upon entering a hospital

FIGURE 13–1
The Circular Organization "Web," Girl Scouts of the USA, January 1988

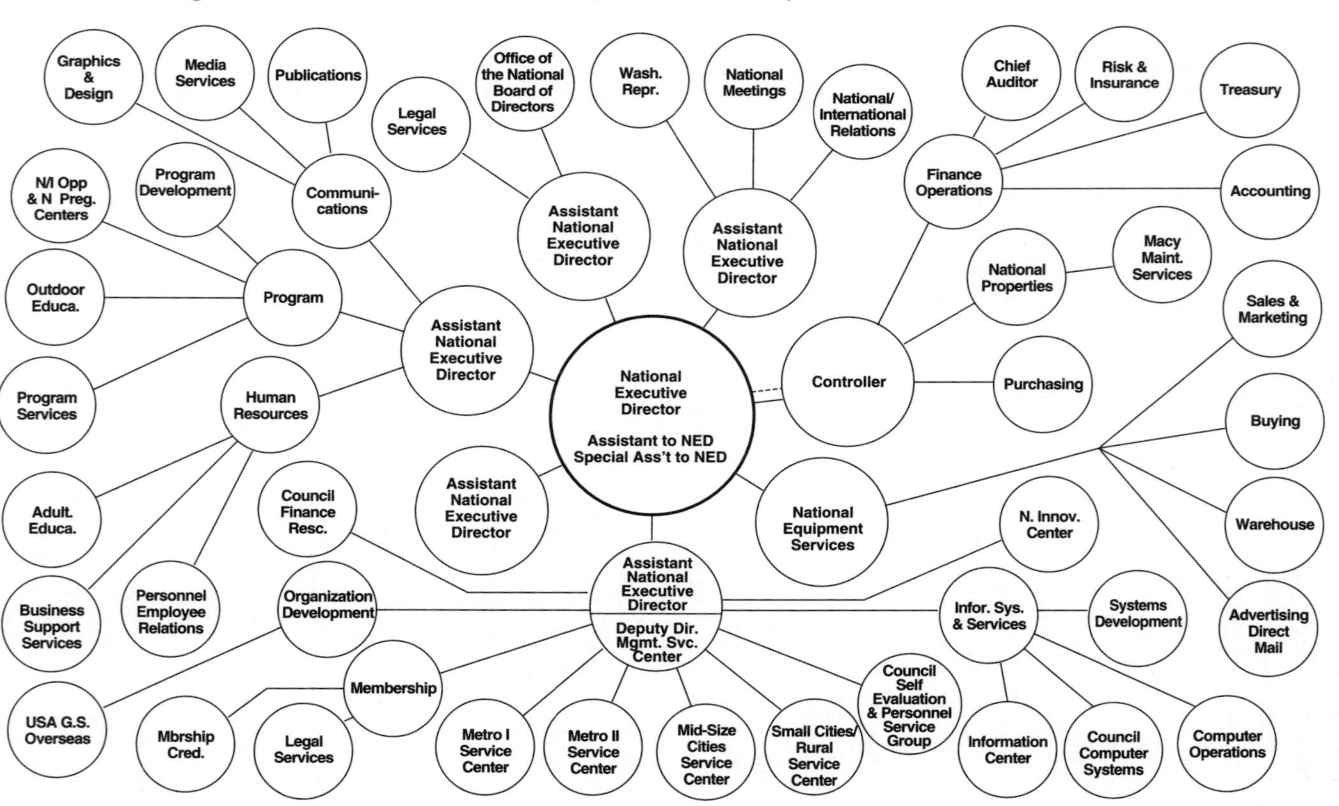

James L. Heskett, Girl Scouts of the U.S.A., Case No. 690-044. Boston: Harvard Business School, 1989, p. 24. Copyright © 1989 by the President and Fellows of Harvard College. Reprinted by permission.

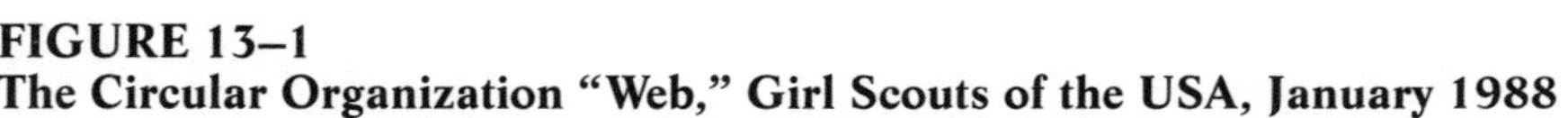

room, inquire about their comfort, and make sure that patients' needs for room cleanliness are met. To support productivity and supply the dignity required to encourage housekeepers to break tradition, Service-Master carefully reengineers work and provides methods, materials, and equipment to insure success and build self-esteem for its charges.

But perhaps the most direct impact of increased job latitude is seen at Southwest Airlines, where it has literally allowed a heavily unionized organization to achieve productivity levels 20 percent higher than the average for its industry. The secret? A tradition of broadly defined jobs in which counter personnel, for example, can be pressed into service to handle bags and cabin attendants regularly perform routine tidying up of the cabin between flights. The tradition is maintained in each successive union negotiation in which the following wording is included in each contract: ". . . those duties historically performed by . . ."[8] Why do employees ratify contracts with such wording? Because of other efforts that the airline's leadership make to insure that on-the-job abuses of the latitude don't occur and that general quality of work life is high.

Reducing Labor Costs by Paying Higher Wages. The beliefs described above lead naturally to support for the idea that the best way in which labor costs in relation to revenues are reduced is to pay higher wages. This philosophy has governed labor relations at Southwest Airlines for years. As one senior executive put it, "We approach negotiations with the viewpoint that we want to pay people as much as we can."[9] The result? A labor bill that is the lowest per seat-mile generated among all major airlines, giving Southwest an almost unassailable competitive advantage.[10]

Similarly, at Taco Bell, as we saw in Chapter 12, by expanding jobs, eliminating entire layers of management, and providing technological and other support to enhance the productivity of frontline managers, Taco Bell has been able to cut its administrative costs in half while, in some cases, more than doubling traditional salaries paid previously for more narrowly defined jobs, creating what Bill Bensyl, former Vice President of Human Resources, has called "irreplaceable value."[11]

In organizations managed by service profit chain tenets, efforts to make employees more successful at what they do and increase their continuity on the job are regarded as the primary means to insure that customers will be served well.

Investing in Customers

Belief in the service profit chain leads to unusually high investments in efforts to both identify customers and understand customers' needs, defined in terms of the value equation, and to retain valued customers longer.

Identifying Needs. The reengineering of Taco Bell's entire organizational structure and strategy was preceded by a marketing research effort to identify the chain's target customers, HFFU's (high-frequency fast-food users), and their needs, FACT (fast food fast, accuracy of orders, cleanliness, and temperature control). ServiceMaster, in an effort to meet the needs of hospital administrators for continuity in the management of support functions, redefined frontline management jobs to encourage adjacent hospitals to "share" outstanding managers, thereby allowing ServiceMaster to reward good performance and keep good managers at a particular facility longer. The Girl Scouts of the USA has funded extensive studies of the needs of girls confronted with the increasing pressures of modern society, a reflection of the vast organization's effort to help each girl reach her full potential.

These organizations and others in our sample identify customer needs in terms of results sought by customers, process quality, product/service package price, and access costs—in short, along dimensions suggested by the value equation. The objective, clearly understood by the leadership of these organizations, is to insure a substantial overlap between customer needs and the capabilities of the organization itself, as illustrated in Figure 13–2.

Insuring Customer Retention. At Taco Bell they're called "safety nets," periodic surveys of customer satisfaction. At ServiceMaster, they are annual customer reviews at which the results of frequent inspections, productivity measures, and overall costs against budget are reviewed with the company's institutional customers. At Wal-Mart, they include senior-citizen greeters at the door and low-price guarantees for the Company's retail customers. At the Girl Scouts of the USA they include audits of Girl Scout councils designed to insure that councils adhere to the policies of the organization in serving the needs of girls. Whatever they're called, they represent investments in efforts to retain customers. There is little question about the importance of spending money for them. The leaders of these organizations understand clearly that it is much less costly to do this than to invest in replacing departing target customers.

Such efforts don't always have to involve formal programs. At Southwest Airlines, they take the form of an understanding among employees that they will be recognized by the organization for going out of their way to serve loyal customers. On a routine basis, it involves what we observed at the Austin terminal when a frequent flyer arrived late for his fully loaded flight, the doors of which had just been closed. Upon observing the customer's distress, the station manager without hesitation quickly boarded the aircraft, purchased someone's seat, and

FIGURE 13–2

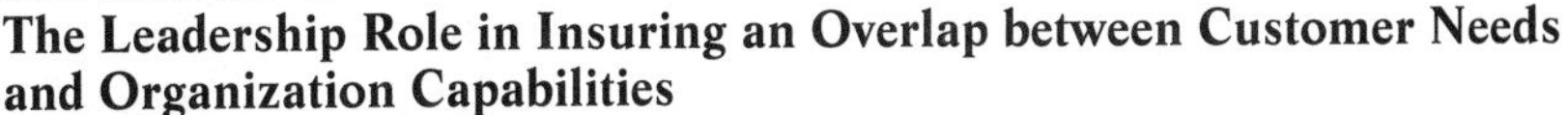

The Leadership Role in Insuring an Overlap between Customer Needs and Organization Capabilities

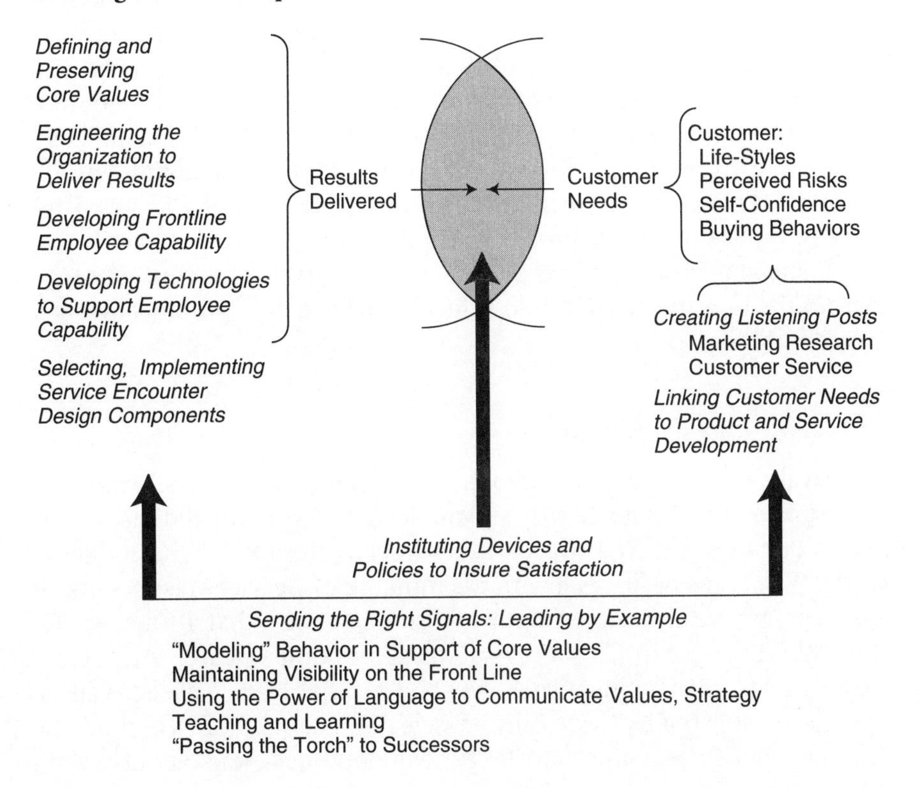

sent the loyal customer on his way. On what basis did he decide to spend the Airline's money in this way? A personal acquaintance with the customer and a knowledge that he flew about 300 flight segments a year with Southwest. It was an investment that will have a large payoff in that customer's loyalty and in favorable word-of-mouth publicity (such as this).

Maintaining Measures and Rewards That Influence Behavior

Service profit chain leadership insures that measures and rewards reflect drivers of growth and profitability to a greater degree than the results themselves. As a result, we are seeing a slow, but steady transformation from traditional performance measures such as return on investment, revenue growth, and profitability to the more highly relevant measures of customer and employee satisfaction and loyalty. The transformation has not been easy in organizations that have employed "dollar for dollar" performance measures for decades. As we have seen, the credibility of nonmonetary measures has been a challenge to establish.

If measures and rewards are to be consistent from the top to the bottom of the organization, the "balanced scorecard" measures that we discussed in Chapter 10 have to be applied to performance measurement at all levels. This helps insure that top management doesn't preach the importance of customer service and satisfaction to customers and frontline employees alike while actually practicing "profit worship." There is an implicit belief among the leaders of the organizations in our sample that profits will follow good performance on the nonfinancial measures, and that the result is worth waiting for. It helps explain the long-term growth in value for investors so graphically portrayed in Figure 1–3.

Communicating the Message

Sam Walton proclaimed to anyone who would listen at Wal-Mart the importance of the manager as "servant leader." Not only did managers listen, but they led Wal-Mart's ascension to the top of the retailing world. The concept fits well with the thinking of ServiceMaster's management, where the most important characteristic that former-CEO Bill Pollard sought in his successor was a "servant's heart." At Southwest Airlines, management seeks to achieve what Herb Kelleher calls a "patina of spirituality" not only in selecting new employees into its "family," but in reaching equally fundamental decisions about which cities to serve.

Of the leaders in our sample, perhaps Frances Hesselbein, during her tenure as Executive Director of the GSUSA, characterized best the ways in which leadership sets an example for the rest of the organization and finds subtle ways to communicate its values.[12] Recognizing that role models were important to her organization, Hesselbein paid particular attention to her appearance, speaking ability, and leadership bearing. She understood the importance of symbols and language as a part of effective service "profit" chain leadership (in a not-for-profit organization), particularly in her efforts to transform what was perceived as a traditional, increasingly irrelevant organization into one perceived as meeting the needs of contemporary urban as well as suburban girls. According to Hesselbein:

> The power of language is so important in this job. People often refer to us as a traditional organization. I try to remind them that we're a contemporary organization with a great tradition. When people say Scouts, I point out that we're the Girl Scouts, not to be confused with the Boy

> Scouts. When people, including those in our own organization, refer to cookie sales as a business activity, somebody has to remind them that it's a girl's program activity. All of us have to constantly remind ourselves that the bottom line in this organization is changed lives.[13]

As part of this effort, Hesselbein repeated the three cornerstones of the organization's management, "mission-focused, values-based, and demographically-driven," several times a day, each time with a voice conveying strong conviction. To provide real meaning to these words, efforts were redoubled to create new programs in computer usage and math to reflect the modern interests and needs of girls characteristic of the "new" Girl Scouts. The third of these cornerstones was communicated more subtly to the public through advertisements that always were designed to show racial diversity whenever girls were pictured in various activities. It took time, but double-digit annual increases in minority participation in the organization slowly began to be realized; the face of the organization literally changed.

A growing amount of evidence suggests that the behaviors described above are more than intuitively appealing. They do, in fact, contribute to longer-term financial performance.

LINKING ORGANIZATION CULTURE, PERFORMANCE, AND THE SERVICE PROFIT CHAIN

Several years ago, one of us completed a study intended to identify linkages between organization culture and performance.[14] It encompassed 200 firms in nineteen industries and was begun with the belief, based on interviews with a number of CEOs, that an organization's performance is related directly to the strength of its culture. What began as an unpromising examination of this relationship resulted in reinforcing the importance of ideas embedded in the service profit chain and influenced our thinking about the leadership task in organizations led by tenets implied by the chain.

To measure the strength of culture, we surveyed the opinions of the top six managers in each of our firms' major competitors. Performance was measured in terms of sales growth, return on investment, and market value over a ten-year period prior to the study.

Having spent a year collecting this vast array of data, we eagerly awaited the results of our analysis. We found, to our dismay, no measurable relationship between culture, as we had defined it, and performance.

Rather than throw out the data and write off a year's worth of work, we decided instead to examine ten pairs of competing firms in as many industries, all with strong cultures but with greatly different levels of performance between the companies in each pair. What we found has led us to conclude that our time was well spent after all.

The clear differentiator between high and low performing firms, all with strong cultures, was the ability of each firm to adapt to changing environments, whether legal, technological, social, or competitive. And the single most important indicator of adaptability was the adherence by management to a clear set of core values stressing the importance of delivering results to various constituencies, especially customers and employees, as part of an effort to deliver profits to owners. Our observations from company documents and interviews were checked and corroborated with the views of expert financial analysts covering each of the industries we studied. They led us to conclude the following: (1) strong cultures don't win as consistently as adaptable ones, (2) adaptability is a "state of the management mind" resulting from a set of core values that include an emphasis on the importance of change, and (3) organizations that vigorously practice these core values and install devices for maintaining adaptability not only greatly improve their chances of sustaining high performance over time, they increase their chances of achieving successful transitions from one leader to another.

In many organizations, the device of choice for maintaining adaptability is continuous quality improvement, forcing an organization to compare itself with the best performers and generally become less insular in its thinking. In others, as we have seen, it is a devotion to listening to customers and "mainlining" their views into the product and service development process. Indeed, both fit comfortably into the framework of service profit chain management, suggesting that this philosophy provides an important means of achieving an adaptable, and therefore high-performance, organization culture.

QUESTIONS FOR MANAGEMENT

Leaders' behaviors described here provide benchmarks against which others' beliefs and deeds can be compared. But with one caveat. The personal styles by which our leaders have both lived and communicated core values and objectives couldn't be more different. To be effective, leadership style has to be natural and one with which a leader is comfortable. The lowest-ranking member of an organization can sense leadership artifice or posturing in a moment. Having said this, however, the common threads in our various descriptions suggest that what leaders do and how they do it is more important than any one personal style, posing several important questions for managers, among which are:

1. Have core values (those shared widely) in the organization been clearly identified?
2. Do these core values emphasize sufficiently the need to be responsive to customers and employees?
3. Is everything that is said or done by the organization's leadership carefully designed to convey the importance of detecting the needs and insuring the loyalty of targeted customers, as well as giving employees the latitude and support needed to meet customers' needs?
4. What steps have been taken to insure that the core values are "used" on a day-to-day basis (for example, through the use of information from "listening posts" in new product design), as well as in making more strategic decisions?
5. What is done to communicate these core values through means such as leadership by example, slogans, ads, and even the decor of physical facilities?
6. To what extent does leadership understand the importance of its responsibility to insure that the organization focuses on just a few important service profit chain concepts, including an emphasis on results for customers and the provision of latitude and support for frontline employees who deliver the results?
7. What is done to encourage all senior managers to spend significant amounts of time with customers and employees?
8. To what extent is teaching, listening, and learning (vs. "telling," commanding, or controlling) emphasized in the attitudes and behaviors of the organization's leaders?
9. Is there sufficient recognition at all levels for those individuals whose actions characterize the core values and the resulting behaviors implied by the service profit chain?

In total, the questions we have posed throughout this book constitute a formidable list. All are not equally important. And some have no importance at all for some managers. To help in making judicious use of these questions, we address last the matter of auditing an organization's progress in achieving service profit chain management.

14

Auditing Service Profit Chain Management Success

The ideas practiced by managers featured in this book constitute, we believe, no less than a complete paradigm for success. It is a comprehensive view or "model" of how a few outstanding service organizations achieve performance levels that far overshadow their "merely good" competitors. The model comprises many complex relationships. Proof that they can be understood and used as the basis for action, however, is provided by leaders and managers of organizations described earlier.

Our first task in this final chapter is to bring together in one place the most important of the relationships describing this paradigm for management. They link the strategic service vision; the cycle of employee capability, value equation, and cycle of customer loyalty of the service profit chain; and the profit model, and are outlined in Figure 14–1.

Many more managers "talk" service profit chain management than actually practice it. Why? In some cases, those who don't walk the talk don't really believe the talk in the first place. It's fashionable to mouth the words. Others, saddled with an organization founded on a "merely good" strategic service vision and an unfocused set of policies and practices for achieving it, don't have the willpower or patience to manage the transition necessary for outstanding performance. In publicly

FIGURE 14–1
Outline of Service Profit Chain Management Relationships

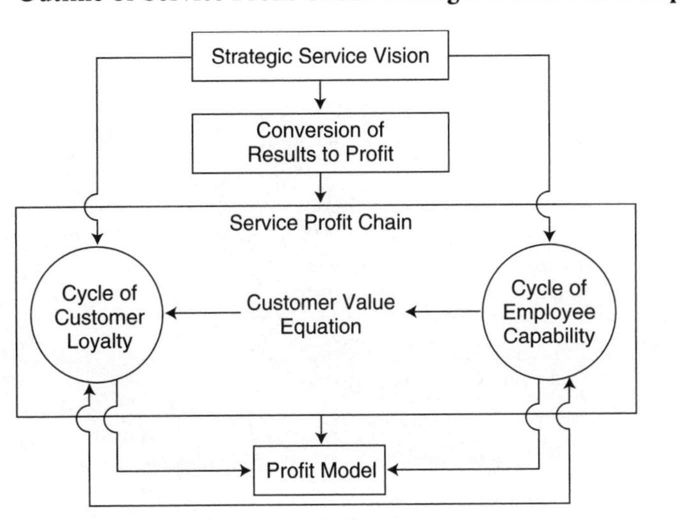

owned companies, it may be shareholders who don't have the patience necessary for change.

Still other leaders have not had comprehensive "levers" with which to institute change. Benchmarks provide such levers, suggesting to managers their most important opportunities for improvement and providing the basis for establishing priorities for action.

That's why we end the book by describing benchmarks suggested by the accomplishments of organizations practicing service profit chain management and by offering a way of auditing progress against the benchmarks.

The paradigm for success starts, as we have seen, with leadership.

LEADERSHIP = FOCUS

A few visionaries, usually no more than one or two in an industry, have been able to envision a comprehensive version of the service profit chain model shown in Figure 14–2. They are the ones who "get it." Many of their competitors never will. Instead these competitors waste time explaining why their highly successful counterparts are able to do things they cannot.

Scott Cook at Intuit, Hal Rosenbluth at Rosenbluth International, Bill Pollard at ServiceMaster, John McCoy at Banc One, Sir Colin Marshall at British Airways, and Herb Kelleher at Southwest Airlines are among those who can recite the service profit chain model in one

FIGURE 14–2
Detailed Service Profit Management Relationships

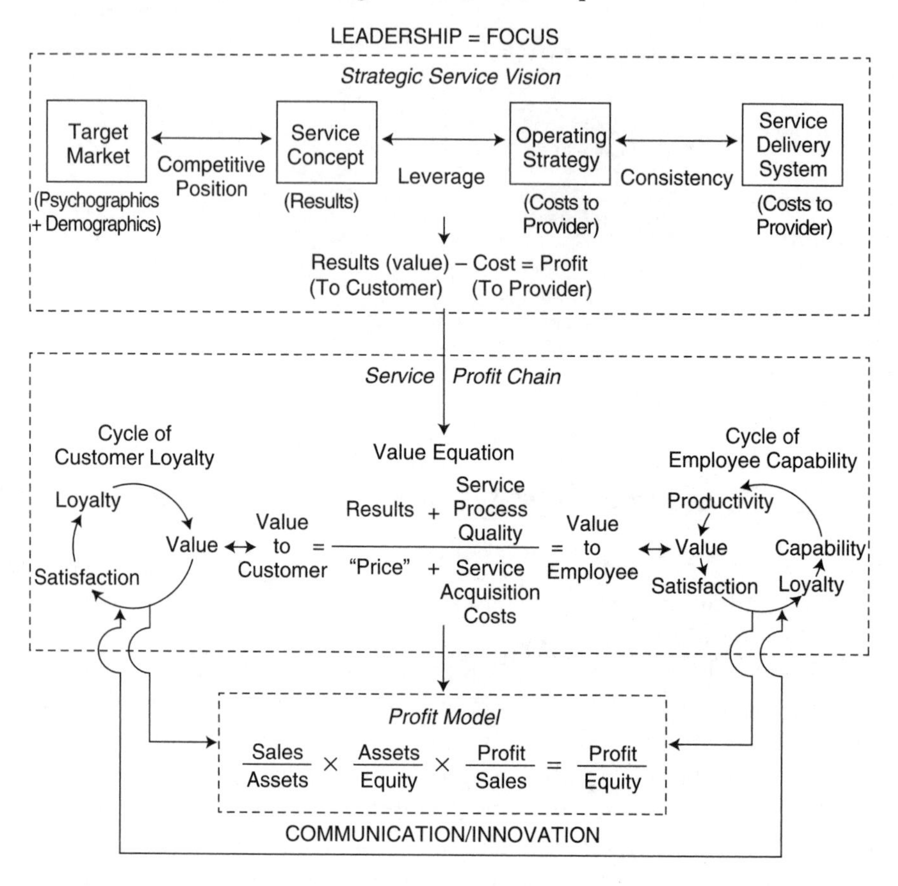

form or another backward and forward. It enables them to know what is and is not important. And they only focus on the important. As Herb Kelleher says, his most important job is to make sure everyone else at Southwest Airlines does too.

STRATEGIC SERVICE VISION = POSITIONING, LEVERAGE, AND CONSISTENCY

There is little question about who the targeted customer is and is not in the minds of managers of these organizations. For example, Intuit does not produce personal financial software for the computer nut interested in the most arcane applications. This enables it to create products for those with limited self-confidence in their use of personal computers. In this manner, it has differentiated itself even from its much larger competitor, Microsoft, by positioning itself to meet the needs of this subset of potential users. It then leverages value to customers over costs of production and distribution by: (1) hiring hard-to-find software engineers who actually enjoy making product that is understandable to novice users, (2) carefully researching the market so they are knowledgeable about customer needs, (3) providing outstanding after-sale service, and (4) relying principally on relatively inexpensive word-of-mouth recommendations from existing users to sell the product. Consistently high-quality service is achieved only by creating an attractive working environment that attracts technical (service) representatives who will stay on the job longer.

Similarly, Rosenbluth International has targeted the corporate travel market where customer organizations need not only good service for traveling employees but also rapid ticketing, the means to control expenses, and, when necessary, preferential treatment in getting limited accommodations for its managers. These are the results sought. They are delivered by efforts at Rosenbluth to leverage results over costs by developing state-of-the-art travel account management capabilities, maintaining affiliations with airline and other reservation systems, and carrying out extensive ongoing training initiatives for its travel representatives. The representatives themselves are encouraged to provide consistently high quality service through careful selection, development, recognition, and reward systems. As a result of a carefully thought-out strategic service vision, Rosenbluth has been able to create a distinct competitive position for itself in an industry with few barriers to entry and limited means of building customer loyalty.

Sir Colin Marshall literally turned around British Airways by restating the organization's strategic service vision around results to be provided to the international business traveler. These included not only core results such as on-time performance, but also a number of amenities, including airport showers and in-flight services, that served to distinguish British Airways from its competitors. Most important of all, however, were efforts to retrain employees to reemphasize the importance of customer service and ways in which it is achieved, to provide frontline employees with greater latitude and support to enable them to deliver better service at lower cost and with greater "leverage" for the British Airways organization. Recognition and reward programs were designed to increase employee satisfaction with, and loyalty on, their jobs. As a result, the organization was able to reposition itself in the minds of formerly dissatisfied customers and, by linking its new strategy to service profit chain actions to back it up, provide the consistently high service levels needed to build customer satisfaction and make British Airways customers some of the most loyal in the industry.

SERVICE PROFIT CHAIN = VALUE, SATISFACTION, AND LOYALTY

Leverage in the strategic service vision translates into profit for the service provider. Because it is based in part on the value of results created for the customer, it provides a direct link to the value equation at the core of the service profit chain, as shown in more detail in Figure 14–2. There is a clear understanding of this in the organizations we have described earlier.

For example, Banc One is not the lowest-cost bank in the U.S. In targeting retail and small-to-medium-sized commercial customers, it seeks to deliver the results sought by individuals desiring good service, rapid loan decisions based on long-term relationships, and convenient banking and related services. By placing an unusual amount of responsibility in the hands of local managers, especially for retail banking decisions, it has been able to understand what customers need and take actions locally to provide it. More recently, with the need to achieve greater economies in handling information and greater consistency in the services provided in competition with rapidly-consolidating competitors, Banc One has centralized some functions that allow for greater economies of scale in an effort to leverage results to customers over costs of service. In doing so, it is attempting to enhance the value delivered to its targeted customers. This value is achieved as well through a loyal cadre of managers who are able to establish and maintain long-term relationships with the kind of customers targeted by the organization.

John McCoy and other senior managers at Banc One have long understood the need for employee capability, including the latitude to make decisions and the support needed to do so successfully, at the local level, even in a bank with more than $90 billion in assets. As a result, the cycle of capability generated by these policies has contributed directly to employee satisfaction and loyalty. They provide direct links to the cycle of customer satisfaction, largely fueled by the high value of services provided by the bank to customers who in the past have desired good service more than the lowest cost. As we see in Figure 14–2, the direct linkages between employee and customer satisfaction and loyalty are once again critical to successful service profit chain management.

Similarly, in ServiceMaster's institutional services division, facility managers, responsible for the package of support services provided to hospitals, schools, and industrial firms, are provided with the latitude to run their own businesses. As we saw earlier, in an effort to expand their jobs while maintaining longer relationships with the organizations they serve, ServiceMaster has given its most outstanding facility managers responsibility for two or more customer facilities. This has extended the relationship between manager and customer, enhanced value to customers, and increased customer satisfaction and loyalty. As a result, greater continuity on the job has enabled ServiceMaster to seek new ways of delivering its services with higher quality, lower cost, and greater productivity, all results sought by customers. This has resulted in an almost impregnable position for the company in serving selected customers in an industry in which the price of entry is a bucket and mop.

PROFIT MODEL = VALUE TO CUSTOMERS VERSUS COSTS TO PROVIDERS

The prices customers are willing to pay for the results delivered by means of the strategic service vision and the value equation in the service profit chain are major determinants of profit model results, as suggested in Figure 14–2. This helps explain why Banc One repeatedly has been among those banks with highest return on assets in the United States, why ServiceMaster's average profit on equity is the highest among major corporations over the past twenty years, why British Airways has been the most profitable of international air carriers in recent years, and why Southwest Airlines has been the most consistently profitable U.S. airline during the same period of time.

These organizations are not necessarily the largest in their respective industries, just the most profitable. It's further proof of the profit impact provided by a clear understanding of the linkages between employee and customer satisfaction and loyalty embodied in service profit chain management thinking.

PERFORMING THE SERVICE PROFIT CHAIN MANAGEMENT AUDIT

The audit shown in Figure 14–3 is organized according to dimensions of the model diagrammed in Figure 14–2. For each dimension, practices we've observed in literally hundreds of service organizations are described in a way intended to help managers calibrate current practice in any one organization. Not all are of equal importance for every organization. For this reason, our experience in applying the audit suggests that it should be performed in five steps.

Identifying the Organizational Unit

The audit can be applied to an entire organization or any one of its divisions or units. Where divisions or units are stand-alone businesses, the audit may have more meaning if applied more specifically. In some cases, it may be useful to apply it to both the entire organization and its individual units in separate audits.

Assessing Importance

Before benchmarking an organization against the practices of others, it is important to "customize" the audit by asking manager-respondents to rank the importance to their organization of each dimension of the audit, using a scale (for example) of 7 (most important) to 1 (least important). A "forced choice" approach to this step often yields the most useful results. It requires that managers be allowed to give any one ranking to only a limited number of dimensions. (For example, of the forty-four dimensions described in Figure 14–3, allow managers to give no more than seven 7's, seven 6's, etc.)

Assessing Current Practice

Benchmarks are provided for each dimension shown in Figure 14–3. Those associated with the value of 7 reflect the practices described earlier in the book. Statements associated with 4's on our scales are roughly equivalent to what we would describe as "merely good" practices. These as well as statements describing "poor" practices (shown opposite the "1's" on our scales) are based on our observations in other organizations.

Each manager completing the audit should be asked to provide his or her views regarding current practice in the organization under study, once again rating practice on a scale of 7 (very high) to 1 (very low).

Measuring the Gaps

Once assessments of importance and current practice have been completed, the averages (and deviations from averages) of results for each dimension can be computed. Those items ranking low in terms of importance can be eliminated from further consideration unless there is some disparity in the opinions of respondents, as shown by calculations of average deviations. Where wide disparity in views concerning any dimension occurs, it is wise to assemble the surveyed managers to learn more about why the disparity exists.

Dimensions on which managers rate their organizations' practices highly also may be given only limited attention.

Establishing Priorities and Taking Action

Focus should be placed on those items ranked as important on which the organization is perceived as performing poorly, those producing the largest negative numbers when ratings for importance are subtracted from those for current performance. Each of these dimensions may warrant further study, discussion, and action of the kind discussed earlier.

A FINAL WORD

Outstanding service management, designed to deliver high levels of value to designated customers, is within the reach of any organization. Some will have to reach much further than others to achieve it. Few will actually do it. Why are we so convinced that this is the case?

We have had a unique opportunity to observe a wide range of practice in hundreds of service firms over a collective period of fifty-plus years in the process of both managing service organizations and developing case materials for the educational ventures with which we have been associated. Our teachers have been literally hundreds of managers who have provided the inspiration for this book. In the spirit of the teacher/learner so often sought after in organizations described earlier, we have passed their lessons on to our students, most often practitioners who have been able to subject them to the most stringent of tests provided by the real world.

The successes achieved by our "students" have convinced us that the ideas embodied in the service profit chain can be replicated. Their accomplishments are reflected in growth and profit levels to which others aspire. But more important, the means by which they have achieved these goals, including high levels of customer and employee satisfaction and loyalty, insure that they will be able to continue to deliver outstanding results in the future. They will continue to "teach" the rest of us as we learn more about the changing terrain of service profit chain management.

FIGURE 14–3
Service Profit Chain Management Audit

The following items reflect important points covered in the book. They are designed to enable you to benchmark your organization's service profit chain management practices against those in other organizations. For each item, descriptions of management practices associated with ratings of 1 (very low), 4 (middle), and 7 (very high) on a seven-point scale are designed to enable you to: (1) calibrate your ratings for your organization and (2) develop a sense of improvement opportunities.

Developing a Strategic Service Vision

Item	Practice	Rating
1. Targeting customers:	Managers use a variety of adjectives to describe targeted customers.	1
	Most managers can describe targeted customers in terms of demographic characteristics.	4
	Most managers can describe targeted customers *in the same* psychographic and demographic terms.	7
2. Business definition:	Most managers describe the business in terms of services or products.	1
	Most managers describe the business in terms of results provided to customers.	4
	Most managers describe the business in terms of results produced for customers, employees, investors, and other important constituents.	7
3. Operating strategy:	Strategies, policies, organization, and controls reflect industry practice.	1
	In designing the operating strategy, an effort is made to create value for customers.	4
	Only those initiatives that leverage results for customers over costs are approved.	7
4. Focus of operations:	All customers are sought; an effort is made to create value for all of them.	1
	An effort is made to create greater value for targeted customers than for others.	4
	Potential customers not fitting the target profile are discouraged from using the service/product package.	7

Managing by the Value Equation

5. Customer segmentation:

There is general consensus that not all customers have the same needs, behaviors.

Extensive marketing research is employed to identify needs and behaviors of various customer segments.

Needs and behaviors of customer segments are identified and analyzed in terms of value equation components.

1 — 4 — 7

6. Service design:

Employees are encouraged to provide good service.

Facilities and systems are designed to help employees provide good service within budgets and profit plans.

All aspects of the operating strategy and service delivery system are designed with the value equation in mind.

1 — 4 — 7

7. Service improvement:

Service is improved whenever possible in response to customer complaints and feedback.

Service is improved to reflect results of marketing research.

Changing customer needs are tracked in terms of elements of the value equation, with service changes implemented on the basis of results.

1 — 4 — 7

8. Value enhancement:

To enhance value, prices are reduced to the lowest possible level.

To enhance value, service is improved as much as possible to avoid price reductions.

All value enhancements are weighed in terms of the degree to which enhancements are leveraged over cost.

1 — 4 — 7

Practicing Potential-based Marketing

9. Lifetime customer value:

No (or little) effort has been made to identify the lifetime value of customers.

The lifetime value of customers has been calculated in terms of purchases over the length of a customer's relationship with the company.

The lifetime value of customers has been calculated in terms of purchases over the length of a customer's relationship with the company plus the value of referrals made by loyal customers to nonusers.

1 — 4 — 7

(Continued)

FIGURE 14–3 *(Continued)*

Practicing Potential-based Marketing (Continued)

Item	Description	Scale
10. Effort to attract/retain customers:	The entire marketing budget is devoted to attracting new customers.	1
	A small portion (20 percent or less) of the marketing budget is devoted to retaining existing customers.	4
	Substantial portions of the marketing budget (40 percent or more) are devoted to both attracting new customers and retaining existing ones.	7
11. Use of listening posts:	Data is collected by a number of people in contact with customers, but little effort is made to organize it.	1
	Customer service provides the most organized source of information about customer concerns and satisfaction, which is communicated to others.	4
	Data from sales reps, customer service, complaint letters, and other sources is organized into information about loyal customers.	7
12. Proportion of customer potential realized:	There is no knowledge of the share of a customer's potential purchases that are being realized by the organization.	1
	Some effort is made to identify potential customer purchases in terms of frequency or size of purchase.	4
	Efforts are made to increase the share of potential customer purchases by increasing transaction frequency, size, and profitability as well as the length of a relationship with a customer.	7

Managing the Cycle of Customer Satisfaction

Item	Description	Scale
13. Primary goals:	The primary "external goal" of the organization is maximizing some measure of profit.	1
	The primary "external goal" of the organization is maximizing current customer loyalty.	4
	The primary "external goal" of the organization is maximizing customer satisfaction in ways that favorably influence future customer loyalty.	7
14. Definition and goals:	Customer satisfaction and loyalty have not been defined; goals have not been set for them.	1
	Customer satisfaction and loyalty have been defined, but no goals have been set for them.	4
	Customer satisfaction and loyalty have been defined, and clear goals exist for both.	7

15. Measurement:	Neither customer satisfaction nor loyalty is measured.	1
	Customer satisfaction is measured, but no effort has been made to link it to customer loyalty.	4
	Both customer satisfaction and loyalty are measured, and linkages between them have established.	7
16. Rewards and recognition:	Employees are not explicitly recognized and rewarded for achieving high customer satisfaction.	1
	Employees achieving above-average customer satisfaction are regularly recognized and rewarded.	4
	Only employees achieving perfect or "top box" customer satisfaction are regularly recognized and rewarded.	7

Building Frontline Capability

17. Management communication and action:	Management emphasizes the importance of customer service, but frontline employees don't feel they have the latitude to deliver on the promise.	1
	Management has embraced the idea of frontline employee "empowerment," but employees don't understand what it means.	4
	Management emphasizes the importance of customer service and is attempting to build the capability to deliver it.	7
18. Establishing appropriate levels of frontline capability:	Little effort has been made to determine the right amount of frontline capability called for by the organization's customer service strategy.	1
	Attention has been given to frontline capability, but employees neither have a clear understanding of their latitude and limits nor feel they have adequate support.	4
	Frontline capability, including latitude, limits, supporting technology, training, and recognition, has been calibrated with the strategy, communicated clearly to employees, and implemented.	7
19. Frontline employee selection:	Frontline employees are selected primarily on the basis of their skills; a small proportion (less than 10 percent) are recommended by current employees.	1
	Frontline employees are selected primarily on the basis of their attitudes; a small proportion (less than 10 percent) are recommended by current employees.	4
	Frontline employees are selected primarily on the basis of their attitudes; a large proportion (more than 20 percent) "select themselves" into the organization based on recommendations from employees.	7

(Continued)

FIGURE 14–3 *(Continued)*

Building Frontline Capability (Continued)

20. Frontline employee support:

Job tasks and limits are clearly defined; support is defined in terms of technology and training necessary to operate it, which are provided. — 1

Frontline employees are given latitude to deliver results for customers; they are provided with the support needed (technology and training) to succeed. — 4

Frontline employees are given wide latitude to deliver results for customers; support is broadly defined to include technology, training, and pay for performance; employees review and help design the support program. — 7

Improving Processes

21. Extent and scope of effort:

To date, no major initiatives have been undertaken to improve process quality in our organization. — 1

Initiatives to improve quality have concentrated on the redesign or reengineering of processes. — 4

The scope of quality improvement initiatives reflects the goal of enhancing value for customers; this includes results delivered, customer access to the service, cost, and ultimately price. — 7

22. Leadership and sustained effort:

Process and quality improvement initiatives in our organization have not been sustained; changes in leadership or a loss of interest among leaders is one of the reasons. — 1

Process and quality improvement efforts continue in our organization although they do not receive the recognition that they once did. — 4

Process and quality improvement has become a part of daily life in this organization; managers constantly urge that it be a consideration in every important decision. — 7

23. Getting "buy-in":

Our process and improvement initiatives were mandated by top management; little was done to get frontline employees and middle managers "on board." — 1

Our process and quality improvement initiative has had limited success because middle managers were not sufficiently involved in its design and implementation. — 4

Every effort was made to obtain "buy-in" from frontline employees and middle managers; assurances were given that no one would lose his or her job because of process quality improvement. — 7

24. Objectives of the effort:

Quality process improvement initiatives have been focused on changing specific ways we do things. — 1

Quality process improvement initiatives are intended to encourage us to change the way we solve problems and work together. — 4

Quality process improvement initiatives are intended to change the very culture of our organization, including a greater sensitivity to best practice anywhere. — 7

Managing Multisite Networks

25. Service delivery system review:

Little systematic thought is given to the design of a service delivery system from the standpoint of enhancing service providers' effectiveness and morale. — 1

Service delivery systems have been redesigned, with an emphasis on insuring quality by the introduction of technology that restricts the service provider's choices and need for judgment. — 4

Service delivery systems constantly are monitored for ways in which to make service providers more effective and satisfied in their jobs. — 7

26. Standardization in multisite networks:

Our organization has had difficulty in achieving standardization of operations in our various operating units. — 1

The limits beyond which service providers may not go in our operating units are clearly specified and controlled. — 4

Core elements of the service have been identified and are required in every operating unit; beyond them, employees or franchisees are free to innovate and are rewarded for doing so. — 7

27. International networks:

Little attention has been given to the degree of standardization required or achieved in international operating sites. — 1

The degree and nature of international standardization required by the business have been established, but the desired goals have not yet been achieved. — 4

The degree of standardization being achieved in international operating sites reflects the cultural sensitivities of the service being delivered. — 7

(Continued)

FIGURE 14–3 *(Continued)*

Managing Multisite Networks (Continued)

28. Franchising:

Frequent conflicts with franchisees continue in spite of efforts to discourage them. (1)

Franchising agreements clearly establish expectations and provide incentives that are designed to encourage franchisee behavior that is good for the network. (4)

Franchising agreements clearly establish expectations and are backed up with a stream of franchiser services designed to remind franchisees of the value of their network relationships. (7)

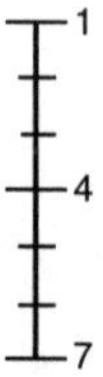

Achieving Total Customer Satisfaction

29. Eliciting customer feedback:

Customer feedback reaches the organization through a number of channels; the most organized is the receipt and processing of complaint letters. (1)

Efforts have been made to coordinate the receipt of information about customer concerns and satisfaction. (4)

Every effort has been made to encourage customers to provide feedback; such information from all sources is consolidated, analyzed, and fed to managers who can act on it. (7)

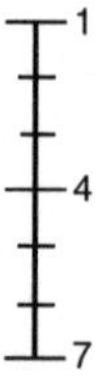

30. Latitude to respond:

Frontline employees are instructed how to respond to customer complaints but given little latitude to do so. (1)

Frontline employees are trained in how to respond to customer complaints; they are allowed to do so within carefully delineated limits. (4)

Frontline employees are provided with training, information, and other support designed to allow them to use their best judgment in responding to customer complaints. (7)

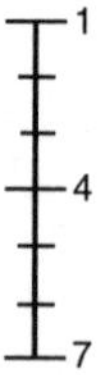

31. Service recovery:

Responses to customer complaints are handled whenever time permits. (1)

Established procedures, usually employing carefully worded letters, are employed in handling customer complaints within well-established time limits. (4)

Responses to customer complaints are made as fast as possible and give more emphasis to personal and customized content than to format or appearance. (7)

32. Guarantees:

Our organization does not guarantee its services or products. — 1

Guarantees are provided for all of our services or products; they are carefully worded to describe conditions for which the guarantees apply. — 4

Unconditional guarantees accompany all of our services, whether they are implicit or explicit; the customer decides whether service or product performance is satisfactory. — 7

Measuring Service Profit Chain Progress

33. Measurement of profit chain components:

Of the profit chain components, only profit and sales growth are tracked regularly and used for management purposes. — 1

Of the profit chain components, profit, sales growth, customer satisfaction, and employee satisfaction are tracked regularly and used for management purposes. — 4

All profit chain components are tracked regularly and used for management purposes. — 7

34. Determination of component relationships:

No effort has yet been made to establish relationships between service profit chain components. — 1

Efforts have been made to establish relationships between service profit chain components, but results do not yet warrant use for management purposes. — 4

Relationships have been established between all or most service profit chain components, and the results are used regularly by managers. — 7

35. Use of balanced scorecard:

Financial measures, such as return on investment and assets employed, are the sole measures used for measuring performance. — 1

Customer satisfaction is now used, along with financial measures, to measure performance. — 4

A balanced scoreboard, comprising measures of financial performance, customer satisfaction, employee satisfaction, and other relevant nonfinancial measures are used to measure performance. — 7

36. Use of measures:

Service profit chain measures, other than profit and growth, are not used as the basis for determining compensation. — 1

Customer satisfaction has been incorporated into the set of measures used to compensate managers. — 4

Financial as well as customer and employee satisfaction and loyalty measures are used as the basis for compensating managers. — 7

(Continued)

FIGURE 14–3 *(Continued)*

Reengineering the Organization

Item	Description	Scale
37. Establishing the need for change:	There is little perception of a need for reengineering the organization.	1
	There is a general sense that there is a need for reengineering the organization, but no evidence has been produced to support it.	4
	There is a strong sense of the need for reengineering the organization, based on measures of customer and employee satisfaction.	7
38. Leadership for change:	Top management is not yet convinced that it is necessary to engage in organization reengineering.	1
	Top management is convinced of the need for organization reengineering, but other levels of management are not.	4
	All levels of management are convinced of the need for organization reengineering.	7
39. Selection of the "vehicle" for change:	No vehicle, such as continuous quality improvement, has been identified as a theme, rationale, and method for achieving organization reengineering.	1
	Several techniques are in use that could be used as the basis for organization reengineering, but no strategy is in place to use them as the means to accomplish it.	4
	A vehicle, such as continuous quality improvement, has been selected and is in use as a method for achieving organization reengineering.	7
40. Implementing change:	The organization is unprepared to pay the price, including the possible loss of many high-performing "command and control" managers, of organization reengineering.	1
	One or more layers of management have been eliminated, although frontline jobs and compensation have been altered significantly.	4
	One or more layers of management have been eliminated, and frontline jobs and compensation have been altered significantly to reflect increased latitude and decision-making responsibility.	7

Leading Service Profit Chain Management

Item	Description	Scale
41. Identifying and communicating core values:	No significant effort has been made to identify the core (shared) values of the organization.	1
	Core values of the organization were established some time ago, but little effort has been made to emphasize them to new and existing members of the organization.	4
	Core values of the organization have been established and are communicated regularly by the leadership of the organization.	7
42. Nature of core (shared) values:	Core values make little reference to the need to listen and respond to the needs of all constituencies important to the organization.	1
	Core values make reference to the need to listen and respond to the needs of important constituencies, but make no reference to these as a way of maintaining an adaptive organization culture.	4
	Core values are stated in a way that stresses the need to listen and respond to the needs of important constituencies as a means to foster an adaptive culture.	7
43. Use of core values:	Little or no use is made of the organization's core (shared) values.	1
	Core values are used regularly in describing the organization to shareholders, prospective employees, and others.	4
	Core values are used regularly in making strategic decisions.	7
44. Leadership behavior:	The leadership of the organization maintains limited contact with frontline service providers.	1
	The leadership of the organization maintains regular contact with frontline service providers, but there is a feeling among the latter that little results from it.	4
	The leadership of the organization maintains regular contact with the frontline and uses it as an opportunity to listen, learn, and teach the use of core values to employees.	7

Notes

Chapter 1. Setting the Record Straight

1. Michael E. Porter, *Competitive Strategy* (New York: Free Press, 1980).
2. James C. Collins and Jerry I. Porras, *Built to Last* (New York: HarperBusiness, 1994).
3. Carl Sewell and Paul B. Brown, *Customers for Life* (New York: Doubleday Currency, 1990), p. 24.
4. Michael Hammer quotation from a presentation at *The Hammer Forum,* Cambridge, Mass.
5. James L. Heskett, *Managing in the Service Economy* (Boston: Harvard Business School Press, 1986), pp. 5–43.
6. Robert D. Buzzell and Bradley T. Gale, *The PIMS Principles: Linking Strategy to Performance* (New York: Free Press, 1987).
7. Frederick F. Reichheld and W. Earl Sasser, Jr., "Zero Defections: Quality Comes to Services," *Harvard Business Review,* September-October 1990, pp. 105–11.
8. Frederick F. Reichheld, *The Loyalty Effect* (Boston: Harvard Business School Press, 1996).
9. W. Earl Sasser, Jr. and Thomas O. Jones, "Why Satisfied Customers Defect," *Harvard Business Review,* November-December 1995, pp. 88–99.
10. W. Earl Sasser, Jr., and Lucy N. Lytle, "Au Bon Pain: The Partner/Manager Program," Case No. 9-687-063 (Boston: Harvard Business School Publishing Division, 1987).
11. James L. Heskett and Leonard A. Schlesinger, *Out in Front: Building High Capability Service Organizations* (Boston: Harvard Business School Press, 1997).
12. See, for example, Benjamin Schneider and David E. Bowen, "New Services Design, Development, and Implementation and the Employee," in W. R. George and C. Marshall, eds., *New Services* (Chicago: American Marketing Association, 1985), pp. 82–101, and E. M. Johnson and D. T. Seymour, "The Impact of Cross-Selling on the Service Encounter in Retail Banking," in J. A. Czepiel, M. R. Soloman, and C. F. Suprenant, eds., *The Service Encounter* (Lexington, MA: D. C. Heath, 1985), pp. 225–39.
13. See James L. Heskett, Thomas O. Jones, Gary W. Loveman, W. Earl Sasser, Jr., and Leonard A. Schlesinger, "Putting the Service-Profit Chain to Work," *Harvard Business Review,* March-April 1994, pp. 164–74.
14. Interview with John Reed, November 1991.
15. Interview with David Glass, May 1993.

Chapter 2. Capitalizing on the Service Profit Chain

1. Material in the following section draws heavily on James L. Heskett, Thomas O. Jones, Gary W. Loveman, W. Earl Sasser, Jr., and Leonard A. Schlesinger, "Putting the

Service-Profit Chain to Work, *Harvard Business Review,* March-April 1994, pp. 164–74.

2. Information about Southwest Airlines is based on James L. Heskett and Roger H. Hallowell, "Southwest Airlines: 1993 (A)," Case No. 9-694-023 (Boston: Harvard Business School Publishing Division, 1993).

3. Internal study, American Express, 1995.

4. For more information about the PIMS study, see Robert D. Buzzell and Bradley T. Gale, *The PIMS Principles: Linking Strategy to Performance* (New York: Free Press, 1987).

5. Frederick F. Reichheld and W. Earl Sasser, Jr., "Zero Defections: Quality Comes to Services," *Harvard Business Review,* September-October 1990, pp. 105–11.

6. James L. Heskett and Roger H. Hallowell, *op. cit.,* p. 7.

7. Frederick Reichheld and Keith Aspinall, "Building High-Loyalty Business Systems," *Journal of Retail Banking,* Winter 1993–1994, pp. 21–29.

8. Jody Hoffer Gittell, "Crossfunctional Coordination, Control and Human Resource Systems: Evidence from the Airline Industry," unpublished Ph.D. dissertation, MIT, 1995, p. 172.

9. Jeffrey J. Zornitsky, "Making Effective Human Resource Management a Hard Business Issue," *Compensation & Benefits Management,* Winter 1995, pp. 16–24.

10. Robert Levering and Milton Moskowitz, *The 100 Best Companies to Work for in America* (New York: Currency Doubleday, 1993), pp. 412–16.

11. Leonard A. Schlesinger and Jeffrey J. Zornitsky, "Job Satisfaction, Service Capability, and Customer Satisfaction: An Examination of Linkages and Management Implications," *Human Resource Planning,* Volume 14, Number 2, pp. 141–49.

12. Internal company study, Waste Management, Inc., June,1995.

13. Internal company study, Chick-Fil-A, October 1993.

14. Internal company study, 1994.

15. Schlesinger and Zornitsky, *op. cit.*

16. Internal company study, MCI, 1991.

17. Leonard A. Schlesinger and Roger Hallowell, "Taco Bell Corp.," Case No. 9-692-058 and Leonard A. Schlesinger and Dena Votroubek, "Taco Bell 1994," Case No. 9-694-076 (Boston: Harvard Business School Publishing Division, 1991 and 1994, respectively).

18. Interview with John Martin, CEO, Taco Bell, January 1992.

19. Robert S. Kaplan and David P. Norton, "Putting the Balanced Scorecard to Work," *Harvard Business Review,* September-October 1993, pp. 134–49.

20. Hugo Uyterhoeven and Myra M. Hart, "Banc One-1993," Case No. 9-394-043, and Rosabeth Moss Kanter and Paul S. Myers, "Banc One Corporation, 1989," Case No. 9-390-029 (Boston: Harvard Business School Publishing Division, 1993 and 1989, respectively).

21. Personal conversation with John B. McCoy, August 1993.

22. Leonard A. Schlesinger and James L. Heskett, "Customer Satisfaction Is Rooted in Employee Satisfaction," *Harvard Business Review,* November-December 1991, pp. 148–49.

Chapter 3. Managing by the Customer Value Equation

1. See, for example, Paul C. Weiler, Howard H. Hiatt, Joseph P. Newhouse, William G. Johnson, Troyen A. Brennan, and Lucian L. Leape, *A Measure of Malpractice* (Cambridge, MA: Harvard University Press, 1993), p. 71.

2. A. Parasuraman, Valerie A. Zeithaml, and Leonard Berry, "SERVQUAL: A Multiple-Item Scale for Measuring Consumer Perceptions of Service Quality," *Journal of Retailing,* Spring 1988, pp. 12–40.

3. J.A. Miller, "Studying Satisfaction, Modifying Models, Eliciting Expectations, Posing Problems, and Making Meaningful Measurements," in H.K. Hunt (ed.), *Con-*

ceptualization and Making Meaningful Measurements (Cambridge, MA: Marketing Science Institute, 1977), pp. 72–91; and Valarie A. Zeithaml, A. Parasuraman, and Leonard L. Berry, *Delivering Quality Service: Balancing Customer Perceptions and Expectations* (New York: Free Press, 1990).

4. Information about USAA presented here is based on James L. Heskett and Roger Hallowell, "USAA: Business Process Review for The Great Lakes Region," Case No. 9-694-024 (Boston: Harvard Business School Publishing Division, 1994) and interviews with company executives.

5. Based on information presented in "Saving Customers With Service Recovery," a video prepared and distribution as part of the series, "People, Service, Success," (Boston: Harvard Business School Management Productions, 1994) and W. Earl Sasser and Norman Klein, "British Airways: Using Information Systems to Better Serve the Customer," Case No. 9-395-065 (Boston: Harvard Business School Publishing Division, 1994).

6. Roland T. Rust, Anthony J. Zahorik, and Timothy L. Keiningham, "Return on Quality (ROQ): Making Service Quality Financially Accountable," *Journal of Marketing,* April 1995, pp. 58–70.

7. James L. Heskett, "The Progressive Corporation Transportation Group," Case No. 9-693-033 (Boston: Harvard Business School Publishing Division, 1992).

Chapter 4. Rethinking Marketing: Building Customer Loyalty

1. Information about Intuit is derived from John Case, "Customer Service: The Last Word," *Inc.,* April 1991, pp. 88–93, and "Listening to Customers," one in a series of videos entitled "People, Service, Success," produced and distributed by Harvard Business School Management Productions, 1994.

2. Robert D. Buzzell and Bradley T. Gale, *The PIMS Principles: Linking Strategy to Performance* (New York: Free Press, 1987).

3. Frederick F. Reichheld and W. Earl Sasser, J., "Zero Defections: Quality Comes to Service," *Harvard Business Review,* September-October 1990, pp. 105–11.

4. Riechheld and Sasser, *op. cit.,* at p. 106.

5. Reichheld and Sasser, *ibid.*

6. For more information about these relationships, see James I. Cash, Jonathan O'Neil, and Keri Ostrofsky, "Otis Elevator: Managing the Service Force," Case No. 9-191-213 (Boston: Harvard Business School Publishing Division., 1991).

7. U.S. Office of Consumer Affairs, *Consumer Complaint Handling in America: An Update Study, Part II* (Washington, D.C.: Technical Assistance Research Programs Institute, April 1, 1986).

8. Personal interview with Phil Bressler, March 1990.

9. Carl Sewell and Paul B. Brown, *Customers for Life* (New York: Doubleday Currency, 1990).

10. W. Earl Sasser Jr., Thomas O. Jones, and Norman Klein, "The Ritz-Carlton: Using Information Systems to Better Serve the Customer," Case No. 9-395-064 (Boston: Harvard Business School Publishing Division, 1994).

11. Quoted from "Listening to Customers," one in a series of video productions entitled "People, Service, Success," (Boston: Harvard Business School Publishing Management Productions, 1994).

12. Reichheld and Sasser, *op. cit.,* at p. 111.

13. Based on internal documentation prepared by SMG, a consultant to Swedbank.

14. See, for example, Regis McKenna, *Relationship Marketing* (Reading, MA: Addison-Wesley, 1991) and Martin Christopher, A. Payne, and D. Ballantyne, *Relationship Marketing* (London: Heinemann, 1991).

15. See Alan W. H. Grant and Leonard A. Schlesinger, "Realize Your Customers' Full Profit Potential," *Harvard Business Review,* September-October 1995, pp. 59–72. The concepts and examples that follow in this section of the chapter are drawn liberally from this source with permission.

16. *Ibid.*, p. 67.
17. Thomas O. Jones, Leonard A. Schlesinger, and Roger Hallowell, "Air Miles Canada," Case No. 9-694-008 (Boston: Harvard Business School Publishing Division, 1993).

Chapter 5. Attaining Total Customer Satisfaction: Not Whether but When

1. See Melvyn A. J. Menezes and Jon Serbin, "Xerox Corporation: The Customer Satisfaction Program," Case No. 9-591-055 (Boston: Harvard Business School Publishing Division, 1991) for a more complete description of Xerox's efforts to achieve total customer satisfaction.
2. Thomas O. Jones and W. Earl Sasser, Jr., "Why Satisfied Customers Defect," *Harvard Business Review,* November-December 1995, pp. 88–99.
3. Frederick Reichheld and Keith Aspinall, "Building High-Loyalty Business Systems," *Journal of Retail Banking,* Winter 1993–1994, pp. 21–29, at p. 26.
4. Personal interview with John Larson, April 1996.
5. Jones and Sasser, *ibid.*

Chapter 6. Managing the Customer-Employee "Satisfaction Mirror"

1. One of the first conferences devoted to an examination of the service encounter is reported in John A. Czepiel, Michael R. Soloman, and Carol F. Surprenant (eds.), *The Service Encounter* (Lexington, MA: D. C. Heath, 1985).
2. For a more complete description of Nordstrom's strategies and policies, see James C. Collins and Jerry I. Porras, *Built to Last* (New York: Harper Business, 1994) and Walter J. Salmon and Manu Parpia, "Nordstrom," Case No. 9-579-218 (Boston: Harvard Business School Publishing Division, 1979).
3. Benjamin Schneider and David E. Bowen, "New Services Design, Development and Implementation and the Employee," in W. R. George and C. Marshall (eds), *New Services* (Chicago: The American Marketing Association, 1985), pp. 82–101.
4. Benjamin Schneider and David E. Bowen, "Human Resource Management Is Critical," *Organizational Dymanics,* 1993, pp. 39–52, at p. 42 (words in brackets are ours). See also the book by the same authors, *Winning the Service Game* (Boston: HBS Press, 1995).
5. This practice is mentioned in Robert Simons and Hilary Weston, "Nordstrom: Dissension in the Ranks? (A)," Case No. 9-191-002 (Boston: Harvard Business School Publishing Division, 1990).

Chapter 7. Building a Cycle of Capability

1. For more information about this company, see a case prepared by William E. Fulmer, "Bugs Burger Bug Killers Inc. (A)," 1990, which in turn was based largely on information and quotes in Tom Richman, "Getting the Bugs Out," *Inc.*, June 1984, pp. 67–72; Annette Kornblum, "Bugs Burger," *Pest Control,* November 1980; and Joan Livingston, "Absolutely Guaranteed," *Nation's Business,* November 1987, pp. 51–52.
2. Much of the remainder of this chapter is based on material in James L. Heskett and Leonard A. Schlesinger, *Out in Front: Building High-Capability Service Organizations* (forthcoming).
3. From a study by The Forum Corporation whose results were published in *The Wall Street Journal,* August 31, 1989.
4. James J. Parkington and Benjamin Schneider, "Some Correlates of Experienced Job Stress: A Boundary Role Study," *Academy of Management Journal* 22 (1979), pp. 270–81; Warren G. Bennis, "Beyond Bureaucracy," in Warren G. Bennis (ed.), *Amer-*

ican Bureaucracy (Chicago: Aldine, 1970), pp. 3–17; and Peter M. Blau, *On the Nature of Organizations* (New York: John Wiley and Sons, 1974), pp. 80–84.

5. For more information about this study, see Leonard A. Schlesinger and Jeffrey Zornitsky, "Job Satisfaction, Service Capability, and Customer Satisfaction: An Examination of Linkages and Management Implications," *Human Resource Planning,* Volume 14, Number 2, pp. 141–49.

6. Hal F. Rosenbluth and Diane McFerrin Peters, *The Customer Comes Second* (New York: Morrow Quill, 1992), p. 59.

7. This quote is from a videotaped interview with Herbert Kelleher in 1991, portions of which are contained in the video "Mobilizing People for Breakthrough Service," which is part of the series "People, Service, Success" (Boston: Harvard Business School Management Productions, 1993).

8. Employee selection on the basis of "life themes" is described in greater detail in Leonard A. Schlesinger, "How to Hire By Wire," *Fast Company,* November 1993, pp. 86–91.

9. "Denmark: Clean Machine—ISS," *Management Today,* May 31, 1994.

10. *Op cit.,* "Mobilizing People for Breakthrough Service."

11. Bill Voelker, "Bugs' Burger Boast: Cadillac of Pest Control Trade," *The Times-Picayune,* March 2, 1980.

12. James L. Heskett, "ServiceMaster Industries, Inc.," Case No. 9-388-064 (Boston: Harvard Business School Publishing Division, 1987), p. 6.

13. Robert Simons, "Control in an Age of Empowerment," *Harvard Business Review,* March–April 1995, pp. 50–58.

14. *Ibid.*

15. William E. Fulmer, *op. cit.,* p. 11.

16. "Many Happy Returns," *Inc.*, October 1990, pp. 30–33ff..

17. Op. cit., "Mobilizing People for Breakthrough Service".

18. William E. Fulmer, *op. cit.,* p. 16.

19. Jay Finegan, "Unconventional Wisdom," *Inc.,* December 1994, pp. 44–59.

20. *Ibid.,* p. 56.

Chapter 8. Developing Processes That Deliver Value

1. For more information about various philosophies of process improvement, see W. Edwards Deming, *Quality, Productivity, and Competitive Position* (Cambridge, MA: MIT Center for Advanced Engineering, 1982); Joseph M. Juran, *Juran on Quality by Design: The New Steps for Planning Quality into Goods and Services* (New York: Free Press, 1992); Philip B. Crosby, *Quality Is Free* (New York: McGraw-Hill, 1979); and Michael Hammer and James Champy, *Reegineering the Corporation: A Manifesto for Business Revolution* (New York: HarperBusiness, 1993).

2. James L. Heskett, "Shouldice Hospital Limited," Case No. 9-683-068 (Boston: Harvard Business School Publishing Division, 1983).

3. W. Earl Sasser and John Klug, "Benihana," Case No. 9-673-057 (Boston: Harvard Business School Publishing Division, 1972).

4. Christopher W. L. Hart and Joan S. Livingston, "Florida Power & Light's Quality Improvement Program," Case No. 9-688-043 (Boston: Harvard Business School Publishing Division, 1987).

5. James L. Heskett, W. Earl Sasser, Jr., and Christopher W. L. Hart, *Service Breakthroughs: Changing the Rules of the Game* (New York: Free Press, 1990, p. 8).

6. Christopher W. L. Hart and Joan S. Livingston, *op. cit.,* p. 6.

7. See G. Lynn Shostack, "Designing Services That Deliver," *Harvard Business Review,* January-February 1984, pp. 133–39.

8. Jane Kingman-Brundage, "Service Mapping: Gaining a Concrete Perspective on Service System Design," pp. 148–63 in Eberhard E. Scheuing and William F. Christopher (eds.), *The Service Quality Handbook* (New York: Amacom, 1993).

9. This section is adapted from James L. Heskett and Robert Anthony, "Note on Service Mapping," No. 9-693-065 (Boston: Harvard Business School Publishing Division, 1992).

10. "Summary Description of FPL's Quality Improvement Program," Company Document, 1989.

11. For additional analyses of the Florida Power & Light experience, see Gary Dessler and Dana L. Farrow, "Implementing a Successful Quality Improvement Programming in a Service Company: Winning the Deming Prize," *International Journal of Service Industry Management,* Volume 1, Number 2, 1990, pp. 45–53.

12. *Ibid.,* p. 53.

13. Gary Jacobson and John Hillkirk, "Crazy about Quality," *Business Month,* June 1989, pp. 71–74, at p. 71.

14. Robert Chapman Wood, "A Hero without a Company," *Forbes,* March 18, 1991, pp. 112–14, at pp. 113–14.

15. James L. Broadhead, Internal Company Memorandum, Florida Power & Light, June 19, 1990. Words in brackets are those of the authors.

16. Antonio N. Fins, "Feeling the Heat at a Florida Utility," *Business Week,* November 12, 1990, pp. 94–95.

Chapter 9. Designing Service Delivery Systems That Drive Quality, Productivity, and Value

1. For a more extensive description of MTV's operating strategy and service delivery system, see John Seabrook, "Rocking in Shangri-La," *The New Yorker,* October 10, 1994, pp. 64–78.

2. *Ibid.,* p. 67.

3. See Randy Bright, *Disneyland Inside Story* (New York: Harry N. Abrams, Inc., 1987) for descriptions of the experiences encountered in engineering Disney's first theme park. Brad Sutton, "How Disneyland Works," *Quality* Progress, July 1991, pp. 17–30, presents an extensive discussion of the impact of service delivery system design on the operation of Disneyland. For descriptions of human resource policies at Disney's theme parks, see N. W. Pope, "Mickey Mouse Marketing," *American Banker,* July 25, 1979, pp. 4–14; and N. W. Pope, "More Mickey Mouse Marketing," *American Banker,* September 12, 1979, pp. 4–14.

4. Interview with Jacques Giraud, November 1987. For additional information about Club Med, see Christopher W. L. Hart, "Club Med (A)," Case No. 9-687-046 (Boston: Harvard Business School Publishing Division, 1986).

5. David A. Maister, "The Psychology of Waiting Lines," in John A. Czepiel, Michael R. Soloman, and Carol F. Surprenant, eds., *The Service Encounter* (Lexington, MA: D. C. Heath & Company, 1985), pp. 113–23.

6. James L. Heskett, "The Benetton Group," Case No. 9-396-177 (Boston: Harvard Business School Publishing Division, 1995) provides much of the information about the company used in this chapter.

7. Rahul Jacob, "How One Red Hot Retailer Wins Customer Loyalty," *Fortune,* July 10, 1995, pp. 72–79.

8. For a more extensive discussion of Staples' efforts to build customer loyalty through its information systems, see Frederick F. Reichheld, *The Loyalty Effect* (Boston: Harvard Business School Press, 1996), pp. 239–41.

9. See Richard B. Chase and Douglas M. Stewart, "Make Your Service Fail-Safe," *Sloan Management Review,* Spring 1994, pp. 35–44, and *Mistake Proofing: Designing Errors Out* (Portland, Oregon: Productivity Press, 1995). Many of the examples in this section are drawn from these interesting sources.

10. Shigeo Shingo, *Zero Quality Control: Source Inspection and the Poka-yoke System* (Portland, Oregon: Productivity Press, 1986).

11. A more extensive discussion of Benetton's strategy of building a global network

is contained in James L. Heskett, "Dynamics of a Global Network Corporation: The Benetton Group," unpublished working paper, 1996.

Chapter 10. Attaining Total Customer Satisfaction: Doing Things Right the Second Time

1. Judith H. Dobrzynski, "Yes, He's Revived Sears. But Can He Reinvent It?," *The New York Times,* January 7, 1996, p. 8.

2. For a more extensive description of the UPS culture and practices, see Jeffrey Sonnenfeld and Meredith Lazo, "United Parcel Service (A)," Case No. 9-488-016 (Boston: Harvard Business School Publishing Division, 1987).

3. Much of the material concerning British Airways presented in this chapter is based on W. Earl Sasser and Norman Klein, "British Airways: Using Information Systems to Better Service the Customer," Case No. 9-395-065 (Boston: Harvard Business School Publishing Division, 1994).

4. John Kotter and James Leahy, "Changing the Culture at British Airways," Case No. 9-491-009 (Boston: Harvard Business School Publishing Division, 1990), p. 10.

5. Sasser and Klein, *op. cit.,* p. 5.

6. U.S. Office of Consumer Affairs, *Consumer Complaint Handling in America: An Update Study, Part II* (Washington, D.C.: Technical Assistance Research Programs Institute, April 1, 1986).

7. *Ibid.*

8. Christopher W. L. Hart, James L. Heskett, and W. Earl Sasser, Jr., "The Profitable Art of Service Recovery," *Harvard Business Review,* July–August 1990, pp. 148–56, at p. 152.

9. For a more extensive discussion of service guarantees, see Christopher W. L. Hart, "The Power of Unconditional Service Guarantees," *Harvard Business Review,* July–August 1988, pp. 54–62, and Christopher W. L. Hart, Leonard A. Schlesinger, and Dan Maher, "Guarantees Come to Professional Service Firms," *Sloan Management Review,* Spring 1992, pp. 19–30.

10. A more extensive description of this guarantee and its impact is presented in Robert E. Hunter and Thomas Raffio, "Implementing Service Guarantees—The Delta Dental Plan Story," *Sloan Management Review,* Spring 1992, pp. 21–22, and Christopher W. L. Hart, *Extraordinary Guarantees* (New York: Amacom, 1993).

11. Internal GTE Management Education and Training announcement, July 1, 1990.

12. Based on data from the company and Christopher W. L. Hart, "Hampton Inn's Guests Satisfied with Satisfaction Guaranteed," *Marketing News,* February 4, 1991, p. 7.

13. Michael Rose, "No Strings Attached," *Executive News Brief,* July 19, 1990.

14. Sasser and Klein, *op. cit.,* p. 5.

15. U.S. Office of Consumer Affairs, *op. cit.,* p. 50.

Chapter 11. Measuring for Effective Management

1. Based on Melvyn Menezes and Jon Serbin, "Xerox Corporation: Total Customer Satisfaction Program," Case No. 9-591-055 (Boston: Harvard Business School Publishing Division, 1991) as well as interviews with company executives.

2. Much of the information about AT&T Universal Card Services in this chapter is based on Michael D. Watkins and Susan Rosegrant, "A Measure of Delight: The Pursuit of Quality at AT&T Universal Card Services (A)," (Cambridge, MA: Harvard University, 1993).

3. *Ibid.,* p. 5.

4. Tom Ehrenfeld, "Merit Evaluation and the Family of Measures," *Harvard Business Review,* September–October 1991, p. 122.

5. W. Earl Sasser, Jr. and Lucy Lytle, "Au Bon Pain Partner/Manager Program," Case No. 9-687-063 (Boston: Harvard Business School Publishing Division, 1987).

6. James L. Heskett and Kenneth Ray, "Fairfield Inn," Case No. 9-689-092 (Boston: Harvard Business School Publishing Division, 1989).

7. Company documents, Swedbank, 1993.

8. See Robert S. Kaplan and David P. Norton, "Putting the Balanced Scorecard to Work," *Harvard Business Review,* September–October 1993 pp. 134–47; "Using the Balanced Scorecard as a Strategic Management System," *Harvard Business Review,* January–February 1996, pp. 75–85; and *The Balanced Scorecard* (Boston, Harvard Business School Press, 1996.)

Chapter 12. Reengineering the Service Organization for Capability: Gains and Pains

1. This model is described in more detail in Michael Beer, "Leading Change," pp. 424–431, in John J. Gabarro (ed.), *Managing People and Organizations* (Boston: Harvard Business School Press, 1992), and Richard Beckhard, *Organization Development: Strategies and Models* (Reading, MA: Addison-Wesley, 1969).

2. Information about Taco Bell is drawn largely from Leonard A. Schlesinger and Roger Hallowell, "Taco Bell Corp.," Case No. 9-692-058, and Leonard A. Schlesinger and Dena Votroubek, "Taco Bell 1994," (Boston: Harvard Business School Publishing Division, 1991 and 1994, respectively).

3. See James L. Heskett, "NYPD New," Case No. 9-396-293 (Boston: Harvard Business School Publishing Division, 1996) for a more detailed description of processes described here.

4. Sources for information about Sears used in this chapter include Judith H. Dobrzynski, "Yes, He's Revived Sears. But Can He Reinvent It?" *The New York Times,* January 7, 1996, Money & Business, pp. 1, 8, and 9.

5. James Q. Wilson and George L. Kelling, "Broken Windows: The Police and Neighborhood Safety," *The Atlantic Monthly,* March 1982, pp. 29–36.

6. James L. Heskett, *op. cit.,* p. 9.

7. *Ibid.,* p. 7.

8. Judith H. Dobrzynski, *op. cit.,* p. 8.

9. *Ibid.*

10. *Ibid.*

11. *Ibid.,* p. 9.

12. See Michael Hammer, "Reengineering Work: Don't Automate, Obliterate," *Harvard Business Review,* July–August 1990, pp. 104–12, and Michael Hammer and James Champy, *Reengineering the Corporation: A Manifesto for Business Revolution* (New York: HarperBusiness, 1993).

13. Chris Smith, "The NYPD Guru," *New York,* April 1, 1996, pp. 28–34, at p. 31.

14. See Leonard A. Schlesinger and James L. Heskett, "The Service-Driven Service Company," *Harvard Business Review,* September–October 1991, pp. 73–81, and "How Does Service Drive the Service Company," *Harvard Business Review,* November–December 1991, pp. 146–58, for an elaboration on these points.

15. James L. Heskett, *op. cit.,* p. 15, based on a personal interview with Deputy Commissioner Maple, February 1996.

Chapter 13. Leading and Living Service Profit Chain Management

1. Descriptions of Wal-Mart are based on field visits as well as material presented in Sam Walton, *Made in America, My Story* (New York: Doubleday, 1992) and James C. Collins and Jerry I. Porras, *Built to Last* (New York: Harper Business, 1994).

2. Quoted from comments by Herbert Kelleher in "Mobilizing People for Breakthrough Service," a video in the series "People, Service, Success" (Boston: Harvard Business School Management Productions, 1994).

3. See Hal F. Rosenbluth and Diane McFerrin Peters, *The Customer Comes Second* (New York: Morrow Quill, 1992).

4. Quoted from comments by William Pollard in "Mobilizing People for Breakthrough Service," a video in the series "People, Service, Success" (Boston: Harvard Business School Management Productions 1994).

5. Peter F. Drucker, "What Business Can Learn from Nonprofits," *Harvard Business Review,* July-August 1989, pp. 88–93.

6. Quoted from correspondence, November 1996.

7. William Pollard, *op. cit.*

8. James L. Heskett and Roger Hallowell, "Southwest Airlines 1993 (A)," Case No. 9-694-023 (Boston: Harvard Business School Publishing Division, 1993), p. 5.

9. James L. Heskett, "Confidential Memorandum," Case No. N1-396-270 (Boston: Harvard Business School Publishing Division, 1996), p. 8.

10. Scott McCartney and Michael J. McCarthy, "Southwest Flies Circles Around United's Shuttle," *The Wall Street Journal,* February 20, 1996, pp. B1 and B9.

11. Quoted from comments by Bill Bensyl in "The Service-Profit Link," a video in the series "People, Service, Success" (Boston: Harvard Business School Management Productions, 1994).

12. For a more complete description of these behaviors, see James L. Heskett, "Girl Scouts of the USA (A)," Case No. 9-690-044 (Boston: Harvard Business School Publishing Division, 1989).

13. *Ibid.*

14. See John P. Kotter and James L. Heskett, *Corporate Culture and Performance* (New York: Free Press, 1992).

Index

About the Authors

JAMES L. HESKETT, the UPS Foundation Professor of Business Logistics at the Harvard Business School, and W. EARL SASSER, JR., the UPS Foundation Professor of Service Management at the Harvard Business School, are co-authors of *Service Breakthroughs* and *The Service Management Course*. Heskett is also a co-author of *Corporate Culture and Performance*. LEONARD A. SCHLESINGER is the former COO of a restaurant-chain Au Bon Pain, George F. Baker, Jr. Professor of Business Administration at the Harvard Business School, and Chair of the Service Management Group.